AUSTRALIAN
POETRY
IN THE
TWENTIETH
CENTURY

AUSTRALIAN POETRY IN THE TWENTIETH CENTURY

Edited by
Robert Gray
and
Geoffrey Lehmann

MINERVA

Published 1993 by Minerva Australia
a part of Reed Books Australia
22 Salmon Street, Port Melbourne, Victoria 3207
a division of Reed International Books Australia Pty Limited

First published in Australia in 1991 by William Heinemann Australia

Typeset in Bembo by Bookset
Printed and bound in Australia by Australian Print Group

National Library of Australia
cataloguing-in-publication data:

Australian poetry in the twentieth century.
Includes index.

ISBN 1 86330 184 4.

1. Australian poetry—20th century.
I. Gray, Robert, 1945–   .
II. Lehmann, Geoffrey, 1940–   .

A821.008

Publication of this title was assisted by the Australia Council,
the Federal Government's arts funding and advisory body.

Every effort has been made to trace and acknowledge copyright material, but should
an infringement or incorrect acknowledgement have occurred, the editors
and publisher tender their apologies and would be grateful to receive
corrected information.

CONTENTS

Contents

INTRODUCTION

THERE IS ONLY need for a brief introduction to this book, since the biographical and critical notes that preface each poet's selection make up a history of our subject.

We have read again every poet of the period we could find, have chosen the poems we like most, and have let the proportional outcome amongst writers be as it may. We felt that by pleasing ourselves, and then each arguing against those choices that seemed to have been made out of private association or personal obsession, we had the best chance of pleasing others, and of arriving close to something objectively valid.

We have not tried to include poets on the basis of regional or any other prescriptive demands. It cannot be productive to pretend things are other than we have found them to be.

This book has been compiled over years and the only imposition upon us has been that of space. Since we have not wanted to truncate our selections from the major writers, nor to miss out on using longer poems, we have needed to be harsh toward a number of poets who might have found a place here. We had no hesitation, however, in cutting back at the more doubtful rather than the more assured end of our material. A particular ambition has been to avoid that last vice of anthologists, especially of those from small literary communities, friendship.

The choice of each editor's poems was made by the other, consulting with whomever he wished. Each of us has acquiesced in that choice, without necessarily agreeing or disagreeing.

We expect poetry to appeal to the senses and to affect the emotions. Poetry is not primarily about ideas, although these can and should be assimilated by it (and revealed at their origin, in feeling). The resources of poetry are all adapted to emotive expression. Work that is basically intellectualising, if presented as poetry, has assumed a decorative, redundant form.

We do not believe literary innovation is necessarily more admirable than an individual, revitalised use of tradition. But neither can we accept the complacencies of much formalism. Beneath both the open and formal approaches, the same qualities of feeling and intellect, and the same visceral abilities, finally justify a poem. Whatever the form used, this must be part of the poem's meaning.

The recent example of the English poet Philip Larkin proves for us that a major, unavoidable talent can make ludicrous all Hegelian, modernist contentions about literature having to 'progress' in a certain direction. Larkin has shown what the freedom of the writer in the modern western world really means.

Ideally we have wanted to produce a book in which can be found together the best achievements of modern Australian poetry; a book for those interested in writing itself.

CHRISTOPHER BRENNAN

———— ❧ ————

B ORN IN SYDNEY in 1870, the son of an Irish brewery worker, Brennan was educated by Jesuits as a scholarship boy, and at the University of Sydney. He obtained an MA with honours in philosophy at twenty-two, and went on a fellowship to the University of Berlin. There he became engaged to his landlady's daughter and also fell in love, more lastingly, with the poetry of Mallarmé. On returning to Sydney he could only find work as a cataloguer in the public library. His German fiancée, who was awaited with expectations of mystical experience in his earlier poems, delayed coming to Australia for four years because of his lack of income. Eventually she arrived and they married.

Brennan's scholarship was such that 'he could have graced the chairs of philosophy, classics or modern languages' in any institution, but it was more than a decade before he was appointed to a lectureship at Sydney University. This was because of his 'immoral' poems and his already noticeable drunkenness. Ultimately he became an associate professor of German and comparative literature, although by this time he was so much an alcoholic that his lectures, which were notoriously erratic, but to which people flocked from outside the university, had to be scheduled for early in the day. Christina Stead was among those inspired by hearing him speak.

Brennan's wife was unsympathetic to his interests. He in turn neglected and tyrannised his household, which eventually included four children and a mother-in-law (recruited by her daughter as an ally in domestic war). Outside his family, in Sydney's bohemia, Brennan was feted for his wit, erudition and ebullience—quoting from, and conversing in, six languages. He was a massive figure, with his great hooked nose complemented by a meerschaum pipe. The student introduced into his study at Sydney University would often find the room in darkness, lit only by the red glow of a beaker of claret over a flame. Brennan was dismissed from the university in 1925 when it became known that he had been living with a much younger woman, Violet Singer. The sacking occurred three months after she was killed, when struck by a tram.

Brennan had ceased living at his home some years before, staying at sailors' hotels and cheap boarding houses around the city. His daughter, Anne, the only one of his family to share any of his intellectual interests, was an habitué of this world also. She became a prostitute for a time. With the 'fun-loving' Vi Singer, Brennan had discovered a capacity for love, and he degenerated rapidly after her death, becoming more and more filthy and gross. He was supported by subscriptions, was bought meals and drinks for his often still brilliant conversation, and moved between the prostitutes and the nuns in Kings Cross. He completed a gradual return to the Church as he was dying in 1932.

Brennan is essentially a poet of the 1890s; by 1902 the main body of his work had been written. We have represented him here because he is a major gateway to modern Australian poetry, his influence reflected in poets as diverse as Hope and Roland Robinson. Despite his archaisms and portentous generalising, which are everywhere in his work, there is a real grandeur at times, as in his masterpiece 'The Wanderer', which is based on his restless trampings at night along the then isolated coastal heath beyond Newport, north of Sydney, where he lived with his family. We have reproduced here the slightly abbreviated form of this poem used by H.M. Green in his classic 1946 anthology *Modern Australian Poetry*.

Brennan's work records his Symbolist quest for an absolute reality—at first through sexual love, and after disillusionment there, through turning inwards, away from the world, to a pure poetic state. (This experience was symbolised by the dark, mysterious Lilith, Adam's first and true wife in Hebraic myth.) He was in his theory a disciple of Mallarmé, with whom he corresponded, and who admired his work ('Poet, marvellous poet').

Brennan claimed that a poem is 'not a way of saying something but a mode of that something's being'. Claims such as this—that artists experience a super-reality—were later rejected in 'The Wanderer'. Chastened by the philosophy of F.C.S. Schiller and other pragmatists, he accepted that the quest, in itself, is all there is.

All of Brennan's earlier search may be seen as an endeavour to create an intellectual substitute for the Catholicism of his youth: Symbolism can be seen as Catholicism theosophised, his Lilith as an inverted Maryology. Stylistically, too, Brennan's poetry is imbued with Catholicism, in its sonorous and theatrical quality. The bardic robes he drew on had always a touch of the purple.

AUBADE

We woke together on a gusty dawn
in the dim house amid the level waste
and stared in anguish on the stretch of years
filled with grey dawn and ever-weeping wind.

For as the hour hung still 'twixt night and day
we whom the dark had drawn so close together
at that dead tide as strangers saw each other
strangers divided by a sea of years.

We might not weep out our passion of despair
but in lorn trance we gazed upon each other
and wonder'd what strange ways had brought our hands
together in that chamber of the west.

We felt the dumb compulsion of the hour
to wander forth in spirit on the wind
and drift far apart in undiscover'd realms
of some blank world where dawn for ever wept.

'THE GRAND CORTÈGE . . .'

The grand cortège of glory and youth is gone
flaunt standards, and the flood of brazen tone:
I alone linger, a regretful guest,
here where the hostelry has crumbled down,
emptied of warmth and life, and the little town
lies cold and ruin'd, all its bravery done,
wind-blown, wind-blown, where not even dust may rest.
No cymbal-clash warms the chill air: the way
lies stretch'd beneath a slanting afternoon,
the which no piled pyres of the slaughter'd sun,
no silver sheen of eve shall follow: Day,
ta'en at the throat and choked, in the huge slum

o' the common world, shall fall across the coast,
yellow and bloodless, not a wound to boast.
But if this bare-blown waste refuse me home
and if the skies wither my vesper-flight,
'twere well to creep, or ever livid night
wrap the disquiet earth in horror, back
where the old church stands on our morning's track,
and in the iron-entrellis'd choir, among
rust tombs and blazons, where an isle of light
is bosom'd in the friendly gloom, devise
proud anthems in a long forgotten tongue:
so cozening youth's despair o'er joy that dies.

THE WANDERER

Quoniam cor secretum concupivi
  factus sum vagus inter stellas huius revelationis:
Atque annus peregrinationis meae
  quasi annus ventorum invisibilium.

When window-lamps had dwindled, then I rose
and left the town behind me; and on my way
passing a certain door I stopt, remembering
how once I stood on its threshold, and my life
was offer'd to me, a road how different
from that of the years since gone! and I had but
to rejoin an olden path, once dear, since left.
All night I have walk'd and my heart was deep awake,
remembering ways I dream'd and that I chose,
remembering lucidly, and was not sad,
being brimm'd with all the liquid and clear dark
of the night that was not stirr'd with any tide;
for leaves were silent and the road gleam'd pale,
following the ridge, and I was alone with night.
But now I am come among the rougher hills
and grow aware of the sea that somewhere near

is restless; and the flood of night is thinn'd
and stars are whitening. O, what horrible dawn
will bare me the way and crude lumps of the hills
and the homeless concave of the day, and bare
the ever-restless, ever-complaining sea?

• • •

Each day I see the long ships coming into port
and the people crowding to their rail, glad of the shore:
because to have been alone with the sea and not to have known
of anything happening in any crowded way,
and to have heard no other voice than the crooning sea's
has charmed away the old rancours, and the great winds
have search'd and swept their hearts of the old irksome thoughts:
so, to their freshen'd gaze, each land smiles a good home.
Why envy I, seeing them made gay to greet the shore?
Surely I do not foolishly desire to go
hither and thither upon the earth and grow weary
with seeing many lands and peoples and the sea:
but if I might, some day, landing I reck not where
have heart to find a welcome and perchance a rest,
I would spread the sail to any wandering wind of the air
this night, when waves are hard and rain blots out the land.

• • •

I am driven everywhere from a clinging home,
O autumn eves! and I ween'd that you would yet
have made, when your smouldering dwindled to odorous fume
close room for my heart, where I might crouch and dream,
of days and ways I had trod, and look with regret
on the darkening homes of men and the window-gleam,
and forget the morrows that threat and the unknown way.
But a bitter wind came out of the yellow-pale west
and my heart is shaken and fill'd with its triumphing cry:
You shall find neither home nor rest; for ever you roam
with stars as they drift and wilful fates of the sky!

• • •

Once I could sit by the fire hourlong when the dripping eaves
sang cheer to the shelter'd, and listen, and know that the woods
    drank full,
and think of the morn that was coming and how the freshen'd leaves
would glint in the sun and the dusk beneath would be bright and
    cool.

Now, when I hear, I am cold within: for my mind drifts wide
where the blessing is shed for naught on the salt waste of the sea,
on the valleys that hold no rest and the hills that may not abide
and the fire loses its warmth and my home is far from me.

•   •   •

How old is my heart, how old, how old is my heart,
and did I ever go forth with song when the morn was new?
I seem to have trod on many ways: I seem to have left
I know not how many homes; and to leave each
was still to leave a portion of mine own heart,
of my old heart whose life I had spent to make that home
and all I had was regret, and a memory.
So I sit and muse in this wayside harbour and wait
till I hear the gathering cry of the ancient winds and again
I must up and out and leave the embers of the hearth
to crumble silently into white ash and dust,
and see the road stretch bare and pale before me: again
my garment and my home shall be the enveloping winds
and my heart be fill'd wholly with their old pitiless cry.

•   •   •

You, at whose table I have sat, some distant eve
beside the road, and eaten and you pitied me
to be driven an aimless way before the pitiless winds,
how much ye have given and knew not, pitying foolishly!
For not alone the bread I broke, but I tasted too
all your unwitting lives and knew the narrow soul
that bodies it in the landmarks of your fields,

and broods dumbly within your little seasons' round,
where, after sowing, comes the short-lived summer's mirth,
and, after harvesting, the winter's lingering dream,
half memory and regret, half hope, crouching beside
the hearth that is your only centre of life and dream.
And knowing the world how limitless and the way how long,
and the home of man how feeble and builded on the winds,
I have lived your life, that eve, as you might never live
knowing, and pity you, if you should come to know.

• • •

I cry to you as I pass your windows in the dusk;
Ye have built you unmysterious homes and ways in the wood
where of old ye went with sudden eyes to the right and left;
and your going was now made safe and your staying comforted,
for the forest edge itself, holding old savagery
in unsearch'd glooms, was your houses' friendly barrier.
And now that the year goes winterward, ye thought to hide
behind your gleaming panes, and where the hearth sings merrily
make cheer with meat and wine, and sleep in the long night,
and the uncared wastes might be a crying unhappiness.
But I, who have come from the outer night, I say to you
the winds are up and terribly will they shake the dry wood:
the woods shall awake, hearing them, shall awake to be toss'd and
    riven,
and make a cry and a parting in your sleep all night
as the wither'd leaves go whirling all night along all ways.
And when ye come forth at dawn, uncomforted by sleep,
ye shall stand at amaze, beholding all the ways overhidden
with worthless drift of the dead and all your broken world:
and ye shall not know whence the winds have come, nor shall ye
    know
whither the yesterdays have fled, or if they were.

• • •

Come out, come out, ye souls that serve, why will ye die?
or will ye sit and stifle in your prison-homes
dreaming of some master that holds the winds in leash
and the waves of darkness yonder in the gaunt hollow of night?
nay, there is none that rules: all is a strife of the winds
and the night shall billow in storm full oft ere all be done.
For this is the hard doom that is laid on all of you,
to be that whereof ye dream, dreaming against your will.
But first ye must travel the many ways, and your close-wrapt souls
must be blown thro' with the rain that comes from the homeless
    dark:
for until ye have had care of the wastes there shall be no truce
for them nor you, nor home, but ever the ancient feud;
and the soul of man must house the cry of the darkling waves
as he follows the ridge above the waters shuddering towards night,
and the rains and the winds that roam anhunger'd for some heart's
    warmth.
Go: tho' ye find it bitter, yet must ye be bare
to the wind and the sea and the night and the wail of birds in the sky;
go: tho' the going be hard and the goal blinded with rain
yet the staying is a death that is never soften'd with sleep.

          • • •

Dawns of the world, how I have known you all,
so many, and so varied, and the same!
dawns o'er the timid plains, or in the folds
of the arm'd hills, or by the unsleeping shore;
a chill touch on the chill flesh of the dark
that, shuddering, shrinks from its couch, and leaves
a homeless light, staring, disconsolate,
on the drear world it knows too well, the world
it fled and finds again, its wistful hope
unmet by any miracle of night,

that mocks it rather, with its shreds that hang
about the woods and huddled bulks of gloom
that crouch, malicious, in the broken combes,
witness to foulnesses else unreveal'd
that visit earth and violate her dreams
in the lone hours when only evil wakes.

• • •

What is there with you and me, that I may not forget
but your white shapes come crowding noiselessly in my nights,
making my sleep a flight from a thousand beckoning hands?
Was it not enough that your cry dwelt in my waking ears
that now, seeking oblivion, I must yet be haunted
by each black maw of hunger that yawns despairingly
a moment ere its whitening frenzy bury it?
O waves of all the seas, would I could give you peace
and find my peace again: for all my peace is fled
and broken and blown along your white delirious crests!

• • •

O desolate eves along the way, how oft,
despite your bitterness, was I warm at heart!
not with the glow of remember'd hearths, but warm
with the solitary unquenchable fire that burns
a flameless heat deep in his heart who has come
where the formless winds plunge and exult for aye
among the naked spaces of the world,
far past the circle of the ruddy hearths
and all their memories. Desperate eves,
when the wind-bitten hills turn'd violet
along their rims, and the earth huddled her heat
within her niggard bosom, and the dead stones
lay battle-strewn before the iron wind
that, blowing from the chill west, made all its way
a loneliness to yield its triumph room;
yet in that wind a clamour of trumpets rang,

old trumpets, resolute, stark, undauntable,
singing to battle against the eternal foe,
the wronger of this world, and all his powers
in some last fight, foredoom'd disastrous,
upon the final ridges of the world:
a war-worn note, stern fire in the stricken eve,
and fire thro' all my ancient heart, that sprang
towards that last hope of a glory won in defeat,
whence, knowing not sure if such high grace befall
at the end, yet I draw courage to front the way.

 . . .

The land I came thro' last was dumb with night,
a limbo of defeated glory, a ghost:
for wreck of constellations flicker'd perishing
scarce sustain'd in the mortuary air,
and on the ground and out of livid pools
wreck of old swords and crowns glimmer'd at whiles;
I seem'd at home in some old dream of kingship:
now it is clear grey day and the road is plain,
I am the wanderer of many years
who cannot tell if ever he was king
or if ever kingdoms were: I know I am
the wanderer of the ways of all the worlds,
to whom the sunshine and the rain are one
and one to stay or hasten, because he knows
no ending of the way, no home, no goal,
and phantom night and the grey day alike
withhold the heart where all my dreams and days
might faint in soft fire and delicious death:
and saying this to myself as a simple thing
I feel a peace fall in the heart of the winds
and a clear dusk settle, somewhere, far in me.

SHAW NEILSON

JOHN SHAW NEILSON'S PARENTS were Scots, his father an immigrant. The eldest of five children, Neilson was born in South Australia in 1872. The family was always poverty-stricken, struggling to make a living on various selections in the Wimmera and Mallee regions of Victoria, hampered by poor soil, dust storms, rabbit plagues and drought. Neilson spent two and a half years at school before becoming an itinerant labourer. From the age of thirteen, his life was one of backbreaking work, as a road-mender, ditch-digger, quarryman, farmhand, or fruit-picker, moving about Victoria. A congenital defect of his sight meant that after his early thirties he was unable to read for himself. Because of his poverty and his shyness, he never married, nor had any close relationships, although he was always an admirer of women, a worshipper of the 'feminine principle'.

Neilson was influenced to write in boyhood by his father, a self-educated poet. Some unknown quantity of his early work was destroyed in a plague of mice that moved across Victoria in the 1890s. His later poetry had to be dictated to his brother or sisters, or to sometimes incredulous workmates, of an evening. Devaney's biography of Neilson has a story recounted by the poet of this kind of session: it is of a quarryman who had agreed to act as amanuensis, exclaiming 'Jesus!' at regular intervals throughout the task, and warning, with real concern, that Jock was 'off his onion'.

Neilson's way of making a living contrasts utterly with the delicate, musical poetry he wrote, about children and colour, girls and light, and at times of some seemingly numinous thing, manifested through nature. He is a rare example in the modern world of a genuine primitive poet of quality. In the tradition (or 'non-tradition') of Burns, Clare and W.H. Davies, he was perhaps even more handicapped than they were, and further removed from the stream of literature. It is claimed that Neilson only knew, from his youth, some old Scots and Irish songs, the poems of Burns and Hood, a little Coleridge, and 'The Rubaiyat of Omar Khayyam' (the scepticism of which was to become more and more attractive to him as he grew older). Later, he heard or read isolated nineteeth century poems and the bush balladists. Also perhaps accessible to him from the *Bulletin*, which he and his father read whenever they could afford it, were essays about the French Symbolists, and examples of their work in translation. Neilson did not speak of this possible influence, and some admirers have claimed that his use of synaesthesia and colour symbolism, so common in French Symbolist poetry, is entirely independent. This is not at all clear.

From the nineties, when he began sending poems to the *Bulletin* in Sydney, Neilson came under the mentorship of the paper's literary editor, A.G. Stephens, who published his work, edited it (though not well, encouraging him to continue in his worst habits of archaism and sentimentality), brought it out in book form, and campaigned on its behalf. Their relationship lasted for nearly forty years.

Neilson met 'A.G.' only once, in 1926, on a trip that he made to Sydney. He was also introduced to Brennan during this visit, and to other leading literary personalities of the city, at a dinner given for him. He recounted later how impressed he was that most of the conversation that evening was in French, and remarked, innocently, that it seemed he was the only one present who could not understand the language.

Neilson suffered several nervous breakdowns, as did other members of his family, in his case caused not only by the poverty, deaths and illnesses among them, but by his crises of religious belief.

In 1928, when his health was failing, a position was found for him as a messenger with a government department in Melbourne. He died in 1942.

In this selection we have removed one poor stanza from 'You, and Yellow Air' and another from 'Eva has Gone'.

Neilson is admired above all other Australian poets by writers as remote from him as Peter Porter; for many, as for A.D. Hope, he has been 'one of the beacons'.

MAY

Shyly the silver-hatted mushrooms make
  Soft entrance through,
And undelivered lovers, half awake,
  Hear noises in the dew.

Yellow in all the earth and in the skies,
  The world would seem
Faint as a widow mourning with soft eyes
  And falling into dream.

Up the long hill I see the slow plough leave
  Furrows of brown;
Dim is the day and beautiful; I grieve
  To see the sun go down.

But there are suns a many for mine eyes
  Day after day:
Delightsome in grave greenery they rise,
  Red oranges in May.

THE HOUR OF THE PARTING

Shall we assault the pain?
  It is the time to part:
Let us of Love again
  Eat the impatient heart.

There is a gulf behind
  Dull voice and fallen lip,
The blue smoke of the mind,
  The gray light on the ship.

Parting is of the cold
  That stills the loving breath,
Dimly we taste the old
  The pitiless meal of Death.

SCHOOLGIRLS HASTENING

Fear it has faded and the night:
   The bells all peal the hour of nine:
The schoolgirls hastening through the light
   Touch the unknowable Divine.

What leavening in my heart would bide!
   Full dreams a thousand deep are there:
All luminants succumb beside
   The unbound melody of hair.

Joy the long timorous takes the flute:
   Valiant with colour songs are born:
Love the impatient absolute
   Lives as a Saviour in the morn.

Get thou behind me Shadow-Death!
   Oh ye Eternities delay!
Morning is with me and the breath
   Of schoolgirls hastening down the way.

SUNDAY EVENING

Homeward, still homeward
   The calm folk ride,
And the unsoiled children
   In dreams abide.

Homeward, still homeward
   Fond arms display
Flowers and calm children—'tis
   A holy day.

The love will uphold them:
  Softly they bear
Green leaves and children with
  The falling hair.

As stars on the darkness
  Console the eye,
So do the deep children
  Bring down the sky.

As flowers at the nightfall
  Give silence fair,
So give the white children
  With falling hair.

YOU, AND YELLOW AIR

I dream of an old kissing-time
  And the flowered follies there;
In the dim place of cherry-trees,
  Of you, and yellow air.

It was an age of babbling,
  When the players would play
Mad with the wine and miracles
  Of a charmed holiday.

Bewildered was the warm earth
  With whistling and sighs,
And a young foal spoke all his heart
  With diamonds for eyes.

You were of Love's own colour
  In eyes and heart and hair;
In the dim place of cherry-trees
  Ridden by yellow air.

It was the time when red lovers
  With the red fevers burn;
A time of bells and silver seeds
  And cherries on the turn.

Out of your eyes a magic
  Fell lazily as dew,
And every lad with lad's eyes
  Made summer love to you.

It was a reign of roses,
  Of blue flowers for the eye,
And the rustling of green girls
  Under a white sky.

I dream of an old kissing-time
  And the flowered follies there,
In the dim place of cherry-trees
  Of you, and yellow air.

THE WAYS OF THE WILDFLOWER

It is but a wildflower untamed by man;
It is one of all outcasts of the berry clan.

It will not be staying where the good flowers abide;
It will be burning and crying on the bare hillside.

In the hopeless desert it will strive to grow;
It will not be the servant in a quiet row.

In the sweet garden it will make the moan;
It will be crying and crying to go out alone.

It will go to the dark lane, it will live in woe;
It will be in places where the weeds are ashamed to grow.

It will turn bitter all the heart of man;
It is the wild thing that grows with the berry clan.

THE LOVING TREE

Three women walked upon a road,
   And the first said airily
'Of all the trees in all the world,
   Which is the loving tree?'

The second said, 'My eyes have seen
   No tree that is not fair;
But the Orange tree is the sweetest tree,
   The loving blood is there.'

And the third said, 'In the green time
   I knew a loving tree
That gave a drink of the blood-red milk,
   It was the Mulberry.'

Then the first one said, 'Of all the trees
   No sweetest can I name;
Ask her who yonder slowly comes—
   That woman lean and lame.'

Grief like a hideous suckling hung
   Along her hollow breast,
Pain was upon her as she walked,
   And as she stooped to rest.

'Why will you question so?' she said,
   'Is it to mock at me?
For how should I, who walk in Hell,
   Know of a loving tree?

'My eyes are not as woman's eyes,
  They hope not east or west:
Dull famine my bed-mate is,
  And loneliness my guest.

''Tis not the most delicious flower
  That leaves the scent of Spring,
Nor is it yet the brightest bird
  That loads his heart to sing.

'A tree may dance in the white weather
  Or dream in a blue gown,
A tree may sing as a sweetheart
  To bid the stars come down:

'Some trees are slim and lovable
  And some are sleek and strong,
But the tree that has the cripple's heart
  Will know the cripple's song.

'The sweetest death is the red death
  That comes up nakedly,
And the tree that has the foiled heart
  It is the loving tree.

'While ever lip shall seek for lip,
  While ever light shall fall,
The tree that has the ruined heart
  Is tenderest of all.

'Oh, ye may have your men to kiss,
  And children warm to hold,
But the heart that had the hottest love
  Was never yet consoled.'

The women three walked on their way,
  Their shamed eyes could see
How well the tree with the foiled heart
  Is still the loving tree.

Eva Has Gone

The women they tell how it all began,
And the men that her face was sunny.
Eva has gone with the sailor-man;
She has taken the ready money.

She said 'I am off in a leaky boat;
What a fool was I to marry!
But the ten-pound note and the five-pound note
Are easy enough to carry.'

Her husband toiled as a slow man can
To put those notes together.
He had stuck to his work when many a man
Would never have faced the weather.

The sailor-man he was six foot high
And of the salt sea smelling.
On earth or in hell there was never a lie
That he was not proud of telling.

Some dark things out on the line she hung;
'Twas a fine warm day for drying.
Oh, cruel was she, for her child was young,
And the neighbours found it crying.

'Now,' they said, 'she has lost her all;
Not even her God can pity.'
And they heavily talked of her dreadful fall
And her open shame in the city.

'She might have gone by the night,' said they,
'When the lovers creep together.
'Twas a shameful way that she went by day,
Like a wild thing off the tether.'

The women they speak of her laziness,
And the men that her mouth was honey.
Eva has gone with a sailor-man;
She has taken the ready money.

The women they say that her eyes were hard,
The men that her mouth was pretty;
And some will say they have gone to the Bush,
And some say into the City.

Her husband said as he worked one day
With his old mate in the quarry,
'The women, they make the worst of it;
And the sailor will soon be sorry.'

THE BIRDS GO BY

Westward at even . . . yet never, never to die!
Surely they live as ever the laugh and the sigh:
After the fight and the fall, the defeat of the pilgrim,
        The birds go by.

No, not for dying like all the sweet flowers are they,
—Flowers giving hope to mankind on their little stay.
Failing only as love fails at the end of the day.

Green earth and water have gladdening out of their cry,
Lifting the eyes of the heart to the height of the sky:
I dream that they bear to the dead the thoughts of the living . . .
        The birds go by.

TELL SUMMER THAT I DIED

When he was old and thin
And knew not night or day,
He would sit up to say
Something of fire within.
How woefully his chin
Moved slowly as he tried
Some lusty word to say:
Tell Summer that I died.

When gladness sweeps the land,
And to the white sky
Cool butterflies go by,
And sheep in shadow stand;
When Love, the old command,
Turns every hate aside,
In the unstinted days
Tell Summer that I died.

TWO LIMERICKS

A charming young lady named Brewster
Trimmed her hat with the head of a rooster.
    When they asked 'Can it crow?'
    She smiled and said 'No—
It can't do that now but it used to.'

· · ·

They were hanging a man up at Bright.
He had been a temperance light.
    When they showed him the rope,
    He said 'I do hope
That it isn't inclined to get tight.'

HUGH McCRAE

———— 🐚 ————

H UGH McCRAE WAS born in Melbourne in 1876. His father was a high civil servant, a poetaster, and a person of apparently great charm who was able to invite into his home all the leading literary figures of the day. McCrae, after leaving school early, decided on a career as a freelance writer and illustrator. At twenty-one he met Norman Lindsay, then an art student. Lindsay, three years the junior, always acknowledged the debt of of his graphic art and painting to McCrae's verse, with its historical pantomime and whimsical caricatures of Greek mythology. McCrae and Lindsay can each be seen as influenced by the *fin de siècle* paganism of the *Yellow Book*, but with the strange addition of an Australian healthiness; of a jaunty, larrikin quality.

McCrae moved to Sydney at about the same time as Lindsay, in 1901, and settled with his wife's parents, wealthy graziers who had recently sold their country property. Lindsay remembered visiting him at that time:

> We usually found him lolling on the back veranda, very hearty and gay, but suffering, he assured us from a peculiar physical infirmity. If he ventured beyond the front gate, he lost his equilibrium and fell down . . . Nearly all the *Satyrs and Sunlight* poems were written in a burst of inspiration at that Wahroonga home.

Lindsay saw in McCrae what he called 'a gift, the capacity for idleness without the stress of thought.' McCrae's preferred occupation between his brief outbursts of inspiration was practical joking. His contribution to the First World War, while employed at the censor's office, was to spend 'most of his time driving its officials distracted, by devising evidence of German espionage', through fake telephone calls in Teutonic accents, messages in coded gibberish, and letters arranging assignations after midnight.

McCrae lived in the United States for a few years from 1914, working as an actor and illustrator, but spent the last twenty-five years of his life beside the river at Camden, outside Sydney. He had a family of three daughters. His constant womanising, at least in his younger days, is said to have given his wife 'a worn and worried look'. McCrae was immensely popular amongst his friends. Douglas Stewart remembered him visiting the *Bulletin* offices and standing in the room 'tall and handsome as the sunlight'.

McCrae and Lindsay (the latter as theorist) were the source of the Sydney school of Nietzschean 'vitalists', associated with the magazine *Vision*. McCrae brought to Australian verse a proto-form of Imagism, in the poems of his main work, *Satyrs and Sunlight*, collected in 1909. Both he and Lindsay insisted that poetry should only deal in clear images which embody life-enhancing values, and should remain uncontaminated by abstractions. McCrae's work was an affront to the wowsers, the conventional, the narrowly mercantile in the society of his time. His sensuousness, his 'pure poetry', prepared the way for the acceptance of modernity in his main disciple, Kenneth Slessor.

JUNE MORNING

The twisted apple, with rain and magian fire
   Caught in its branches from the early dawn,
I, from my bed, through the fogged pane see and desire
   Of its sharp sweetness, something. Green the lawn
And stiff with pointed spears of daffodils run wild:
   The sluggard sun draws the drowned daphne back to life—
And all the drowsy doves, brown sparrows, husband, wife,
   Are stirring on the housetops—child to early child
Cooeeing and calling; blind windows open eyes,
   And in the air the bitter fragrance floats
Of someone's gardener's pipe. I will arise
   And in the stinging shower forget gold motes,
Thick pillows, blankets, books; travel the wholesome road
   And give my body to the sun.

THE WATCHERS

We sat beside the water
   And we saw the ringdoves fly
Against the cloudy castles
   Of the Genie in the sky . . .

And, from the hazel copses,
   Where the night was coming in,
We heard the sound of voices
   And of harp and violin . . .

We saw the hounds and huntsmen
   Go in couples past the moon,
With giant shadows waving
   On the motionless lagoon.

They went into the distance,
    Through faded flower and tree,
Like thin transparent phantoms,
    On an ancient tapestry.

. . . . . .

Then, silver-sweet and flowing
    Across the sleeping corn
We heard their bugles blowing
    Amid the stars at morn.

AMBUSCADE

Or the black centaurs, statuesquely still,
    Whose moving eyes devour the snuffling mares,
And watch with baneful rage their nervous strides
    Whip the dark river white, lest, unawares,
Some danger seize them . . . Statuesquely still,
    Behind the waving trellises of cane,
The centaurs feel their hearts—besieged with blood—
    Stagger like anvils when the sled-blows rain
Shower on shower in persistent flood . . .

Now Cornus, he, the oldest of the group,
    With many wounds, strong arms, and clay-rolled hair,
Coughs for a signal to his dreadful troop
    And springs, wide-fingered, from the crackling lair.
Loudly the victims neigh, they thrash the stream,
    They tear their foemen's beards with frothy teeth,
And fill the banks with sparkling spires of steam
    That heavenward roll in one tumultuous wreath.

Within the branches of an ancient oak,
    A mother-satyr, sleeping with her young,
Smit by a sudden stone, upbraids the stroke;
    Then turns to see from whence it has been flung.
Scarce does she mark the cursed centaur pack,
    Than, standing clear, she blows a whistle shrill,
Which, like an echo, straight comes flying back
    Louder and louder down the empty hill.

A roar of hooves, a lightning view of eyes
    Redder than fire, of long straight whistling manes,
Stiff crests, and tails drawn out against the skies,
    Of angry nostrils, webbed with leaping veins,
The stallions come!

MARY GILMORE

———— ❧ ————

BORN NEAR GOULBURN, New South Wales in 1865, to Gaelic-speaking parents, Mary Cameron finished her schooling as a student teacher in various inland towns around the state. It was while she was working at a mining settlement near Broken Hill that her life-long devotion to the militant labour movement was aroused. From 1890 to 1895 she taught in Sydney, and in this time became a close friend of Henry Lawson, and knew A.G. Stephens, both of whom helped reinforce her radical politics. In 1896 she went to Paraguay to join a utopian socialist community called New Australia, and there married a shearer, William Gilmore. The community failed and the couple came back to an isolated farming existence in western Victoria. In 1908 she became initial editor of the women's page of the *Worker* in Sydney. In 1910 she collected her poems in a first book, much of which is about the joys of married life; however in 1912 she and her husband separated, he going to work in northern Queensland, and she keeping their son.

Throughout her life she campaigned on behalf of the working class, children, Aborigines, and the aged. Her eight books of verse express this passionate concern. Nostalgic domesticity is another recurring theme. Her poetry is often simplistic, in both technique and content, but the commitment and strong, plain lyricism of her best work prefigure much in the poetry of Judith Wright. Her prose, *Old Days: Old Ways* and *More Recollections*, evokes her childhood in the bush and gathers pioneer lore and memories of the Aborigines.

Mary Gilmore wrote some of her best poetry into her nineties. When she died in 1962, aged ninety-eight, having long peered down and commented on the spiritual condition of the country from a tiny flat above Kings Cross, she was given a state funeral through the streets of Sydney—as a Dame Commander of the Order of the British Empire who had regularly written for a communist newspaper, the *Tribune*.

DEDICATORY

In memory of my Father

I have known many men, and many men
In the quick balance of the mind have weighed,
And even as Abram found his score was ten,
His ten was one, so was my hope betrayed.
But though the tale is told, and fallen spent
Is the first fiction of a great man's name,
Eminent amid the uneminent
He still stands tall; a lonely mark for fame.
So, too, where truth sweeps out time's dusty floor
I have seen names, long praised, flung out as naught;
And I have seen one, whom the world called poor,
Walking amid the mountains of his thought.

EVE-SONG

I span and Eve span
A thread to bind the heart of man;
But the heart of man was a wandering thing
That came and went with little to bring:
Nothing he minded what we made,
As here he loitered, and there he stayed.

I span and Eve span
A thread to bind the heart of man;
But the more we span the more we found
It wasn't his heart but ours we bound.
For children gathered about our knees:
The thread was a chain that stole our ease.
And one of us learned in our children's eyes
That more than man was love and prize.
But deep in the heart of one of us lay
A root of loss and hidden dismay.

He said he was strong. He had no strength
But that which comes of breadth and length.
He said he was fond. But his fondness proved
The flame of an hour when he was moved.
He said he was true. His truth was but
A door that winds could open and shut.

And yet, and yet, as he came back,
Wandering in from the outward track,
We held our arms, and gave him our breast,
As a pillowing place for his head to rest.
I span and Eve span,
A thread to bind the heart of man!

THE WARADGERY TRIBE

Harried we were, and spent,
    Broken and falling,
Ere as the cranes we went,
    Crying and calling.

Summer shall see the bird
    Backward returning;
Never shall there be heard
    Those, who went yearning.

Emptied of us the land,
    Ghostly our going,
Fallen, like spears the hand
    Dropped in the throwing.

We are the lost who went
    Like the cranes, crying;
Hunted, lonely, and spent,
    Broken and dying.

LESBIA HARFORD

---- ❧ ----

LESBIA HARFORD, BORN in 1891 in Melbourne, had a congenital heart defect, which made her life more than usually exhausting, precarious and short. She also had extraordinary will-power, however, and lived fully and self-sacrificingly, before she died at the age of thirty-six.

Harford, whose family name was Keogh, was educated at Catholic boarding schools and the University of Melbourne, from which, in 1916, she was one of the first women graduates in law. As a member of the Industrial Workers of the World (the radical labour movement known as the Wobblies) she chose to work in clothing and textile factories as a sweated labourer. Sometimes a fellow activist had to cover her lack of productivity, caused by her ill health. In 1918 she moved to Sydney to live with and help support the family of a gaoled I.W.W. member. She worked as a machinist, and then as a domestic servant for the Fairfax family, the newspaper proprietors.

In 1920 she married an unsuccessful working class artist, a man remembered as 'charming', but who was an alcoholic, and sometimes violent. The marriage was happy at first, but after a few years they divorced. She drifted away from politics and worked as a school teacher among working class children. She also wrote a novel *The Invaluable Mystery*, about the treatment of Germans and radicals in Australia during the First World War, which was lost for sixty years until it was published in 1987.

By 1925 she was living with her mother again in Melbourne, and had taken a job as an articled clerk. Her health steadily weakened and she collasped and died of a bacterial infection of the heart in 1927. In the last six months of her life, her poems record that she was saying Latin prayers, though undecided whether God exists or not. Some of Harford's poems appeared in radical papers and in a special issue of a literary magazine during her life. After her death a small volume of her work came out, but a definitive collection was not published until 1985.

Harford was a bisexual, who had her first lesbian affair with her philosophy tutor at university, and numerous brief idealistic relationships after that with working class girls. She was opposed to what she thought of as elitist forms of art, and for this reason rejected classical music and only valued brass bands. Her attitude to poetry was similar, and many of her poems are simplistic. But some have a bare and aphoristic force. Her political ideals allowed her to avoid, far more consistently than her contemporaries, the Victorianisms then so prevalent in Australian poetry.

SUMMER LIGHTNING

Just now, as warm day faded from our sight,
Hosts of archangels, fleet
On lightning-wingèd feet
Passed by, all glimmering in the busy night.

Sweet angels, bring no blinding truth to birth,
Give us no messages
From heavenly palaces;
Leave us our dark trees and our starlight earth.

DAY'S END

Little girls—
You are gay,
Little factory girls
At the end of day.

There you stand
Huddled close
On the back of a tram,
Having taken your dose.

And you go
Through the grey
And the gold of the streets
At the close of the day.

Blind as moles:
You are crude,
You are sweet—little girls—
And amazingly rude.

But so fine
To be gay,
Gentle people are dull
At the end of the day.

The Invisible People

When I go into town at half past seven
Great crowds of people stream across the ways,
Hurrying, although it's only half past seven.
They are the invisible people of the days.

When you go in to town about eleven
The hurrying, morning crowds are hid from view.
Shut in the silent buildings at eleven
They toil to make life meaningless for you.

Closing Time: Public Library

At ten o'clock the great gong sounds its dread
Prelude to splendour. I push back my chair,
And all the people leave their books. We flock,
Still acquiescent, down the marble stair
Into the dark where we can't read. And thought
Swoops down insatiate through the starry air.

HARLEY MATTHEWS

———— 🙥 ————

HARLEY MATTHEWS WAS born in 1889 in Sydney and educated at Sydney High School. He was an articled clerk in a solicitor's office until he enlisted in the Australian Imperial Forces in 1914. Matthews was among the Anzacs who landed at Gallipoli beach in a campaign against the Turks which became a legendary disaster. He survived the slaughter there to fight in France. After the war he worked for a Sydney afternoon newspaper, and in 1920 went to the United States, where he was a freelance writer for two years. In 1922 he established a vineyard at Moorebank, outside Sydney. This became a weekend meeting-place for writers, and is referred to by Slessor in 'Five Bells', when he recalls 'The night we came to Moorebank in slab-dark'.

In 1942 Matthews was arrested at midnight and interned in an army prison camp for six months because of his association with members of the Australia First movement (an isolationist, anti-British, quasi-Fascist organisation), although he himself was not a member. During this time his elderly mother died and his vineyard was ruined through neglect. Later he was awarded seven hundred pounds compensation by a Royal Commission. He established another rural property near Sydney, lived there unmarried, and died in 1968.

It was not until twenty years after World War I that Matthews published his poems on Gallipoli. Their tone occasionally suggests

Robert Frost's narrative voice. The long delay in their appearance, which occurred just before World War II, and their being too long for most anthologies, have caused them to be overlooked. 'Women Are Not Gentlemen', rediscovered by Les Murray for *The New Oxford Book of Australian Verse*, and 'Two Brothers', chosen here, are among the outstanding English-language poems of the First World War. Matthews' shorter and less successful poems have, typically, a note of disgruntled patriotism along with their praise of the Australian bush.

Two Brothers

We laughed. Those two were with us still.
Always in camp, on shipboard, they had held
Themselves apart from us. Packed in the boat
Just now, they had sat staring, beyond reach
Of every joke we made to keep our dread
Down. Then we had forgotten them. Instead,
Grinding of keels. Shouts . . . 'Over with you!' The swill
Of water round your body. Your feet jarred
Against stones. Stumblings. Breaths coming hard,
This pack pushing you down. Blankness . . .

                                        Half-afloat
A dead sailor lay sprawled upon the beach.
But no rest for us. On. On. In a cleft
Between the hills the wounded lay or sat.
Some cheered. But most were still. 'Give it to them
For us,' a gash that was a mouth once wailed.
On. Up. Legs, feet heavy—this pack—Up still . . .
Now we lay waiting on the hill,
And with us were those two. They were two brothers.
They kept aloof there even from us others.

    In front, over the ridge some rifles spat;
Beyond, the battle came to life. It rushed
Along unvisioned valleys at a stride,
Roaring its challenge out for us to pit
Our strength against it. Then grew sullen, hushed;
Once more, louder than ever, as over it
The seaplane sailed.
'We'll soon be in it,' someone said. The air
Cracked open over us. Smoke swooped down.
Things fell, fell, fell. A man screamed: 'I'm hit.'
More, more shells shrieked their coming. We lay flat,
But never flat enough. Run! Down the slope.
No. No. Where then? 'Earth take and hide
Me,' all my being cried.
That will fall here. Run! Which way? Too late. 'Earth—'
No. There is no escape from the machine;

Unseeing it picks us out, and strikes unseen.
You are the one hope, Earth. Only a hope . . .
    Then one shell passed us by. Now they all burst
Behind us, spattering the sea below—
Like a storm gone over. The sun shone again,
And slender grasses leaned and swayed.
Patches of ocean toyed with glints and gleams,
Ships swung at anchor unafraid.
We saw men come unhurrying, and go
This way and that down on the beach. 'It seems
More like a holiday,' one brother said.
'Somewhere at home, some seaside place—the sun,
The boats, and all that passing to and fro.'
    The other laughed. 'Colour is all it lacks—
Some women's dresses here and there.' No one
Spoke for a while. We lay against our packs,
Each watching what he saw. 'A prisoner,
Look!' Halfway down the hill
A man stood up. He screamed. 'Kill him! Kill. Kill.
There, bayonet him. Shoot him. Our orders were
Not to take one of them.'
Not an arm lifted. None took up that shout.
The prisoner shambled round the hill. 'He's out
Of it,' we were all thinking.

                                        'He seemed glad
To have been taken,' someone's voice broke in.
'Who could have shot a man like that? Not me.'

    The world had grown to only sky and sea,
To only murmurs from beyond the blue.
'Their orders cannot make us beasts, blood-mad,'
That was the older brother speaking. 'And I say,
The man who took that prisoner, he won
For us the greatest victory to-day.'
    No word more. Sprawl, eyes shut against the sun.
The wind brought rumors up. Deep-stained the glare
Into that inner world of ours pierced through.
    'You wait till we advance and they begin

To shoot at you.' It was the old soldier's voice.
At things it hinted that could not be told,
But only learnt, each for himself. The air
Settled about us. Unseen shadows came
And touched our hearts with cold.
'That will not make me want to kill.' That cry
Rippled across our thoughts.

                  'You'll have no choice
When the order comes to open fire.'

                       'No! No!
I will not. I will not. I will shoot high.'
   New voices crowded out all else. 'Then why
Did you enlist?' . . . 'Traitor to waste
Good ammunition!' . . . 'Let us shoot him here,
Ourselves.' . . . 'Think of the wounded men below.'

   Quick! Flat! Words died. Thought stopped. From out to sea
It came. There. Our own battleships again.
Guns. Guns. Their dark din
Trailed through the sky; then shattered itself on hills
Far over. Earth shuddered. Yes, men embraced
You there, too, Earth; and cried out in the pain
Of their fear, men we called the enemy.
'The bastards!' a man shouted. 'That shell kills
A hundred of them.' The air beat out and in
As though great doors were slammed and opened.

                           'Boys,
I know.' The voice laughed. 'Both came to the war
To please some girl.' We laughed too. In that noise
And tremor we remembered them once more.
We talked, laughed, listened. Still there stirred that thought.
Stories of places, women, men.
Nothing could dull the ache of waiting. How long? When?
Then all at once the word—
And over that hillside there were heard
Hands kissing rifles as they caught
Them up. 'Advance.' Men rising, packs being eased;
It was as though Earth had herself been stirred
To action. 'We are advancing.'

We were going
Along the beach again. But now we turned
Into a valley, banked with bushes growing
So furtive in the sun;
And pools quivered, where water had now ceased
For heaviness to run.
   The path forked. We halted. Now which way
To the edge of this world? Did they both lead there
Sooner or later? Left or right?
Our captain muttered: 'Orders do not say
Which track we are to take.' He turned about
'At least let us go light.
Quick, men, off with these packs and leave them here.
And now I want two men to volunteer
To stay and guard them.' Me! I cannot. Out
At last two men stepped. At this chance they smiled.
We moved off. Up that right-hand track we filed,
Disdainful, at heart envious
Of two men made so sure of living. They
Were not those brothers. They went on with us.

   How near were we now? Would we find it there
In the next valley? Yet it was aware
Of our coming. We heard its anger grow.
Up on the left it stamped, stamped, and the track
Was barred with smoke and noise.
Bullets snarled by, or flicked off leaves. A man
Stumbled . . . 'He's only wounded. Come on, boys,
We can't stop. He must find his own way back.'
   We ran. We crawled. We ran,
And that unseen eye followed all the way;
Always the shells kept bursting just ahead.
Look! Over there. Four men down at once. 'Spread
Out more, you fools.' Spread out? There is no room.
Into the bushes then . . . They clutch and tear,
The ground gives underfoot.
Up! Help me, twig, bough, root.
   Under the ridge at last. Rest. Breathe. The air—
How quiet here. A flower is in bloom.

And then they came, our own men, over the crest,
Bleeding and limping, babbling out their news:
'We've chased them miles ahead' . . . . 'They won't
Stand up and fight like us' . . . 'They're just in front.'
They led one who kept crying: 'I could see
No one. Only green bushes and a hill.'
He would never see so much again. Breathe. Rest.

   'Fix bayonets,' the word comes. 'Charge!' Charge. Kill.
Now go and kill the man who has to wait
For you down there. Legs, bring me to him straight.
Do not falter. All along this had to be,
And just this way. Where is he hiding?
Only green bushes and a hill.

Suppose

There is no man at all. Yes, but there is.
I feel his eye on me. He knows. He knows
I'm on this ridge; I'm crawling through this wheat.
There is no hiding from him anywhere.
'Take cover, men. Lie down. Here in this dip.'

  Behind this bush. Already bullets strip
Off one by one the leaves above me—his.
Dig, fingers, scratch deep in that earth. Down there
Is shelter. See—this root,
The way it goes. And stones know it, too.
'I'm shot,' a man cries. 'Oh! Don't touch me. No,
I can't bear it.' Bullets come, more and more;
Nothing may stir. Fingers, only grip
The ground tighter. He is calling still:
'Don't leave me to them. Shoot me first. Shoot . . .'
The air is turned to lead,
Its weight presses me down and holds me flat.
Now he is crying only to himself.

   'Fire!' The word runs. 'On that ridge ahead.'
Fire. Fire. Shoot. Shoot. Something at last to do,
If only it is to kill.
But no man shows himself. Shoot. Shoot. What at?
Nothing—only green bushes and a hill.

We were back on the ridge again.
At nightfall we'd come in; the crest was lined
With men already digging to entrench.
Not a face there we knew. They cried 'Dig here,
They'll attack soon.' And as we worked they told
Of Turks who'd stood, and Turks who'd run,
Of Turks they'd killed, of men they'd left behind
In fights on far high hills they could not hold.
    We all knew one another now. One fear
Brought us together, made all work as one.
There was no officer to see it done.

    The trench was to our knees when it began.
In front, sparks pricked the darkness. Bullets whined
Again above us. The old soldier took
Command. 'Don't fire. Not yet. Wait till they come.'
Those sparks kept creeping down. Crackling, they ran
Ripping the darkness through from end to end.
The air is combed deeper. I dare not look
Upward. I press my face against this heap
Of earth, and only listen. Rifles crash.
Over me, I could touch that rushing sound.

    'Up! Up! Here they come. Fire!' I see a flash,
I press my finger. There leaps out a flame
From my own rifle. Shouts, flame, crashings smash
The night to pieces. Fire. Re-load. Fire. 'Keep
It up, lads.' Hot. My rifle burns my hand—
'Cease fire.' Is it all over? 'Stop!' Men aim
And shoot into the darkness just the same.
'Cease fire, you fools. Don't waste another round.'
The clamour dies away, to leave at last
Only a whimper on the left. The night
Draws in together. 'Dig,' is the command,
And sometimes words from man to man are passed—
'More stretcher-bearers wanted on the right,'
Or, 'Stand to arms. Stand-to.' We rise and stand.

We heard them gathering on the hills again.
They called and whistled, bugles blew.
'Allah!' they cried. Then feet came thudding on.
'Allah!' Up on the left the firing grew,
In one gust it came down to us. 'Stand-to!
Here they come. Fire!' Once more
We fire at shouts and shadows—and then . . . gone.
They are gone now, all melted as before.
   'Dig!' Now we dig to keep
The cold back. One time it began to rain.
For how long? Did we sleep?
'Stand-to. They're coming.' It was that all night.
   We stood-to, waiting for the dawn.
They would attack before it came, we thought,
But the darkness held only darkness. We heard
No foot stumbling, out on the hills no call.
Far-off a rifle spluttered—that was all.
At last there came the light,
The hills showed motionless. A stray air caught
A bush nearby; its rain-drops kissed the earth.
   'Stand down! Some men may sleep.' The word
Passed gladly on. We saw the day's slow birth,
We who were left to watch. We hoped anew.
The trench was to our breasts. Out came the sun,
And now this glow to warm our tired limbs through;
This stillness made for sleep . . . But we must dig.

   A rifle broke the quiet. A man cried out,
Along the trench a little way.
Now he lay on its floor—
One of those brothers. He gasped, gasped, and then was still.
It was the younger one;
The other kneeled by him. We heard him say:
'Come, Tom. We have to dig now. Only wait,
And we can all sleep soon.' The old soldier said,
'Yes, dig, man. Can't you see that he is dead?'

He got up. From his eyes had gone all doubt.
He threw his rifle up to fire; to shout:
'Kill! Kill them all!' There showed upon the hill
No one. But we knew then that, for a war,
Love they enlisted too, as well as Hate.

KENNETH SLESSOR

K ENNETH SLESSOR WAS born in Orange, New South Wales, in 1901, the elder son of Robert Schloesser, a German-Jewish mining engineer, who Anglicised the family name during the First World War. His mother was the daughter of Scottish immigrants. Slessor was brought up at Chatswood in Sydney, and after leaving school, went into a lifetime career in journalism. He worked for the *Sun* and *Smith's Weekly* (of which he was editor from 1935 to 1939, and editor-in-chief in 1939–40), and after the war for the *Telegraph*, a right-wing 'popular' morning newspaper, where he was leader writer and chief book reviewer almost until his death in 1970. From 1940 to 1944 he was official war correspondent accompanying the Second AIF, in Greece, Crete, Syria, North Africa, and New Guinea. He resigned his commission in a controversy over army censorship of correspondents' reports.

Slessor was the president of the Sydney Journalists' Club from 1956 to 1965, and brought his courtly style (bow ties, waistcoats, portliness) to a scene of hard drinking and hot poker machines above the railway yards in south Sydney. He was, with Douglas Stewart, responsible for government grants to Australian writers, on the Commonwealth Literary Fund, from 1953.

For most of his adult life Slessor lived around the bohemian Kings Cross area of Sydney. He rented for a long period one half of a 'minor mansion' overlooking Sydney Harbour, which he kept shadowy and filled with curios: heavy cedar furniture, hefty silver, china and glassware, pewter tankards, old maps, etchings, tarot cards, watercolours by Norman Lindsay, and a library of antique books.

Slessor's first wife, whom he married when he was twenty-one and she sixteen, died in her thirties of cancer. His second wife became an alcoholic. He won custody, in their divorce, of his son.

In the ten years after 1937, the year of 'Five Bells', he wrote only three poems that he retained, then nothing further. He was already recognised, among those interested, as Australia's finest poet: He was cremated without religious ceremony and his ashes buried with his first wife. In his last years, Slessor, according to accounts like that of Hal Porter in *The Extra*, was privately and stoically depressed; yet despite 'his gout giving him hell, and with his haemorrhoids aflame', he maintained his immaculate manners, his dandyism, and his generosity to young writers.

Slessor's supreme importance to Australian poetry lies in the visual and auditory richness of his style. He brought a European ornateness to a country that had seemed to rebuff such sensuality. Slessor's language is the most original and individual of any Australian poet's. The associative daring of this language is present in his earliest published poems, his youthful fantasias, exotic scenes and allegories, that derive from Hugh McCrae and from a fascination with European high culture.

Slessor was co-editor of the briefly-flaring *Vision* magazine, which was a vehicle for the philosophy of Norman Lindsay. Of the Lindsay credo, he said, 'A lot of it I never agreed with. I did agree on one point of dogma . . . our insistence on the concrete image in art, and our hatred of the abstract.'

The most significant development in Slessor's work is his movement away from Lindsay's Nietzschean vitalism to an attitude that permitted pessimism and pity. All of his poetry is obsessed with the flux of things, with meaninglessness and death. His strategy for dealing with 'the tunnels of nothingness' between the stars, with 'Infinity's trapdoor, eternal and merciless', was to savour the finest pleasures of life—wine and friends, odes and curries, billiards, girls, metaphors, metres, 'every dish that passes', as he puts it in 'To a Friend'.

Next Turn

No pause! The buried pipes ring out,
   The flour-faced Antic runs from sight;
Now Columbine, with scarlet pout,
   Floats in the smoking moon of light.

Now programmes wave, heads bend between—
   The roaring Years go past in file.
Soon there's the Transformation Scene—
   And then the Footmen down the aisle.

For you must wait, before you leave
   This Theatre of Varieties,
Their frozen fingers on your sleeve,
   Their most respectful 'Now, sir, please!'

Out in the night, the Carriage stands,
   Plumed with black trees. The Post-boys grin.
The Coachman beats upon his hands.
   Turn after Turn goes on within.

The Night-Ride

Gas flaring on the yellow platform; voices running up and down;
Milk-tins in cold dented silver; half-awake I stare,
Pull up the blind, blink out—all sounds are drugged;
The slow blowing of passengers asleep;
Engines yawning; water in heavy drips;
Black, sinister travellers, lumbering up the station,
One moment in the window, hooked over bags;
Hurrying, unknown faces—boxes with strange labels—
All groping clumsily to mysterious ends,
Out of the gaslight, dragged by private Fates.
Their echoes die. The dark train shakes and plunges;
Bells cry out; the night-ride starts again.

Soon I shall look out into nothing but blackness,
Pale, windy fields. The old roar and knock of the rails
Melts in dull fury. Pull down the blind. Sleep. Sleep.
Nothing but grey, rushing rivers of bush outside.
Gaslight and milk-cans. Of Rapptown I recall nothing else.

CAPTAIN DOBBIN

Captain Dobbin, having retired from the South Seas
In the dumb tides of 1900, with a handful of shells,
A few poisoned arrows, a cask of pearls,
And five thousand pounds in the colonial funds,
Now sails the street in a brick villa, 'Laburnum Villa',
In whose blank windows the harbour hangs
Like a fog against the glass,
Golden and smoky, or stoned with a white glitter,
And boats go by, suspended in the pane,
Blue Funnel, Red Funnel, Messageries Maritimes,
Lugged down the port like sea-beasts taken alive
That scrape their bellies on sharp sands,
Of which particulars Captain Dobbin keeps
A ledger sticky with ink,
Entries of time and weather, state of the moon,
Nature of cargo and captain's name,
For some mysterious and awful purpose
Never divulged.
For at night, when the stars mock themselves with lanterns,
So late the chimes blow loud and faint
Like a hand shutting and unshutting over the bells,
Captain Dobbin, having observed from bed
The lights, like a great fiery snake, of the *Comorin*
Going to sea, will note the hour
For subsequent recording in his gazette.

But the sea is really closer to him than this,
Closer to him than a dead, lovely woman,
For he keeps bits of it, like old letters,
Salt tied up in bundles
Or pressed flat,
What you might call a lock of the sea's hair,
So Captain Dobbin keeps his dwarfed memento,
His urn-burial, a chest of mummied waves,
Gales fixed in print, and the sweet dangerous countries
Of shark and casuarina-tree,
Stolen and put in coloured maps,
Like a flask of seawater, or a bottled ship,
A schooner caught in a glass botle;
But Captain Dobbin keeps them in books,
Crags of varnished leather
Pimply with gilt, by learned mariners
And masters of hydrostatics, or the childish tales
Of simple heroes, taken by Turks or dropsy.
So nightly he sails from shelf to shelf
Or to the quadrants, dangling with rusty screws,
Or the hanging-gardens of old charts,
So old they bear the authentic protractor-lines,
Traced in faint ink, as fine as Chinese hairs.

Over the flat and painted atlas-leaves
His reading-glass would tremble,
Over the fathoms, pricked in tiny rows,
Water shelving to the coast.
Quietly the bone-rimmed lens would float
Till, through the glass, he felt the barbèd rush
Of bubbles foaming, spied the albicores,
The blue-finned admirals, heard the wind-swallowed cries
Of planters running on the beach
Who filched their swags of yams and ambergris,
Birds' nests and sandalwood, from pastures numbed
By the sun's yellow, too meek for honest theft;
But he, less delicate robber, climbed the walls,
Broke into dozing houses

Crammed with black bottles, marish wine
Crusty and salt-corroded, fading prints,
Sparkle-daubed almanacs and playing cards,
With rusty cannon, left by the French outside,
Half-buried in sand,
Even to the castle of Queen Pomaree
In the Yankee's footsteps, and found her throne-room piled
With golden candelabras, mildewed swords,
Guitars and fowling-pieces, tossed in heaps
With greasy cakes and flung-down calabashes.

Then Captain Dobbin's eye,
That eye of wild and wispy scudding blue,
Voluptuously prying, would light up
Like mica scratched by gully-suns,
And he would be fearful to look upon
And shattering in his conversation;
Nor would he tolerate the harmless chanty,
No '*Shenandoah*', or the dainty mew
That landsmen offer in a silver dish
To Neptune, sung to pianos in candlelight.
Of these he spoke in scorn,
For there was but one way of singing '*Stormalong*',
He said, and that was not really singing,
But howling, rather—shrieked in the wind's jaws
By furious men; not tinkled in drawing-rooms
By lap-dogs in clean shirts.
And, at these words,
The galleries of photographs, men with rich beards,
Pea-jackets and brass buttons, with folded arms,
Would scowl approval, for they were shipmates, too,
Companions of no cruise by reading-glass,
But fellows of storm and honey from the past—
'The Charlotte, Java, '93,'
'Knuckle and Fred at Port au Prince,'
'William in his New Rig,'
Even that notorious scoundrel, Captain Baggs,

Who, as all knew, owed Dobbin Twenty Pounds
Lost at fair cribbage, but he never paid,
Or paid 'with the slack of the tops'l sheets'
As Captain Dobbin frequently expressed it.

There were their faces, grilled a trifle now,
Cigar-hued in various spots
By the brown breath of sodium-eating years,
On quarter-decks long burnt to the water's edge,
A resurrection of the dead by chemicals.
And the voyages they had made,
Their labours in a country of water,
Were they not marked by inadequate lines
On charts tied up like skins in a rack?
Or his own Odysseys, his lonely travels,
His trading days, an autobiography
Of angles and triangles and lozenges
Ruled tack by tack across the sheet,
That with a single scratch expressed the stars,
Merak and Alamak and Alpherat,
The wind, the moon, the sun, the clambering sea,
Sails bleached with light, salt in the eyes,
Bamboos and Tahiti oranges,
From some forgotten countless day,
One foundered day from a forgotten month,
A year sucked quietly from the blood,
Dead with the rest, remembered by no more
Than a scratch on a dry chart—
Or when the return grew too choking bitter-sweet
And laburnum-berries manifestly tossed
Beyond the window, not the fabulous leaves
Of Hotoo or canoe-tree or palmetto,
There were the wanderings of other keels,
Magellan, Bougainville and Cook,
Who found no greater a memorial
Than footprints over a lithograph.

For Cook he worshipped, that captain with the sad
And fine white face, who never lost a man
Or flinched a peril; and of Bougainville
He spoke with graceful courtesy, as a rival
To whom the honours of the hunting-field
Must be accorded. Not so with the Spaniard,
Sebastian Juan del Cano, at whom he sneered
Openly, calling him a fool of fortune
Blown to a sailors' abbey by chance winds
And blindfold currents, who slept in a fine cabin,
Blundered through five degrees of latitude,
Was bullied by mutineers a hundred more,
And woke and found himself across the world.

Coldly in the window,
Like a fog rubbed up and down the glass
The harbour, bony with mist
And ropes of water, glittered; and the blind tide
That crawls it knows not where, nor for what gain,
Pushed its drowned shoulders against the wheel,
Against the wheel of the mill.
Flowers rocked far down
And white, dead bodies that were anchored there
In marshes of spent light.
Blue Funnel, Red Funnel,
The ships went over them, and bells in engine-rooms
Cried to their bowels of flaring oil,
And stokers groaned and sweated with burnt skins,
Clawed to their shovels.
But quietly in his room,
In his little cemetery of sweet essences
With fond memorial-stones and lines of grace,
Captain Dobbin went on reading about the sea.

'AFTER THE CANDLES HAD GONE OUT . . .'

from Five Visions of Captain Cook

After the candles had gone out, and those
Who listened had gone out, and a last wave
Of chimney-haloes caked their smoky rings
Like fish-scales on the ceiling, a Yellow Sea
Of swimming circles, the old man,
Old Captain-in-the-Corner, drank his rum
With friendly gestures to four chairs. They stood
Empty, still warm from haunches, with rubbed nails
And leather glazed, like agèd serving-men
Feeding a king's delight, the sticky, drugged
Sweet agony of habitual anecdotes.
But these, his chairs, could bear an old man's tongue,
Sleep when he slept, be flattering when he woke,
And wink to hear the same eternal name
From lips new-dipped in rum.

'Then Captain Cook,
I heard him, told them they could go
If so they chose, but he would get them back,
Dead or alive, he'd have them,'
The old man screeched, half-thinking to hear 'Cook!
Cook again! Cook! It's other cooks he'll need,
Cooks who can bake a dinner out of pence,
That's what he lives on, talks on, half-a-crown
A day, and sits there full of Cook.
Who'd do your cooking now, I'd like to ask,
If someone didn't grind her bones away?
But that's the truth, six children and half-a-crown
A day, and a man gone daft with Cook.'

That was his wife,
Elizabeth, a noble wife but brisk,
Who lived in a present full of kitchen-fumes
And had no past. He had not seen her
For seven years, being blind, and that of course
Was why he'd had to strike a deal with chairs,
Not knowing when those who chafed them had gone to sleep
Or stolen away. Darkness and empty chairs,
This was the port that Alexander Home
Had come to with his useless cutlass-wounds
And tales of Cook, and half-a-crown a day—
This was the creek he'd run his timbers to,
Where grateful countrymen repaid his wounds
At half-a-crown a day. Too good, too good,
This eloquent offering of birdcages
To gulls, and Greenwich Hospital to Cook,
Britannia's mission to the sea-fowl.

It was not blindness picked his flesh away,
Nor want of sight made penny-blank the eyes
Of Captain Home, but that he lived like this
In one place, and gazed elsewhere. His body moved
In Scotland, but his eyes were dazzle-full
Of skies and water farther round the world—
Air soaked with blue, so thick it dripped like snow
On spice-tree boughs, and water diamond-green,
Beaches wind-glittering with crumbs of gilt,
And birds more scarlet than a duchy's seal
That had come whistling long ago, and far
Away. His body had gone back,
Here it sat drinking rum in Berwickshire,
But not his eyes—they were left floating there
Half-round the earth, blinking at beaches milked
By suck-mouth tides, foaming with ropes of bubbles

And huge half-moons of surf. Thus it had been
When Cook was carried on a sailor's back,
Vengeance in a cocked hat, to claim his price,
A prince in barter for a longboat.
And then the trumpery springs of fate—a stone,
A musket-shot, a round of gunpowder,
And puzzled animals, killing they knew not what
Or why, but killing . . . the surge of goatish flanks
Armoured in feathers, like cruel birds:
Wild, childish faces, killing; a moment seen,
Marines with crimson coats and puffs of smoke
Toppling face-down; and a knife of English iron,
Forged aboard ship, that had been changed for pigs,
Given back to Cook between the shoulder-blades.
There he had dropped, and the old floundering sea,
The old, fumbling, witless lover-enemy,
Had taken his breath, last office of salt water.

Cook died. The body of Alexander Home
Flowed round the world and back again, with eyes
Marooned already, and came to English coasts,
The vague ancestral darknesses of home,
Seeing them faintly through a glass of gold,
Dim fog-shapes, ghosted like the ribs of trees
Against his blazing waters and blue air.
But soon they faded, and there was nothing left,
Only the sugar-cane and the wild granaries
Of sand, and palm-trees and the flying blood
Of cardinal-birds; and putting out one hand
Tremulously in the direction of the beach,
He felt a chair in Scotland. And sat down.

WILD GRAPES

The old orchard, full of smoking air,
Full of sour marsh and broken boughs, is there,
But kept no more by vanished Mulligans,
Or Hartigans, long drowned in earth themselves,
Who gave this bitter fruit their care.

Here's where the cherries grew that birds forgot,
And apples bright as dogstars; now there is not
An apple or a cherry; only grapes,
But wild ones, Isabella grapes they're called,
Small, pointed, black, like boughs of musket-shot.

Eating their flesh, half-savage with black fur,
Acid and gipsy-sweet, I thought of her,
Isabella, the dead girl, who has lingered on
Defiantly when all have gone away,
In an old orchard where swallows never stir.

Isabella grapes, outlaws of a strange bough,
That in their harsh sweetness remind me somehow
Of dark hair swinging and silver pins,
A girl half-fierce, half-melting, as these grapes,
Kissed here—or killed here—but who remembers now?

THE COUNTRY RIDE

*'Of all the Journeys that ever I made, this was the merriest, and I
was in a strange mood for mirth.'*
—Samuel Pepys, 11 April 1661.

Earth which has known so many passages
Of April air, so many marriages
Of strange and lovely atoms breeding light,
Never may find again that lost delight.

In the sharp sky, the frosty deepnesses,
There are still birds to barb the silences,
There are still fields to meet the morning on,
But those who made them beautiful have gone.

Diamonds are flung by other smoking springs,
But where is he that cropped their offerings—
The pick-purse of enchantments, riding by,
Whistling his '*Go and Be Hanged, That's Twice Good-bye*'?

Who such a frolic pomp of blessing made
To kiss a little pretty dairymaid. . . .
And country wives with bare and earth-burnt knees,
And boys with beer, and smiles from balconies. . . .

The greensleeve girl, apprentice-equerry,
Tending great men with slant-eye mockery:
'Then Mr Sam says, "Riding's hot," he says,
Tasting their ale and waving twopences. . . .'

Into one gaze they swam, a moment swirled,
One fiery paintbox of the body's world—
Into Sam's eye, that flying bushranger—
Swinging their torches for earth's voyager.

And how the blood sang, and the senses leapt,
And cells that under tents of horn had slept
Rose dancing, at the black and faceless bale
Of gallows-flesh that had not girl nor ale!

OUT OF TIME

I

I saw Time flowing like the hundred yachts
That fly behind the daylight, foxed with air;
Or piercing, like the quince-bright, bitter slats
Of sun gone thrusting under Harbour's hair.

So Time, the wave, enfolds me in its bed,
Or Time, the bony knife, it runs me through.
'Skulker, take heart,' I thought my own heart said.
'The flood, the blade, go by—Time flows, not you!'

Vilely, continuously, stupidly,
Time takes me, drills me, drives through bone and vein,
So water bends the seaweeds in the sea,
The tide goes over, but the weeds remain.

Time, you must cry farewell, take up the track,
And leave this lovely moment at your back!

II

Time leaves the lovely moment at his back,
Eager to quench and ripen, kiss or kill;
To-morrow begs him, breathless for his lack,
Or beauty dead entreats him to be still.

His fate pursues him; he must open doors,
Or close them, for that pale and faceless host
Without a flag, whose agony implores
Birth, to be flesh, or funeral, to be ghost.

Out of all reckoning, out of dark and light,
Over the edges of dead Nows and Heres,
Blindly and softly, as a mistress might,
He keeps appointments with a million years.

I and the moment laugh, and let him go,
Leaning against his golden undertow.

III

Leaning against the golden undertow,
Backward, I saw the birds begin to climb
With bodies hailstone-clear, and shadows flow,
Fixed in a sweet meniscus, out of Time,

Out of the torrent, like the fainter land
Lensed in a bubble's ghostly camera,
The lighted beach, the sharp and china sand,
Glitters and waters and peninsula—

The moment's world, it was; and I was part,
Fleshless and ageless, changeless and made free.
'Fool, would you leave this country?' cried my heart,
But I was taken by the suck of sea.

The gulls go down, the body dies and rots,
And Time flows past them like a hundred yachts.

North Country

North Country, filled with gesturing wood,
With trees that fence, like archers' volleys,
The flanks of hidden valleys
Where nothing's left to hide

But verticals and perpendiculars,
Like rain gone wooden, fixed in falling,
Or fingers blindly feeling
For what nobody cares;

Or trunks of pewter, bangled by greedy death,
Stuck with black staghorns, quietly sucking,
And trees whose boughs go seeking,
And trees like broken teeth

With smoky antlers broken in the sky;
Or trunks that lie grotesquely rigid,
Like bodies blank and wretched
After a fool's battue,

As if they've secret ways of dying here
And secret places for their anguish
When boughs at last relinquish
Their clench of blowing air—

But this gaunt country, filled with mills and saws,
With butter-works and railway-stations
And public institutions,
And scornful rumps of cows,

North Country, filled with gesturing wood—
Timber's the end it gives to branches,
Cut off in cubic inches,
Dripping red with blood.

SOUTH COUNTRY

After the whey-faced anonymity
Of river-gums and scribbly-gums and bush,
After the rubbing and the hit of brush,
You come to the South Country

As if the argument of trees were done,
The doubts and quarrelling, the plots and pains,
All ended by these clear and gliding planes
Like an abrupt solution.

And over the flat earth of empty farms
The monstrous continent of air floats back
Coloured with rotting sunlight and the black,
Bruised flesh of thunderstorms:

Air arched, enormous, pounding the bony ridge,
Ditches and hutches, with a drench of light,
So huge, from such infinities of height,
You walk on the sky's beach

While even the dwindled hills are small and bare,
As if, rebellious, buried, pitiful,
Something below pushed up a knob of skull,
Feeling its way to air.

FULL ORCHESTRA

My words are the poor footmen of your pride,
Of what you cry, you trumpets, each to each
With mouths of air; my speech is the dog-speech
Of yours, the Roman tongue—but mine is tied
By harsher bridles, dumb with breath and bone.
Vainly it mocks the dingo strings, the stops,
The pear-tree flying in the flute, with drops
Of music, quenched and scattered by your own.

So serving-men, who run all night with wine,
And whet their ears, and crouch upon the floor,
Sigh broken words no man has heard before
Or since, but ravished in the candleshine,
Between the push and shutting of a door,
From the great table where their masters dine.

FIVE BELLS

Time that is moved by little fidget wheels
Is not my Time, the flood that does not flow.
Between the double and the single bell
Of a ship's hour, between a round of bells
From the dark warship riding there below,
I have lived many lives, and this one life
Of Joe, long dead, who lives between five bells.

Deep and dissolving verticals of light
Ferry the falls of moonshine down. Five bells
Coldly rung out in a machine's voice. Night and water
Pour to one rip of darkness, the Harbour floats
In air, the Cross hangs upside-down in water.

Why do I think of you, dead man, why thieve
These profitless lodgings from the flukes of thought
Anchored in Time? You have gone from earth,
Gone even from the meaning of a name;
Yet something's there, yet something forms its lips
And hits and cries against the ports of space,
Beating their sides to make its fury heard.

Are you shouting at me, dead man, squeezing your face
In agonies of speech on speechless panes?
Cry louder, beat the windows, bawl your name!

But I hear nothing, nothing . . . only bells,
Five bells, the bumpkin calculus of Time.
Your echoes die, your voice is dowsed by Life,
There's not a mouth can fly the pygmy strait—
Nothing except the memory of some bones
Long shoved away, and sucked away, in mud;
And unimportant things you might have done,
Or once I thought you did; but you forgot,
And all have now forgotten—looks and words
And slops of beer; your coat with buttons off,
Your gaunt chin and pricked eye, and raging tales

Of Irish kings and English perfidy,
And dirtier perfidy of publicans
Groaning to God from Darlinghurst.

Five bells.

Then I saw the road, I heard the thunder
Tumble, and felt the talons of the rain
The night we came to Moorebank in slab-dark,
So dark you bore no body, had no face,
But a sheer voice that rattled out of air
(As now you'd cry if I could break the glass),
A voice that spoke beside me in the bush,
Loud for a breath or bitten off by wind,
Of Milton, melons, and the Rights of Man,
And blowing flutes, and how Tahitian girls
Are brown and angry-tongued, and Sydney girls
Are white and angry-tongued, or so you'd found.
But all I heard was words that didn't join
So Milton became melons, melons girls,
And fifty mouths, it seemed, were out that night,
And in each tree an Ear was bending down,
Or something had just run, gone behind grass,
When, blank and bone-white, like a maniac's thought,
The naphtha-flash of lightning slit the sky,
Knifing the dark with deathly photographs.
There's not so many with so poor a purse
Or fierce a need, must fare by night like that,
Five miles in darkness on a country track,
But when you do, that's what you think.

Five bells.

In Melbourne, your appetite had gone,
Your angers too; they had been leeched away
By the soft archery of summer rains
And the sponge-paws of wetness, the slow damp
That stuck the leaves of living, snailed the mind,
And showed your bones, that had been sharp with rage,
The sodden ecstasies of rectitude.
I thought of what you'd written in faint ink,

Your journal with the sawn-off lock, that stayed behind
With other things you left, all without use,
All without meaning now, except a sign
That someone had been living who now was dead:
'At Labassa. Room 6 × 8
On top of the tower; because of this, very dark
And cold in winter. Everything has been stowed
Into this room—500 books all shapes
And colours, dealt across the floor
And over sills and on the laps of chairs;
Guns, photoes of many differant things
And differant curioes that I obtained . . .'

In Sydney, by the spent aquarium-flare
Of penny gaslight on pink wallpaper,
We argued about blowing up the world,
But you were living backward, so each night
You crept a moment closer to the breast,
And they were living, all of them, those frames
And shapes of flesh that had perplexed your youth,
And most your father, the old man gone blind,
With fingers always round a fiddle's neck,
That graveyard mason whose fair monuments
And tablets cut with dreams of piety
Rest on the bosoms of a thousand men
Staked bone by bone, in quiet astonishment
At cargoes they had never thought to bear,
These funeral-cakes of sweet and sculptured stone.

Where have you gone? The tide is over you,
The turn of midnight water's over you,
As Time is over you, and mystery,
And memory, the flood that does not flow.
You have no suburb, like those easier dead
In private berths of dissolution laid—
The tide goes over, the waves ride over you
And let their shadows down like shining hair,
But they are Water; and the sea-pinks bend
Like lilies in your teeth, but they are Weed;

And you are only part of an Idea.
I felt the wet push its black thumb-balls in,
The night you died, I felt your eardrums crack,
And the short agony, the longer dream
The Nothing that was neither long nor short;
But I was bound, and could not go that way,
But I was blind, and could not feel your hand.
If I could find an answer, could only find
Your meaning, or could say why you were here
Who now are gone, what purpose gave you breath
Or seized it back, might I not hear your voice?

I looked out of my window in the dark
At waves with diamond quills and combs of light
That arched their mackerel-backs and smacked the sand
In the moon's drench, that straight enormous glaze,
And ships far off asleep, and Harbour-buoys
Tossing their fireballs wearily each to each,
And tried to hear your voice, but all I heard
Was a boat's whistle, and the scraping squeal
Of seabirds' voices far away, and bells,
Five bells. Five bells coldly ringing out.

                                        Five bells.

BEACH BURIAL

Softly and humbly to the Gulf of Arabs
The convoys of dead sailors come;
At night they sway and wander in the waters far under,
But morning rolls them in the foam.

Between the sob and clubbing of the gunfire
Someone, it seems, has time for this,
To pluck them from the shallows and bury them in burrows
And tread the sand upon their nakedness;

And each cross, the driven stake of tidewood,
Bears the last signature of men,
Written with such perplexity, with such bewildered pity,
The words choke as they begin—

'*Unknown seaman*'—the ghostly pencil
Wavers and fades, the purple drips,
The breath of the wet season has washed their inscriptions
As blue as drowned men's lips,

Dead seamen, gone in search of the same landfall,
Whether as enemies they fought,
Or fought with us, or neither; the sand joins them together,
Enlisted on the other front.

El Alamein.

R. D. FITZGERALD

———— ✧ ————

ROBERT D. FITZGERALD was born in 1902 at Hunter's Hill, a Sydney suburb, where he lived most of his life. He was a relative of Mary Gilmore. FitzGerald abandoned a science course at the University of Sydney and became a surveyor, working in Fiji for five years, then returning to Australia where he eventually became the senior surveyor for the New South Wales State Government. He was influenced by the cultural theories of the painter and novelist Norman Lindsay, and published his early work in the Lindsayite journal *Vision*. His long philosophical poem 'Essay on Memory' won a major poetry competition in 1938, and established his reputation.

For many years FitzGerald and Slessor were spoken of in tandem, as Australia's outstanding modern poets. Some critics, Australian and American, saw FitzGerald as belonging to the front rank of contemporary English-language poets. More recently FitzGerald's reputation has declined. His content is still admired: his hard-won optimism; his insistence that activity, despite death and eventual obliteration, is worthwhile for its own sake; and also his ability to deal with large philosophical problems. But his language is felt to be unmusical and laboured. 'The Face of the Waters' is exceptional amongst FitzGerald's work in its freedom of form and unhampered movement. He here successfully gives an imaginative, sensory scope to his preoccupation with the philosopher Whitehead's metaphysical system.

THE FACE OF THE WATERS

Once again the scurry of feet—those myriads
crossing the black granite; and again
laughter cruelly in pursuit; and then
the twang like a harpstring or the spring of a trap,
and the swerve on the polished surface: the soft little pads
sidling and skidding and avoiding; but soon caught up
in the hand of laughter and put back . . .

There is no release from the rack
of darkness for the unformed shape,
the unexisting thought
stretched half-and-half
in the shadow of beginning and that denser black
under the imminence of huge pylons—
the deeper nought;
but neither is there anything to escape,
or to laugh,
or to twang that string which is not a string but silence
plucked at the heart of silence.

Nor can there be a floor to the bottomless;
except in so far as conjecture must arrive,
lungs cracking, at the depth of its dive;
where downward further is further distress
with no change in it; as if a mile and an inch
are equally squeezed into a pinch,
and retreating limits of cold mind
frozen, smoothed, defined.

Out of the tension of silence (the twanged string);
from the agony of not being (that terrible laughter
tortured by darkness); out of it all
once again the tentative migration; once again
a universe on the edge of being born:
feet running fearfully out of nothing
at the core of nothing:
colour, light, life, fearfully
becoming eyes and understanding: sound becoming ears . . .

For eternity is not space reaching
on without end to it; not time without end to it,
nor infinity working round in a circle;
but a placeless dot enclosing nothing,
the pre-time pinpoint of impossible beginning,
enclosed by nothing, not even by emptiness—
impossible: so wholly at odds with possibilities
that, always emergent and wrestling and interlinking
they shatter it and return to it, are all of it and part of it.
It is your hand stretched out to touch your neighbour's,
and feet running through the dark, directionless like darkness.

Worlds that were spun adrift re-enter
that intolerable centre;
indeed the widest-looping comet
never departed from it;
it alone exists.
And though, opposing it, there persists
the enormous structure of forces, laws,
as background for other coming and going,
that's but a pattern, a phase, no pause,
of ever-being-erected, ever-growing
ideas unphysically alternative
to nothing, which is the quick. You may say hills live,
or life's the imperfect aspect of a flowing
that sorts itself as hills; much as thoughts wind
selectively through mind.
The egg-shell collapses
in the fist of the eternal instant;
all is what it was before.
Yet is that eternal instant
the pinpoint bursting into reality,
the possibilities and perhapses,
the feet scurrying on the floor.
It is the suspense also

with which the outward thrust
holds the inward surrender—
the stresses in the shell before it buckles under:
the struggle to magpie-morning and all life's clamour and lust;
the part breaking through the whole;
light and the clear day and so simple a goal.

A. D. HOPE

--- ❧ ---

ALEC DERWENT HOPE was born in 1907 at Cooma, New South Wales, son of a Presbyterian minister, and spent most of his childhood at a manse in rural Tasmania. He was schooled at home in his earlier years, his mother having been a teacher, his father taking him for Latin. At Sydney University he won the university medal in both English and philosophy and went on a scholarship to Oxford, but he was unhappy there and failed to take a degree. Returning to Australia in the Depression, he became a school teacher and later a lecturer at Sydney Teachers' College within the University of Sydney, where he formed a close friendship with James McAuley, ten years his junior. They were strong influences on each other's work, but when McAuley converted to Catholicism their interests began to diverge. Hope moved to the English department at the University of Melbourne and then became professor of English at the Australian National University in Canberra, where he remained until his retirement in 1968.

Hope's first book of poetry was published in 1955, when he was forty-eight and had been writing for many years. The delay is attributable to the explicitly sexual content of much of his early work. Although he quickly became part of the literary 'establishment', when *The Wandering Islands* appeared, Hope was long regarded as a 'wild man' and an outsider, even though a professor. He was also making a reputation as a particularly acerbic reviewer, determined to disrupt the self-cosseting standards of the Australian literary world of the time. He deplored any social purpose in literature, insisting literary values alone should be applied. He was suspicious of the obscurity of experimental modes, believing a good mind can make itself coherent, and opposed surrealism and dissociation as self-indulgence. These ideas—shared with McAuley—were influenced by the classicism of John Anderson of Sydney University, the leading philosopher in Australia of that era. Most notorious of all Hope's criticism was his attack on Patrick White's novels; he also wrote a post mortem on free verse. Both these positions have been rather ruefully modified.

Hope has acknowledged a difficulty in writing about his homeland and directly of his own experience, since his work typically has an intellectual origin and is written 'to illuminate an idea'. Mythology, the classics and European culture often provide the catalyst or reference point for his poems.

The most profound influence on Hope's attitudes has been Nietzsche. A theme is his disgust with those who may be identified with Nietzsche's 'last men'—the self-indulgent, suburban, vicariously-experiencing, technologically-protected modern citizen. Hope's *Ubermensch* is the scientist or intellectually-daring artist who challenges conventional ideas and easy solutions. Poetry is the subjective, value-creating response to a rational, objective picture of the world. Celebration, the proper concern of poetry, includes for him 'an intellectual assent to the causes that make the natural world an order and system, and an imaginative grasp of ... its processes'. He is an addict, he says, of popularised science. He sees the natural world as being entirely physical processes, and humans as continuous with this, as literally beasts, though not necessarily to be despised because of that. We are noble in our capacity to witness to the truth, and to create 'new orders of being' through the imagination, through art.

Though never of Norman Lindsay's circle, it is Hope who best conveys in poetry many of Lindsay's ideas—the individualism, the 'healthy' lustfulness, the admiration for strenuous achieving, the paganism, the caricatured 'classicism'. His women are often only their primary sexual characteristices (although Hope has written in 'Advice to Young Ladies' one of the outstanding feminist poems by an Australian)—they are visualised as in Lindsay's art: great Wagnerian nudes, as white and pink and dolloped with their attributes as meringue. Most likely Hope found his affinity with Lindsay's 'vision' through admiration for the poetry of Hugh McCrae. Of all the influences apparent in Hope's work and acknowledged by him— Byron, Pope, Baudelaire, Yeats—it is that of McCrae which feels most fundamental. There is a similar boisterous, vulgarly energetic quality, a similar neo-classical theatre and caricature. The difference is the much wider scope and intelligence of Hope.

Hope was appropriated by a group of Melbourne academic writers during the 1950s, led by the Catholic poet and critic Vincent Buckley, but, apart from a proselytising formalism and expository style, has little in common with them. ('Ode on the Death of Pius the Twelfth' is a rare agnostic moment in Hope's work.) He values individualism and vigour, and has remained carnal, pluralist, sceptical, and a celebrator of human achievements.

THE DAMNATION OF BYRON

When the great hero, adding to the charms
Of genius and his scandals, left the light
Stamped with the irresistible trade of arms,
The Hell of Women received him as their right.

Through the Infernal Fields he makes his way
Playing again, but on a giant stage,
His own Don Juan; pursuing day by day
Childe Harold's last astonishing pilgrimage.

It is the landscape of erotic dreams:
The dim, brown plains, the country without air
Or tenderness of trees by hidden streams,
But cactus or euphorbia here and there

Thrusts up its monstrous phallus at the sky.
And moving against this silvered, lustrous green
Like a pink larva over the whole dry
Savannah of hell, the bodies of women are seen.

And at his coming all their beauties stir
Mysterious, like the freshening of a rose
As, the incomparable connoisseur,
Pale and serene across their world he goes,

Always there rises glowing in his path,
Superb and sensual, in the light that pours
A tarnished glory on the soil of death,
This leafless nakedness of tropic flowers;

The female body's impersonal charm, the curves
Of a young head poised on its gracious stalk.
The idiom of her gesture he observes,
That tender dislocation of her walk.

Held in his brain's deep lupanar they float,
The tapering trunk, the pure vase of the hips,
The breasts, the breasts to which the hands go out
Instinctive, the adoring finger-tips,

The thighs incurved, the skin misted with light,
The mouth repeating its own rich circumflex . . .
At first he moves and breathes in his delight
Drowned in the brute somnambulism of sex.

He is a kind of symbol of the male:
As a great bull, stiffly, deliberately
Crosses his paddock, lashing his brutal tail,
The sullen engine of fecundity,

So, in his first youth and his first desire,
His air of pride and the immortal bloom,
Once more he sets the feminine world on fire,
Passing in his romantic blaze of gloom.

Prodigious vigour flowers new in him:
Each morning nerves him with heroic lust.
His thoughts are women, he breathes, is clothed with them,
He sinks on something female in the dust.

He has them all, all the menagerie
Of race, the subtle stimulus of shapes:
Negresses in their first nubility
With the sad eyes and muzzles of young apes,

Vast Scandinavian divinities
Superbly modelled, for all their cowlike air,
The pale bread of their bellies' magnificent rise
From the blond triangle of pubic hair,

And slender girls with delicate golden shanks
And elongated skulls from lost Peru . . .
The sensual emphasis of the Spaniard's flanks,
And the callipygous haunches of the Jew . . .

Dancers and whores, blue-stockings, countesses,
Types of La Fornarina and Caroline Lamb,
All the seductions of all mistresses,
The savage, the sentimental and the sham . . .

And yet he is alone. At first he feels
Nothing above the tumult of his blood,
While through his veins like the slow pox there steals
The deep significance of his solitude.

And from this feeling without haste or pause
Vengeance predestined sharpens, bit by bit;
As lust its anaesthesia withdraws
The force of his damnation grows from it.

Grows as the mind wakes inexorably
The critic, the thinker, the invincible
Intelligence at last detached and free
Wakes, and he knows . . . he knows he is in hell.

And there begins in him that horrible thing,
Clairvoyance, the cruel nightmare of escape:
He seeks companions: but they only bring
Wet kisses and voluptuous legs agape . . .

He longs for the companionship of men,
Their sexless friendliness. He cannot live
'Like the gods in Lucretius once again'
Nor ever in woman's wit and charm forgive

The taint of the pervading feminine
Yet always to this nausea he returns
From his own mind—the emptiness within
Of the professional lover. As he learns

How even his own society has become
A horror, a loneliness he cannot bear,
The last stage of Don Juan's martyrdom,
The last supreme resources of despair

Appear, and brutally lucid he descends
Simply to treat them as The Enemy.
His lust becomes revenge, his ardour lends
Insatiable pleasure to his insanity.

As he exhausts himself in the delights
Of torture, gourmandising in their pain,
Hate eats his features out: it seethes and bites
Like a slow acid. It destroys his brain.

Yet this resource betrays him, even this,
For like tormented demons, they adore
Their torment. They revere like savages
The god's ferocity with lascivious awe.

Until, neurotic, hounded by strange fears,
At last his journey changes to a flight.
Delirious, broken, fugitive, he hears
Marching and countermarching in the night,

The panic of vague terrors closing in:
Whichever way he turns he hears them come.
Far off immeasurable steps begin,
Far off the ominous mumble of a drum,

And from the bounds of that dim listening land
Approaches with her grave incessant tread
The Eternal Goddess in whose placid hand
Are all the happy and all the rebellious dead.

Before her now he stands and makes his prayer
For that oblivion of the Second Death . . .
When suddenly those majestic breasts all bare
Riding the tranquil motion of her breath

Reveal the body of her divinity:
The torso spread marmoreal, his eyes
Downwards uncover its mighty line and see
Darkness dividing those prodigious thighs.

There as he stares, slowly she smiles at him . . .
And the great hero, mad with the terrible
Madness of souls, turns fleeing, while the dim
Plains heave with the immense derision of Hell.

THE RETURN FROM THE FREUDIAN ISLANDS

When they heard Sigmund the Saviour in these coasts
The islanders were very much impressed;
Abandoned the worship of their fathers' ghosts
And dedicated temples to their guest,

Shocked and delighted as the saint revealed
The unacknowledged body and made them see,
Suppressed by corsets, morbidly concealed
In cotton combinations, neck to knee,

How it bred night-sweats, the disease of shame,
Corns, fluxions, baldness and the sense of sin,
How clothes to the Analytic Eye became
Fantasies, furtive symbols of the skin.

At first the doctrine took them all by storm;
Urged to be stark, they peeled as they were told;
Forgetting their rags had also kept them warm,
For the island climate is often extremely cold.

And if the old, the wry, the ugly shared
Some natural reluctance to begin it,
Enthusiasts all, the young at once declared
Their Brave Nude World, that had such people in it.

Till some discovered that stripping to the buff
Only exposed the symbol of The Hide:
Its sinister pun unmasked, it must come off,
The saint must preach The Visible Inside!

The saint, though somewhat startled at this view,
Trapped by the logic of his gospel, spent
Some time in prayer, and in a week or two,
To demonstrate the new experiment,

Breastless and bald, with ribbed arms, lashless eyes,
In intricate bandages of human meat,
With delicate ripple and bulge of muscled thighs,
The first skinned girl walked primly down the street.

Though there were many to admire her charms:
The strappings and flexures of twig-like toes, the skeins
And twisted sensitive cables of her arms,
The pectoral fans, the netting of nerves and veins:

Yet those who followed her example found
One lack—till Sigmund undertook to prove
How much their late behaviour centred round
A common skin disease they had called love.

And for a time they thoroughly enjoyed
The brisk intolerance of the purified,
In sects and schisms before The Holy Freud
Self-torn—while lesser saints were deified.

Till Faith, which never can let well alone,
From heresy and counter-heresy
Prompted the saint to bare beneath the bone
The Ultimate Visceral Reality.

Long time he mused before The Sacred Id,
Long prayed, before he finally began
And, purged, impersonal, uninhibited,
Produced at last The Basic Freudian Man.

At the Fertility Festival that year
The skinned men blushed to see the skeleton,
A bone-cage filled with female guts appear
Tottering before them in the midday sun.

Its slats and levering rods they saw, the full
Cogged horseshoe grin of two and thirty teeth,
The frantic eyeballs swivelling in the skull,
The swagging human umbles underneath,

The soft wet mottled granite of the lung
Bulge and collapse, the liver worn askew
Jauntily quiver, the plump intestines hung
In glistening loops and bolsters in their view,

And clear through gut and bowel the mashy chyme
Churn downward; jelled in its transparent sheath
The scowling foetus tethered, and the time-
Bomb tumour set unguessed its budded death.

And while for them with mannequin grace she swayed
Her pelvis, Sigmund, so that none should miss
The beauty of the new world he had made,
Explained The Triumph of Analysis:

Pimples and cramps now shed with pelt and thews,
No dreams to fright, no visions to trouble them,
For, where the death-wish and self-knowledge fuse,
They had at last The Human L.C.M. . . .

Here the saint paused, looked modestly at the ground
And waited for their plaudits to begin.
And waited . . . There was nothing! A faint, dry sound
As first a poet buttoned on his skin.

The Martyrdom of St Teresa

There was a sudden croon of lilies
Drifting like music through the shop;
The bright knives flashed with heavenly malice,
The choppers lay in wait to chop;

And Jesus with his crown of briar
Worn like a little hat in *Vogue*
Picked up her soul of ruby fire
And popped it in his shopping bag.

She was so small a saint, a holy
Titbit upon the butcher's block—
Death chose the cuts with care and slowly
Put on his apron, eyed the clock

And sitting down serenely waited
Beside the plump brown carcass there,
Which kings had feared and the popes hated,
Which had known neither hate nor fear;

While through all Spain mysterious thunder
Woke cannibal longings in the blood,
Inviting man to put asunder
The flesh that had been joined with God.

The little nuns of her foundation
Arrived on foot, by mule or cart,
Each filled with meek determination
To have an elbow, or the heart.

Death with a smile expertly slices
A rib for one, for one the knee,
Cuts back a breast, cuts deeper, prises
Out the raw heart for all to see;

In Sister Philomena's basket
Safe for St Joseph's lies an arm;
The saw shrills on a bone, the brisket
Becomes a miracle-working charm;

At five to six Death drops his cleaver:
The sunset, as the crowd goes home,
Pours down on every true believer
The mystic blood of martyrdom.

THE DOUBLE LOOKING GLASS

See how she strips her lily for the sun:
The silk shrieks upward from her wading feet;
Down through the pool her wavering echoes run;
Candour with candour, shade and substance meet.

From where a wet meniscus rings the shin
The crisp air shivers up her glowing thighs,
Swells round a noble haunch and whispers in
The dimple of her belly. . . . Surely eyes

Lurk in the laurels, where each leafy nest
Darts its quick bird-glance through the shifting screen.
. . . . Yawn of the oxter, lift of liquid breast
Splinter their white shafts through our envious green

Where thuds this rage of double double hearts.
. . . . My foolish fear refracts a foolish dream.
Here all things have imagined counterparts:
A dragon-fly dim-darting in the stream

Follows and watches with enormous eyes
His blue narcissus glitter in the air.
The flesh reverberates its own surprise
And startles at the act which makes it bare.

Laced with quick air and vibrant to the light,
Now my whole animal breathes and knows its place
In the great web of being, and its right;
The mind learns ease again, the heart finds grace.

I am as all things living. Man alone
Cowers from his world in clothes and cannot guess
How earth and water, branch and beast and stone
Speak to the naked in their nakedness.

. . . . A silver rising of her arms, that share
Their pure and slender crescent with the pool
Plunders the braided treasure of her hair.
Loosed from their coils uncrowning falls the full

Cascade of tresses whispering down her flanks,
And idly now she wades a step, and stays
To watch the ripples widen to the banks
And lapse in mossy coves and rushy bays.

Look with what bliss of motion now she turns
And seats herself upon a sunny ledge,
Leans back, and drowsing dazzles, basking burns.
Susannah! . . . . what hiss, what rustle in the sedge;

What fierce susurrus shifts from bush to bush?
. . . . Susannah! Susannah, Susannah! . . . . Foolish heart,
It was your own pulse lisping in a hush
So deep, I hear the water-beetle dart

And trace from bank to bank his skein of light,
So still the sibilance of a breaking bud
Speaks to the sense; the hairy bee in flight
Booms a brute chord of danger in my blood.

What danger though? The garden wall is high
And bolted and secure the garden door;
The bee, bold ravisher, will pass me by
And does not seek my honey for his store;

The speckled hawk in heaven, wheeling slow
Searches the tufts of grass for other prey;
Safe in their sunny banks the lilies grow,
Secure from rough hands for another day.

Alert and brisk, even the hurrying ant
Courses these breathing ranges unafraid.
The fig-tree, leaning with its leaves aslant,
Touches me with broad hands of harmless shade.

And if the urgent pulses of the sun
Quicken my own with a voluptuous heat,
They warm me only as they warm the stone
Or the thin liquid paddling round my feet.

My garden holds me like its private dream,
A secret pleasure, guarded and apart.
Now as I lean above the pool I seem
The image of my image in its heart.

In that inverted world a scarlet fish
Drifts through the trees and swims into the sky,
So in the contemplative mind a wish
Drifts through its mirror of eternity.

A mirror for man's images of love
The nakedness of woman is a pool
In which her own desires mount and move,
Alien, solitary, purposeful

Yet in this close were every leaf an eye,
In those green limbs the sap would mount as slow.
One with their life beneath an open sky,
I melt into the trance of time, I flow

Into the languid current of the day.
. . . . The sunlight sliding on a breathing flank
Fades and returns again in tranquil play;
Her eyelids close; she sleeps upon the bank.

Now, now to wreak upon her Promised Land
The vengeance of the dry branch on the bud.
Who shall be first upon her? Who shall stand
To watch the dragon sink its fangs in blood?

Her ripeness taunts the ignominy of age;
Seethes in old loins with hate and lust alike.
Now in the plenitude of shame and rage
The rod of chastisement is reared to strike.

And now to take her drowsing; now to fall
With wild-fire on the cities of the plain;
Susannah! . . . . Yet once more that hoarse faint call,
That rustle from the thicket comes again?

Ah, no! Some menace from the edge of sleep
Imposes its illusion on my ear
Relax, return, Susannah; Let the deep
Warm tide of noonday bear you; do not fear,

But float once more on that delicious stream.
Suppose some lover watches from the grove;
Suppose, only suppose, those glints, the gleam
Of eyes; the eyes of a young man in love.

Shall I prolong this fancy, now the sense
Impels, the hour invites? Shall I not own
Such thoughts as women find to recompense
Their hidden lives when secret and alone?

Surprise the stranger in the heart, some strong
Young lion of the rocks who found his path
By night, and now he crouches all day long
Beside the pool to see me at my bath.

He would be there, a melancholy shade
Caught in the ambush of his reckless joy,
Afraid to stir for fear I call, afraid
In one unguarded moment to destroy

At once the lover and the thing he loves.
Who should he be? I cannot guess; but such
As desperate hope or lonelier passion moves
To tempt his fate so far, to dare so much;

Who having seen me only by the way,
Or having spoken with me once by chance,
Fills all his nights with longing, and the day
With schemes whose triumph is a casual glance.

Possessed by what he never can possess,
He forms his wild design and ventures all
Only to see me in my nakedness
And lurk and tremble by the garden wall.

He lives but in my dream. I need repel
No dream for I may end it when I please;
And I may dream myself in love as well
As dream my lover in the summer trees,

Suppose myself desired, suppose desire,
Summon that wild enchantment of the mind,
Kindle my fire at his imagined fire,
Pity his love and call him and be kind.

Now think he comes, and I shall lie as still
As limpid waters that reflect their sun,
And let him lie between my breasts and fill
My loins with thunder till the dream be done.

The kisses of my mouth are his; he lies
And feeds among the lilies; his brown knees
Divide the white embraces of my thighs.
Wake not my love nor stir him till he please,

For now his craft has passed the straits and now
Into my shoreless sea he drives alone.
Islands of spice await his happy prow
And fabulous deeps support and bear him on.

He rides the mounting surge, he feels the wide
Horizon draw him onward mile by mile;
The reeling sky, the dark rejoicing tide
Lead him at last to this mysterious isle.

In ancient woods that murmur with the sea,
He finds once more the garden and the pool.
And there a man who is and is not he
Basks on the sunny margin in the full

Noon of another and a timeless sky,
And dreams but never hopes to have his love;
And there the woman who is also I
Watches him from the hollow of the grove;

Till naked from the leaves she steals and bends
Above his sleep and wakes him with her breast
And now the vision begins, the voyage ends,
And the great phoenix blazes in his nest.

. . . . Ah, God of Israel, even though alone,
We take her with a lover, in the flush
Of her desires. SUSANNAH! . . . . I am undone!
What beards, what bald heads burst now from the bush!

ODE ON THE DEATH OF PIUS THE TWELFTH

To every season its proper act of joy,
To every age its natural mode of grace,
Each vision its hour, each talent we employ
    Its destined time and place.

I was at Amherst when this great pope died;
The northern year was wearing towards the cold;
The ancient trees were in their autumn pride
    Of russet, flame and gold.

Amherst in Massachusetts in the Fall:
I ranged the college campus to admire
Maple and beech, poplar and ash in all
    Their panoply of fire.

Something that since a child I longed to see,
This miracle of the other hemisphere:
Whole forests in their annual ecstasy
    Waked by the dying year.

Not budding Spring, not Summer's green parade
Clothed in such glory these resplendent trees;
The lilies of the field were not arrayed
    In riches such as these.

Nature evolves their colours as a call,
A lure which serves to fertilize the seed;
How strange then that the splendour of the Fall
    Should serve no natural need.

And, having no end in nature, yet can yield
Such exquisite natural pleasure to the eye!
Who could have guessed in summer's green concealed
    The leaf's resolve to die?

Yet from the first spring shoots through all the year,
Masked in the chlorophyll's intenser green,
The feast of crimson was already there,
    These yellows blazed unseen.

Now in the bright October sun the clear
Translucent colours trembled overhead
And as I walked, a voice I chanced to hear
    Announced: The Pope is dead!

A human voice, yet there the place became
Bethel: each bough with pentecost was crowned;
The great trunks rapt in unconsuming flame
    Stood as on holy ground.

I thought of this old man whose life was past,
Who in himself and his great office stood
Against the secular tempest as a vast
    Oak spans the underwood;

Who in the age of Armageddon found
A voice that caused all men to hear it plain,
The blood of Abel crying from the ground
    To stay the hand of Cain;

Who found from that great task small time to spare:
—For him and for mankind the hour was late—
So much to snatch, to save, so much to bear
    That Mary's part must wait,

Until in his last years the change began:
A strange illumination of the heart,
Voices and visions such as mark the man
    Chosen and set apart.

His death, they said, was slow, grotesque and hard,
Yet in that gross decay, until the end
Untroubled in his joy, he saw the Word
    Made spirit and ascend.

Those glorious woods and that triumphant death
Prompted me there to join their mysteries:
This Brother Albert, this great oak of faith,
    Those fire-enchanted trees.

Seven years have passed, and still, at times, I ask
Whether in man, as in those plants, may be
A splendour, which his human virtues mask,
    Not given to us to see?

If to some lives at least there comes a stage
When, all the active man now left behind,
They enter on the treasure of old age,
    This autumn of the mind.

Then, while the heart stands still, beyond desire
The dying animal knows a strange serene:
Emerging in its ecstasy of fire
    The burning soul is seen.

Who sees it? Since old age appears to men
Senility, decrepitude, disease,
What Spirit walks among us, past our ken,
    As we among these trees,

Whose unknown nature, blessed with keener sense
Catches its breath in wonder at the sight
And feels its being flood with that immense
    Epiphany of light?

MOSCHUS MOSCHIFERUS

A song for St Cecilia's Day

In the high jungle where Assam meets Tibet
The small Kastura, most archaic of deer,
Were driven in herds to cram the hunter's net
And slaughtered for the musk-pods which they bear;

But in those thickets of rhododendron and birch
The tiny creatures now grow hard to find.
Fewer and fewer survive each year. The search
Employs new means, more exquisite and refined:

The hunters now set out by two or three;
Each carries a bow and one a slender flute.
Deep in the forest the archers choose a tree
And climb; the piper squats against the root.

And there they wait until all trace of man
And rumour of his passage dies away.
They melt into the leaves and, while they scan
The glade below, their comrade starts to play.

Through those vast, listening woods a tremulous skein
Of melody wavers, delicate and shrill:
Now dancing and now pensive, now a rain
Of pure, bright drops of sound and now the still

Sad wailing of lament; from tune to tune
It winds and modulates without a pause;
The hunters hold their breath; the trance of noon
Grows tense; with its full power the music draws

A shadow from a juniper's darker shade;
Bright-eyed, with quivering muzzle and pricked ear,
The little musk-deer slips into the glade
Led by an ecstasy that conquers fear.

A wild enchantment lures him, step by step
Into its net of crystalline sound, until
The leaves stir overhead, the bowstrings snap
And poisoned shafts bite sharp into the kill.

Then as the victim shudders, leaps and falls,
The music soars to a delicious peak,
And on and on its silvery piping calls
Fresh spoil for the rewards the hunters seek.

But when the woods are emptied and the dusk
Draws in, the men climb down and count their prey,
Cut out the little glands that hold the musk
And leave the carcasses to rot away.

A hundred thousand or so are killed each year;
Cause and effect are very simply linked:
Rich scents demand the musk, and so the deer,
Its source, must soon, they say, become extinct.

Divine Cecilia, there is no more to say!
Of all who praised the power of music, few
Knew of these things. In honour of your day
Accept this song I too have made for you.

ON AN ENGRAVING BY CASSERIUS

for Dr John Z. Bowers

Set on this bubble of dead stone and sand,
Lapped by its frail balloon of lifeless air,
Alone in the inanimate void, they stand,
These clots of thinking molecules who stare
Into the night of nescience and death,
And, whirled about with their terrestrial ball,
Ask of all being its motion and its frame:
This of all human images takes my breath;
Of all the joys in being a man at all,
This folds my spirit in its quickening flame.

Turning the leaves of this majestic book
My thoughts are with those great cosmographers,
Surgeon adventurers who undertook
To probe and chart time's other universe.
This one engraving holds me with its theme:
More than all maps made in that century
Which set true bearings for each cape and star,
De Quiros' vision or Newton's cosmic dream,
This reaches towards the central mystery
Of whence our being draws and what we are.

It came from that great school in Padua:
Casserio and Spiegel made this page.
Vesalius, who designed the *Fabrica*,
There strove, but burned his book at last in rage;
Fallopius by its discipline laid bare

The elements of this humanity,
Without which none knows that which treats the soul;
Fabricius talked with Galileo there:
Did those rare spirits in their colloquy
Divine in their two skills the single goal?

'One force that moves the atom and the star,'
Says Galileo; 'one basic law beneath
All change!' 'Would light from Achernar
Reveal how embryon forms within its sheath?'
Fabricius asks, and smiles. Talk such as this,
Ranging the bounds of our whole universe,
Could William Harvey once have heard? And once
Hearing, strike out that strange hypothesis,
Which in *De Motu Cordis* twice recurs,
Coupling the heart's impulsion with the sun's?

Did Thomas Browne at Padua, too, in youth
Hear of their talk of universal law
And form that notion of particular truth
Framed to correct a science they foresaw,
That darker science of which he used to speak
In later years and called the Crooked Way
Of Providence? Did *he* foresee perhaps
An age in which all sense of the unique,
And singular dissolves, like ours today,
In diagrams, statistics, tables, maps?

Not here! The graver's tool in this design
Aims still to give not general truth alone,
Blue-print of science or data's formal line:
Here in its singularity he has shown
The image of an individual soul;
Bodied in this one woman, he makes us see
The shadow of his anatomical laws.
An artist's vision animates the whole,
Shines through the scientist's detailed scrutiny
And links the person and the abstract cause.

Such were the charts of those who pressed beyond
Vesalius their master, year by year
Tracing each bone, each muscle, every frond
Of nerve until the whole design lay bare.
Thinking of this dissection, I descry
The tiers of faces, their teacher in his place,
The talk at the cadaver carried in:
'A woman—with child!'; I hear the master's dry
Voice as he lifts a scalpel from its case:
'With each new step in science, we begin.'

Who was she? Though they never knew her name,
Dragged from the river, found in some alley at dawn,
This corpse none cared, or dared perhaps, to claim;
The dead child in her belly still unborn,
Might have passed, momentary as a shooting star,
Quenched like the misery of her personal life,
Had not the foremost surgeon of Italy,·
Giulio Casserio of Padua,
Bought her for science, questioned her with his knife,
And drawn her for his great *Anatomy*;

Where still in the abundance of her grace,
She stands among the monuments of time
And with a feminine delicacy displays
His elegant dissection: the sublime
Shaft of her body opens like a flower
Whose petals, folded back expose the womb,
Cord and placenta and the sleeping child,
Like instruments of music in a room
Left when her grieving Orpheus left his tower
Forever, for the desert and the wild.

Naked she waits against a tideless shore,
A sibylline stance, a noble human frame
Such as those old anatomists loved to draw.
She turns her head as though in trouble or shame,
Yet with a dancer's gesture holds the fruit

Plucked, though not tasted, of the Fatal Tree.
Something of the first Eve is in this pose
And something of the second in the mute
Offering of her child in death to be
Love's victim and her flesh its mystic rose.

No figure with wings of fire and back-swept hair
Swoops with his: Blessed among Women!; no sword
Of the spirit cleaves or quickens her; yet there
She too was overshadowed by the Word,
Was chosen, and by her humble gift of death
The lowly and the poor in heart give tongue,
Wisdom puts down the mighty from their seat;
The vile rejoice and rising, hear beneath
Scalpel and forceps, tortured into song,
Her body utter their magnificat.

Four hundred years since first that cry rang out:
Four hundred years, the patient, probing knife
Cut towards its answer—yet we stand in doubt:
Living, we cannot tell the source of life.
Old science, old certainties that lit our way
Shrink to poor guesses, dwindle to a myth.
Today's truths teach us how we were beguiled;
Tomorrow's how blind our vision of today.
The universals we thought to conjure with
Pass: there remain the mother and the child.

Loadstone, loadstar, alike to each new age,
There at the crux of time they stand and scan,
Past every scrutiny of prophet or sage,
Still unguessed prospects in this venture of Man.
To generations, which we leave behind,
They taught a difficult, selfless skill: to show
The mask beyond the mask beyond the mask;
To ours another vista, where the mind
No longer asks for answers, but to know:
What questions are there which we fail to ask?

Who knows, but to the age to come they speak
Words that our own is still unapt to hear:
'These are the limits of all you sought and seek;
More our yet unborn nature cannot bear.
Learn now that all man's intellectual quest
Was but the stirrings of a foetal sleep;
The birth you cannot haste and cannot stay
Nears its appointed time; turn now and rest
Till that new nature ripens, till the deep
Dawns with that unimaginable day.'

The Ballad of Dan Homer

O, me name is Dan Homer; I'm blind as the Jews
And I travels about with me head full of news;
But the gods call me Danny and teach me the rhymes,
Though I've never been home since the Classical Times.

Now all yez young women from Dublin to Greece,
Gather round me and take home a warnin' apiece:
There's a terrible feller called Zeus-Take-the-Lot
And yez never can tell if he's up yez or not.

Ye'll not see him come and ye'll not see him go,
But he'll have the drawers off yez before ye sez no.
Sure, a girl may be walkin' as trim as a queen
And the next thing she knows she's arse-up on the green.

O, the girls that he's ruined, yez wouldn't believe,
And each time, bedad, a new trick up his sleeve;
And none of your Mollys-Come-Roll-on-the-Grass,
But fine, genteel girls of the good social class.

Europa was keepin' the cows from the corn
When a well-spoken bull comes up dippin' his horn:
'Would yez care for a turn, Ma'am?' She gets up astride
And I gives yez one guess, then, who had the last ride.

There was Danaë's dad, just as cunnin' as mean,
Shuts her up in the top of a brazen machine.
'Twas no trouble at all, sure, for Zeus-Take-the-Lot
He soon found a penny to place in the slot.

There was Leda was takin' a bath in the brook
When a bloody great bird paddles up for a look.
Sez she: 'Where's the harm?', never thinkin' of Zeus;
So she goes for a tickle and gets the whole goose.

There was Semele set with her back to the fire,
For the ease of her arse lifts her petticoats higher;
When the hearth gives a heave and the fire gives a crack
And it's Zeus gives her beautiful bottom a smack.

There was Io mistook him for love-in-a-mist;
Alcmene—But there now, to tell the whole list,
Callisto, Antiope, girls by the score
Would take me a month, faith, and still there'd be more.

So every young woman that walks out alone,
If a stone sez: 'Good-day Ma'am!', don't sit on that stone;
If Barney's bull speaks to yez, hurry indoors
And never go out without two pairs of drawers.

If he knocks on your door, girls, don't answer at all
For he'll not wait to hang up his hat in the hall,
And once yez allow him a dip in the pot,
Ye'll be rockin' a cradle for Zeus-Take-the-Lot.

So here's to the lass with the big, meltin' heart
And the pretty mavourneen that thinks herself smart.
Faith, the run of the mill boys is easy to fix,
But a girl can't keep up with a god and his tricks.

EVE LANGLEY

———— ✢ ————

B ORN IN FORBES, New South Wales, in 1908, Eve Langley
is known for one novel, *The Pea-Pickers*, although she also
published a sequel to this, *White Topee*. Langley went to New Zea-
land, married there, and had three children by her husband and one
illegitimately. She spent several years in New Zealand in a mental
hospital.

Returning to Australia, she tried to enter the Sydney literary scene,
but soon withdrew to a shack in the bush of the Blue Mountains
and worked on what eventually amounted to another eleven novels.
Despite the sympathy of editors at Angus and Robertson, such as
Beatrice Davis and Douglas Stewart, who regarded *The Pea-Pickers*
as a classic, these later novels could not be published, because of
the uncontrolled elaborateness of their style and their illegibility.
It seems Langley continued to type long after her typewriter ribbons
had worn out.

At the age of fifty Langley adopted the name Oscar Wilde by deed
poll, and something of his persona and dress. She always wore men's
clothes, to which she added a sheath knife in her belt, and a white
topee, and she was obsessed with guns. When she died her house
was found to be full of brown paper parcels which contained only
folded chicken wire, stones or feathers. Steve, the boisterous heroine
of her two published novels discovers in *White Topee* that, 'What I
really wanted to be was a man.'

Langley wrote only a few poems, which are not collected.

NATIVE BORN

In a white gully among fungus-red
Where serpent logs lay hissing at the air,
I found a kangaroo. Tall, dewy, dead,
So like a woman, she lay silent there,
Her ivory hands, black-nailed, crossed on her breast,
Her skin of sun and moon hues, fallen cold.
Her brown eyes lay like rivers come to rest
And death had made her black mouth harsh and old.
Beside her in the ashes I sat deep
And mourned for her, but had no native song
To flatter death, while down the ploughlands steep
Dark young Camelli whistled loud and long,
'Love, liberty and Italy are all.'
Broad golden was his breast against the sun.
I saw his wattle whip rise high and fall
Across the slim mare's flanks, and one by one
She drew the furrows after her as he
Flapped like a gull behind her, climbing high,
Chanting his oaths and lashing soundingly,
While from the mare came once a blowing sigh.
The dew upon the kangaroo's white side
Had melted. Time was whirling high around,
Like the thin woomera, and from heaven wide
He, the bull-roarer, made continuous sound.
Incarnate, lay my country by my hand:
Her long hot days, bushfires and speaking rains,
Her mornings of opal and the copper band
Of smoke around the sunlight on the plains.
Globed in fire bodies the meat-ants ran
To taste her flesh and linked us as we lay,
For ever Australian, listening to a man
From careless Italy, swearing at our day.
When, golden-lipped, the eaglehawks came down
Hissing and whistling to eat of lovely her,
And the blowflies with their shields of purple brown
Plied hatching to and fro across her fur,

I burnt her with the logs, and stood all day
Among the ashes, pressing home the flame
Till woman, logs and dreams were scorched away,
And native with night, that land from where they came.

RONALD McCUAIG

———— ⚘ ————

RONALD McCUAIG WAS born at Newcastle, New South Wales, in 1908. He has been a journalist all his working life, employed by *Wireless Weekly* from 1928 to 1938, and later by the Australian Broadcasting Commission, *Smith's Weekly*, the *Bulletin* (for which he wrote light verse under the name 'Swilliam'), and the Department of Information. McCuaig's 'serious' poetry, which is light in tone, is far more successful than his topical verse, though its supposed lightness has caused his neglect. His own modesty may also have contributed—it has persuaded him to pass himself off to fellow writers in his later years as a public servant, seemingly without irony. McCuaig was a friend of Slessor, who admired his acerbic love poems, written from the viewpoint of a clerk living in the high-rise dilapidation of Sydney's Kings Cross during the 1930s. His best poetry, apart from the outstanding examples here, is most often colloquial, and satirises the plight, ploys and manoeuvrings of the sexes, in their relations to each other. A *Selected Poems*, which appeared in 1992, has no work more recent than that of the late fifties.

MRS AGNES MCCUAIG AT THE PIANO

(Études, Op. 25, No. 2: Chopin)

Fluttering like leaves, the flickering triplets
Replace the hands that play with hands that played
In music's kinematic light and shade.
Creating you, the music begets
Chopin, your composer, for me, your composition,
Muttering, 'These young women fill me with contrition,
Studying my studies without thought of recognition
Endlessly, endlessly, endlessly, endlessly. . . .'

'No, no, no, Chopin. This time you are mistaken.
I shall avenge her, I am a poet. She had me taught to speak,
And I shall use my elocution in praise of her technique:
The grave will open! The dead will awaken!'
'She is well-spared your second-rate critique.
What had she that biographers might seek?'
                    'She read me books, she gave me toys,
                    She sang of comical negro boys;
                    She cried and cried when Judy died
                    With a broken back
                    On a book bush-track;
If she turned you could see the flames of her brilliant eyes—'
'Let her face the keys. We die when music dies.
Elusive as my music she will soon be gone,
Wavering on and on, and on and on. . . .'

Ghost of gaiety, guest of grief,
I have grown older, now, because of you
Than you, because of me, could manage to;
Soon you will be beyond belief,
And no one left who knew you, or could say
How you threw all that ecstasy away:

Enchant me with the void where we belong,
My mother of memory,
My man of melody,
My child of song.

Au Tombeau de mon Père

I went on Friday afternoons
Among the knives and forks and spoons
Where mounted grindstones flanked the floor
To my father's office door.

So serious a man was he,
The Buyer for the Cutlery. . . .
I found him sketching lamps from stock
In his big stock-records book,

And when he turned the page to me:
'Not bad for an old codger, eh?'
I thought this frivolous in him,
Preferring what he said to them:

They wanted reparations paid
In German gold and not in trade,
But he rebuked such attitudes:
'You'll have to take it out in goods.'

And what they did in time was just,
He said, what he had said they must:
If Time had any end in sight
It was, to prove my father right.

The evening came, and changed him coats,
Produced a rag and rubbed his boots,
And then a mirror and a brush
And smoothed his beard and his moustache;

A sign for blinds outside to fall
On shelves and showcases, and all
Their hammers, chisels, planes and spades,
And pocket-knives with seven blades.

Then, in the lift, the patted back:
'He's growing like you, Mr Mac!'
(The hearty voices thus implied
A reason for our mutual pride.)

And so the front-door roundabout
Gathered us in and swept us out
To sausage, tea in separate pots,
And jellies crowned with creamy clots.

And once he took me on to a
Recital, to hear Seidel play,
And Hutchens spanked the piano-bass,
Never looking where it was.

When I got home I practised this,
But somehow always seemed to miss,
And my cigar-box violin,
After Seidel's, sounded thin.

And once he took me to a bill
Of sporadic vaudeville.
A man and woman held the stage;
She sneered in simulated rage,

And when he made a shrewd reply
He'd lift his oval shirt-front high
And slap his bare and hairy chest
To celebrate his raucous jest.

Then, as the shout of joy ensued,
Uniting mime and multitude,
And mine rang out an octave higher,
A boy-soprano's in that choir,

My father's smile was half unease,
Half pleasure in his power to please:
'Try not to laugh so loudly, Ron;
Those women think you're catching on.'

But far more often it was to
The School of Arts we used to go;
Up the dusty stairway's gloom,
Through the musty reading-room

And out to a veranda-seat
Overlooking Hunter Street.
There in the dark my father sat,
Pipe in mouth, to meditate.

A cake-shop glowed across the way
With a rainbow-cake display;
I never saw its keeper there,
And never saw a customer,

And yet there was activity
High in the south-western sky:
A bottle flashing on a sign
Advertising someone's wine.

So, as my father thought and thought
(Considering lines of saws he'd bought,
Or, silence both his church and club,
Feeling close to Nature's hub,

Or maybe merely practising
Never saying anything,
Since he could go, when deeply stirred,
Months, at home, without a word,

Or pondering the indignity
Of having to put up with me),
I contemplated, half awake,
The flashing wine, the glowing cake:

The wine that no one can decant,
And the cake we didn't want:
As Mr Blake's Redeemer said,
'This the wine, and this the bread.'

ELIZABETH RIDDELL

———— ✤ ————

E LIZABETH RIDDELL WAS born in 1910 in New Zealand, and came to Australia immediately she left school, invited by a Sydney newspaper editor to work as a journalist on the strength of some schoolgirl verses she had published in a magazine. 'They thought that a poet might make a journalist,' she has remarked, adding 'It was terrible poetry.' Her fare was paid, and her rent for two weeks, and she immediately had to produce a theatre page. She has since become one of Australia's most respected newspaper women, a career she has greatly enjoyed, in which she has 'done everything', and which has brought her the prestigious Walkley Award. In 1942 she went to New York for eighteen months, to open an office for her Sydney employer, and was then transferred to London as a war correspondent, and later to Paris. After her return to Australia, in 1945, she worked on a national women's magazine; and now, supposedly retired, continues to work as a book reviewer for the *Bulletin* magazine and for a television programme. Her marriage to the journalist E.N. Greatorex was a notably happy one. They had no children, and 'never meant to'.

Elizabeth Riddell has published four collections of poetry, the latest in 1989, and a selected volume, in 1991. Her poetry, she has said, has been strongly influenced both in style and content by her career as a journalist. It is occasional poetry, not driven to explore overriding themes, but it has an admirable readability, and a sureness in finding the emotional depth in a seemingly ordinary subject. Her work has, in tension with its spareness, a very unjournalistic aestheticism.

WAKEFUL IN THE TOWNSHIP

Barks the melancholy dog,
Swims in the stream the shadowy fish.
Who would live in a country town
If they had their wish?

When the sun comes hurrying up
I will take the circus train
That cries, cries once in the night
And then not again.

In the stream the shadowy fish
Sleeps below the sleeping fly.
Many around me straitly sleep
But not I.

Near my window a drowsy bird
Flickers its feathers against the thorn.
Around the township's single light
My people die and are born.

I will join the circus train
For mangy leopard and tinsel girl
And the trotting horses' great white haunches
Whiter than a pearl.

When to the dark blue mountains
My captive pigeons flew
I'd no heart to lure them back
With wheat upon the dew.

When the dog at morning
Whines upon the frost
I shall be in another place.
Lost, lost, lost.

OCCASIONS OF BIRDS

I

I heard on the radio how birds in Assam
lifted like a cloud over the camellia forest
and flew to a village in the last light.
There it was warm and filled with other wings
transparent and flickering.
They dashed themselves against the smoking lamps and fell
into the street
onto the trodden stems of water hyacinth.

Women who had been picking tea
all day on the hillside
came down to the village
holding their baskets against their muslin skirts
and their skirts away from the bleeding feathers
in fear and surprise. There was hardly a sound
when the wings ceased to beat.

It was south of the Kahsi hills where the Brahmaputra flows
the birds flowed to their death in the soft night.

II

In Dar-es-Salaam the morning lay on us like wet silk.
We bought fruit in thin slices and yellow bead rings,
waiting for the news of the tornado, the hurricane,
the cyclone, the typhoon
crouched in the opaque sky.

We ran before the hurricane
to Malagasy, to Réunion, to Mauritius
where it caught us, cast us on the beach
beside the tourist cabins and the sugar cane,
both with rats.

Port Louis was under water, we saw with dismay.
The corpses of duck dinners
floated in the gutter under blind windows
and past the closed doors of schools.

Reflected in this aberrant lake, old cool houses
suitable for provincial nobles and for slaves
brooded under wisteria. Their columns were erected
in memory of the Loire.

I recalled reading about the pink pigeons of Mauritius.
They had tiny heads and supplicating voices,
poor flakes of pink driven out when the forest was felled
to make way for the chateaux.
There is not one left to complain.

III

Governor Hunter despatched
many a live bird to England
to bleach in the fog, attempt a trill
in Hove or Lockerbie
and marvel through the bars
at rain on the pale honeyed flowers
and at honeyeaters dancing on the rain.

As Governor Hunter and his men marched west
the sun struck gold from epaulettes
and sparkled on the cages ready for the feather,
the bright eye, the tender claw, the beak
of the lyrebird and the cockatoo
(the rosy one, the sulphur-crested screamer, the shining black)
and the paradise parrot of which Leach says
'it is an exquisite creature,
in general green below and blue above'
(like forest, like sky)
'with red shoulders'
(at sunset out-sparkling the Governor's gold)
'and a red forehead. It nests in sandhills.'

One hundred and eighty years later
a man is out there in the dunes
searching for the paradise parrot.
Listen as he walks, crab-scuttle on the sand.
He has not much to offer this bird
which saw the gold and heard the sound of fife and drum.

IV

We were in a foreign country
reading in a newspaper about another foreign country—
well, hardly foreign at all
since once we saw it from a deck,
a smudge of cloud on cloud, Mangere Island in the lonely Chathams
twelve thousand miles away in the long fall
of grey seas. Reading about the five black robins
last of their race,
news because they were about to die.
As with a few Indians along the Amazon,
robins and Indians, the only news,
small items because so far away and small
and about to die.

Rain sluiced the colonnades
where they sold the International Herald Tribune
(how to rent a palazzo, share a car to Munich, learn Chinese)
with baseball scores from home.
Rare robins, the item said,
rare black robins, three females and two males.
The usual ratio, we're used to it.

It's cold on Mangere. The waves swing in across the rocks
great shawls of kelp.
Three men were on Mangere
with tents and paperbacks and Tarot cards
a radio, tinned butter, binoculars
to watch the robins, and suddenly spied
after fifteen years the orange-breasted parakeet
risen again, a flame rekindled from the phoenix fire.
What next? The black stilt or the kakapo?
The parrot like an owl that walks, stately, instead of flying?
We doubt if they'll turn up.

The birds will be reprogrammed. Not much to do
with chirping, building nests or catching gnats
or even flying. It's cold on Mangere
for orange-breasted parakeets and such.

WILLIAM HART-SMITH

———— ❧ ————

B ORN IN ENGLAND in 1911, Hart-Smith emigrated to New
Zealand with his parents as a boy, and first came to Australia
when he was twenty-five. After serving with the Australian army
within Australia during World War II, he returned to New Zealand
until the early sixties, then settled back in Australia, first in Sydney
and later in Perth. He worked mainly in advertising or as a radio
broadcasting technician in Australia, and in adult education in New
Zealand. Most of his poetry is set on this side of the Tasman, and it
is here that his main collections have been published.

After a nervous collapse and hospitalisation in Perth, where he had
taught creative writing, Hart-Smith returned once more to live in
New Zealand in 1978. He died in Auckland of a stroke, aged seventy-
nine, leaving a dozen books of poetry and four children.

Hart-Smith was one of the principal contributors to the nationalist
Jindyworobak movement of the late thirties and the forties (see Roland
Robinson's biography), out of his fascination with the outback, where
he travelled during his war service. In technique his imagist free
verse shows the influence of D. H. Lawrence (although nowhere
more than in 'Nullarbor' which remains a genuinely personal poem)
and also of William Carlos Williams, in its tightly-controlled, impro-
vised rhythms, and its expressive use of enjambment. Hart-Smith's
is the earliest application of the Williams poetic in Australia. Unlike
Williams he often makes use of impromptu rhyming.

Hart-Smith's work is detracted from by a *faux-naif* tone of voice
and by whimsy. It too often plays at being charming, along the edge
of the trivial and the cute. He does have a satisfying austerity and, in
many poems, striking imagery.

NULLARBOR

Here earth and sky are reduced to an ultimate simplicity,
The earth to a completely flat circle,
An ocean-circle of red soil with flecks of white limestone,
Patches of dead brown grass and stiff dead bushes
And tuft-like clumps and knots of dwarf bushes
That look dead,
But really grip their lives tightly away from the sun,
Grip hold of their lives with little hard fists.
The leaves
Are leathery tongues with a small spittle of salt in them.
And the sky is a pure thing,
A flawless cover of glass,
An inverted glass cover upon a table.

When the train stopped I swung my legs over the side,
jumped down from the roped truck and sat on the dry hot boards of
    the flat-top,
My feet dangling over, idly swinging, my hands behind me,
The palms taking a print from the rough wood
And the cinders and grit,
Making up my mind to take the next jump, the leap to the track,
And curiously examining a reluctance to do so . . .
Sleepers, a slope of cinders and metal, then
The desert, the miraculous, empty, utterly pure desert,
The clean desert and the clean bright wind,
The rim out there
Not abruptly ending, but broken,
An undercutting and a flowing into,
The sky running into the earth and the earth running into the sky,
Long liquid lines of sky, opaque, making inroads into the rim,
The edge of the world,
And long low islands floating . . .
Mirage.
It is the hot air rising.
The air becoming hot and beginning to tremble and throb and dance,
Destroys the abruptness, the clean cut-off.

And then you appeared. There you were, suddenly there in the
    desert
Beyond the train, beyond the line of waiting trucks,
As if you had suddenly appeared out of nothing,
With your black body, your brush of sun-bleached hair
And the stick stuck in your belt
Behind you, sticking out like a tail.
You were not looking at us. You were walking away from us when
    you appeared,
Walking away in a queer loping fashion
Going off at an angle with your back to us.
My legs stopped swinging and I stared at you, fascinated,
Looked into your back and wondered what it was you were after,
You, boy . . .
I saw you were a boy.
You stopped then, turned back and ran a little distance,
Then turned again and walked straight towards me,
Closer and closer, till I could see into your eyes,
Closer, without stopping; then you swung yourself up onto the flat-
    top beside me
And sat there looking out over the desert.

How long did we sit there? How long was it we sat there saying
    nothing?
Perhaps an eternity. Sat there saying nothing.
I could hear your breathing. Your body had a familiar strong smell,
An earth smell, a special earth smell;
And I thought of the leaves with the taste of brine in them,
The spicy tang of them, the gnarled old bushes,
Life bunched up in their fists.

I changed. Slowly I changed. I became a grotesque thing.
I became white-skinned, a human being with a white skin . . .
Grotesque!
A thin being with a sharp nose and a strong reek,
Huddled into myself, covered up, cowering away from life,
A distorted thing with my senses only half awake,
My eyes only half opened, my nostrils clogged with a numbing
    deadness,

My ears with a pressure on the drums,
Only partly sensitive.

It was an eternity. I know it was.

Did you break it because of me? Did you speak at last because you
    knew what was happening to me?
Did you do it to save me?
You moved,
You pointed upward with your finger at a bird, a solitary great bird
    with white wings tipped with brown,
Spiralling, making circles, great wide circles and spirals with
    motionless huge wings
High over our heads . . .
'Eaglehawk,' you said. 'Eaglehawk.'

It's funny, but you accepted me then. We used the code of stranger
    approaching stranger.
You came and sat down beyond the limits of my camp,
The camp of my personality and the small fire of my heart,
Waiting with your back to it before my thoughts sent out their
    women
With food and drink, went out and brought you in. We talked.
You asked for a cigarette. I gave you one and lit it for you.
I can see my white hands cupped against the brown skin of your
    face.
The deep ridge of brows as you bent over my hands and sucked in
    the flame; the tuft of beard on your chin.
A boy.
I remarked to myself on the rich body quality of your voice
And unconsciously deepened the tones of my own.
You talked as you smoked, the cigarette looking silly and pathetic in
    your fingers,
Held between ball of thumb and forefinger.

Then my own world broke in. It came
Out of the future, out of the future from a terrible distance,
Roared down on me and shrieked, and pounded fists on my heart.
The clash of jerked couplings shattered something in my head.

You jumped down. I heard above the noise the soft crunch of your
    feet as they hit the ground
And you looked at me over your shoulder, then turned away,
Turned your back on me and walked away
With that queer loose-swinging lope of yours,
That straight-backed, loose-limbed walk full from the hips.
You walked away and never looked back.

I sat there as the train moved
And the ground began to slide sideways under my feet,
Sideways under my boots,
Until the blur made me giddy and sick.
And when I looked up you had gone.
I looked back, but you had gone.
The desert was flowing away to the left
Bringing the clean wind strong on the right side of my head;
And the stones and low bushes were flowing away, faster and faster,
Faster. Only the desert remained itself, remained unchanged,
Flowing away from itself,
Yet continually renewing itself from right to left, faster, faster,
And the wind a gale,

And under me a grind and clatter of wheels.

from MAN INTO TREES

for Caroline Kalmar

Here, nothing is ever folded
and put away:

leaf, stick, twig, shards
of bark, like shed garments,

are simply dropped when finished with,
and turn to compost where they lie.

Pollen is spilled upon the glass
of a dressing-table top;

earring petals drop
and rust where they are fallen.

The floors and walls are damp,
tier upon tier of shelves of stone descend

scattered with gritty pebbles
and glittering sand.

But not a tidy notion troubles
the innocent conscience of this land,

a sweet, sweet odour rises,
a lovely fragrance comes

of spilled unguents, spices,
and aromatic gums.

ROLAND ROBINSON

————— 🙰 —————

B ORN IN IRELAND of English parents in 1912, Roland
Robinson was nine years old when he came to Australia. At
fourteen he was already working on a sheep station in outback
NSW, first as a houseboy and then as a rouseabout and boundary
rider. Later in his working life he was a horse-trainer, jockey, fencer,
dam builder, factory worker, railway fettler, cleaner, art school
model, member of a ballet company, gardener, helped catch croco-
diles and snakes for a menagerie, and in his last job was the green-
keeper of a golfcourse in Sydney. During the Second World War, as
a conscientious objector, he had to labour on railway lines in the
Northern Territory. It was here that he had his first contact with
tribal Aborigines, having already sought out detribalised blacks on
the south coast of NSW. Until very recently he has been the only
white poet to listen to, and collect, the anecdotes and oral traditions
of these people, which he has set down in verse and prose.

Intensely attracted by the Australian landscape and the bushman's
ethos, always a radical, Robinson joined whole-heartedly from its
beginning in the Jindyworobak programme—to write out of the
uniqueness of the Australian environment, and to incorporate Abo-
riginal culture—after meeting the group's founder, Rex Ingamells,
in Adelaide. He has come to be seen as the Jindyworobaks' most
successful poet.

Robinson wrote eight small volumes of poetry, five prose works on Aboriginal myths and legends, a book of stories about the relationships of Aborigines and whites, and three volumes of autobiography. These last reveal an extremely emotional, driven nature. He regularly fled to the bush to escape routine, or what he felt as emotional demands. A man of striking looks, his relationships with women were difficult and twice ended tragically. He died in 1992.

Robinson was devoted to the poetry of Edward Thomas, for the purity of its impulse and style, and he valued Brennan's 'The Wanderer' above all other Australian poems. These influences show as both naturalness and elevation in his work, but he has an intensity that is all his own—his best poems 'burn and gleam' with the colours of the outback and of the coastal bush. His poems can have a rather *fin de siècle* lushness of emotion at times, but this appears so unexpectedly in their landscape that it is appealing. His work has been undervalued because it is small in scope and lacks any intellectual scheme, but its vividness and emblematic force amply compensate.

DRIFTING DUG-OUT

Now that the fig lets fall her single stars
of flowers on these green waters I would be
withdrawn as Gul-ar-dar-ark the peaceful dove
sending his callings over the many springs,
over the fountains and the jets of song
of Nin the finch and Geek-keek the honeyeater.
I would be withdrawn as Gul-ar-dar-ark calling
out of the distant sky and tresses of the leaves,
now that the fig lets fall her single flowers
like stars to pass beyond my trailing hand.

TO A MATE

He was a man who, with his hand,
would make the language of the sand
that showed where piccaninny walked,
where emu trod or dingo stalked.

Euro's pad or writhe of snake,
or brolga's imprint he could make.
And he was one to booze and brawl
and lie beside the fire asprawl.

He was a man, when moved, who spoke
of how at Innaminka soak,
when the molten west grew dim,
the creatures from the desert's rim

came in to drink and play as he
lay watching by a hakea tree,
where stars and dingo howls, he swore
were solitude not known before.

Wherever now with swag outspread
he camps by soak or river-bed,
would that I saw his camp-fire's sparks
and hailed him through the paper-barks.

CASUARINA

The last, the long-haired casuarina
stands upon the hillside where
against the turquoise night of those first
yellow stars, she shakes her hair.

She shakes her hair out in her singing
of cliffs and caves and waterfalls,
and tribes who left the lichened sandstone
carved in gods and animals.

This is her country: honeyeaters
cry out its Aboriginal name
where on her ridges still the spear tall
lilies burn in flame and flame.

I listen, and our legend says not
more than this dark singing tree,
although her golden flowering lover
lies slain beside the winter sea.

THE DROVERS

Over the plains of the whitening grass
and the stunted mulga the drovers pass,
and in the red dust cloud, each side
of the cattle, the native stockmen ride.

And day after day lays bare the same
endless plains as the way they came,
and ever the cloven ranges lie
at the end of the land and the cloudless sky.

With creak of pack and saddle leather,
and chink of chain and bit together,
with moan of the herd, with hobble and bell
they come to the tanks at the tea-tree well.

And through corroding blood–red hills,
by sanded rivers the Gulf rain fills,
far, where the morning star has shone
and paled above, their tracks are gone.

THE PRISONERS

After our labouring train had passed
through those red sandridges at last
and, straightening out, went racing for
dark mountains in the desert's floor,
I saw, in that red-purple land,
the bearded Italian prisoners stand
beside the line until our train
should pass to let them toil again.
Then, clinging to the rushing car,
I leaned out, shouting: Come sta!
And, from blurred faces by the track,

heard: Bene! Bene! shouted back.
I looked and saw them where they stood
against those ridges red as blood,
looked and saw them lessen and
be lost in spinifex and sand.
There, we were carried northward while
my vision stayed and shared exile
with those men whom, I believed,
the blood deep desert had received.

NORTHERN ORIOLE

The tumult ends, the downpour stops.
On broad palm leaves the large warm drops
cling. That bird calls out again
as though his throat were filled with rain.
From tree to tree he glides among
the dripping leaves and makes his song.
Now from the poinciana's bough
sounds his echoing song, and now
deep within the banyan's shade,
that bell like, flute cool call is made.
High in the orange flowering gum
his voice is heard, but where I come
he makes no more that blended note
as though the rain had filled his throat.
Swooping, with folded wings he goes
over the far tree tops for those
mountains of the clouds and where
the storms let down their purple hair.

Deep Well

I am at Deep Well where the spirit trees
writhe in cool white limbs and budgerigar
green hair along the watercourse carved out
in deep red earth, a red dry course that goes
past the deep well, past the ruined stone
homestead where the wandering blacks make camp
(their campfire burning like a star at rest
among dark ruins of the fallen stone)
to find the spinifex and ochre red
sandhills of a land inhabited by those
tall dark tribesmen with long hair and voices
thin and far and, deepening, like a sea.
I am at Deep Well where the fettlers' car
travels towards the cool blue rising wave
that is the Ooraminna Range, and starts
those pure birds screaming from the scrub to swerve,
reveal their pristine blush in wings and breasts,
to scatter, settle and flower the desert-oak.
Here I have chosen to be a fettler, work
to lay the red-gum sleepers, line and spike
the rails with adze and hammer, shovel and bar,
to straighten up and find my mates, myself
lost in the spinifex flowing down in waves
to meet the shadow-sharpened range and know
myself grown lean and hard again with toil.
Here, in the valley camp where hills increase
in dark blue depths, the desert hakea stands
holding the restless finches and a single star.

YOOLA AND THE SEVEN SISTERS

related by Minyanderri

Yoola, always wanting women,
women run from him,
sees seven women, seven sisters,
and chases after them.

The seven sisters are frightened.
Whirring, they leave the ground.
They travel down the sky and at
a rock-hole come down.

From that place the seven women
look back and see that man
coming still, and to another
waterhole they run.

Yoola walks all round that place.
Steep cliffs rise
all round the sisters. The cliffs
echo their cries.

Through the only gap comes Yoola.
At him the sisters run.
Yoola, grasping at the sisters,
misses every one.

The sisters run into the desert.
Among waterless sands,
they make ritual with song and
dance and clapping hands.

Yoola, tired in the desert,
drags his spear along
behind him. Sandhills rise
at his ritual song.

Yoola camps. There, he stands
his spear upright.
In that place a sacred gum-tree
grows up in the night.

Yoola camps. He lays his spear
down on the ground.
In that place he leaves a
stone spear behind.

From waterhole to waterhole
the seven sisters run.
Yoola, carrying his spear,
thinks of them one by one.

The seven sisters are running
between two ranges' walls.
Yoola, on a rearing cliff,
sings his rituals.

The sisters rest beside a soak.
Yoola comes again.
The sisters scatter, come together
far out on the plain.

At Wankareenga waterhole
cliffs rise all about
the seven sisters. Yoola comes.
There is no way out.

'The waterhole,' the sisters shriek.
They plunge, and swimming down,
with Yoola swimming after them,
one by one they drown.

The spirits of the sisters
went up into the sky.
And Yoola followed after
running hard close by.

The sisters are those seven stars
running away in fright.
Yoola is the big star close
beside them in the night.

MAPOORAM

related by Fred Biggs

Go out and camp somewhere. You're lying down.
A wind comes, and you hear this 'Mapooram'.
'What's that?' you say. 'Why, that's a "Mapooram".'
You go and find that tree rubbing itself.
It makes all sorts of noises in the wind.
It might be like a sheep, or like a cat,
or like a baby crying, or someone calling,
a sort of whistling-calling when the wind
comes and swings and rubs two boughs like that.

A Wirreengun, a clever-feller, sings
that tree. He hums a song, a 'Mapooram':
a song to close things up, or bring things out,
a song to bring a girl, a woman from that tree.
She's got long hair, it falls right down her back.
He's got her for himself. He'll keep her now.

One evening it was sort of rainy-dark.
They built a mia-mia, stripping bark.
You've been out in the bush sometime and seen
them old dry pines with loose bark coming off.
You get a lot of bark from them dry pines,
before they rot and go too far, you know.
That woman from the tree, she pulled that bark.
It tore off, up and up the tree. It pulled
her up into the tree, up, up into the sky.
Well, she was gone. That was the end of it.
No more that Wirreengun could call her back.

'Mapooram. Mapooram.' 'What's that?' you say.
Why, that's two tree boughs rubbing in the wind.

THE STAR-TRIBES

related by Fred Biggs

Look, among the boughs. Those stars are men.
There's Ngintu, with his dogs, who guards the skins
of Everlasting Water in the sky.
And there's the Crow-man, carrying on his back
the wounded Hawk-man. There's the Serpent, Thurroo,
glistening in the leaves. There's Kapeetah,
the Moon-man, sitting in his mia-mia.

And there's those Seven Sisters travelling
across the sky. They make the real cold frost.
You hear them when you're camped out on the plains.
They look down from the sky and see your fire
and, 'Mai, mai, mai!' they sing out as they run
across the sky. And, when you wake, you find
your swag, the camp, the plains all white with frost.

JOHN BLIGHT

———— 🐚 ————

J OHN BLIGHT WAS born in 1913 and has spent almost all of his life in Queensland. During the Depression in the 1930s he tramped the coastline of that state looking for work. In 1939 he took up an accountant's job in Bundaberg. For a while during World War II he was a prices inspector for the Commonwealth Government, and later became part owner of a timber mill at Maryborough. He is married, with a family. In 1968 he retired and went to live in Brisbane.

Blight's work first appeared in the *Bulletin*, and he became widely appreciated when he began to publish his remarkable 'sea sonnets', which have been collected in two volumes, *A Beachcomber's Diary* (1963) and *My Beachcombing Days* (1968). The sonnet, inventively manhandled, was the ideal form to concentrate Blight's sinewy, untidy, flashing and wry meditations on life. His sonnets, as they strain to break out of their framework, are about the mind being as rich and strange as the ocean.

In later poems, mainly on urban subjects and not represented here, Blight has rejected fixed form. His intention is now often obscure and his lines routinely end on a preposition or an article—a device used so reiteratively it loses any expressive function. Disgust about urban humanity, anger at old age, and lust are recurring themes. Never complacent, Blight has become more uncomfortable over time.

NOR'-EASTER

The straw broom of the nor'-east sweeps the beach.
Yellow, raking straws of sand, stinging, cleansing, scratch
my raw legs; but no woman can I see,
my head hung low, while she is ranting at me.
Not my day; not a day for dogs, or gulls,
or canvas flapping. Cleaning the beach, squalls
threatening, cumulus cumbersome in the hills
of the sea-littoral; this wind kills
all joy of the beach, is a steamroller wife
of a man by the sea. All my life
I have been sullenly subdued when she blows.
Only some little good in all her bluster shows:
she cleans the beach, sweeps, beats the sand.
For the white strand of her morning, I once took her hand.

FISHERMAN AND JETTY

Old jetty, wade with me out into the sea
and there let us watch ship and shag pass;
knee-deep I, thigh-deep you. We
with our reasons to be there: standing in the glass
sea, rod in hand, crane on deck;
each under scrutiny, looking a wreck,
yet part of the scene which people on shore
come here, long hours, to gaze at . . .
'Will he catch a fish?' 'The jetty is more
like Japanese torii with that
missing wood decking.' They're speaking of us.
If we were on land, they'd never discuss
two such old derelicts. So—the sea honours all,
the quick and the dead, that age in its thrall.

STINGRAY BAY

I live at a place where the seasons change each day,
where the tide comes in, goes out, in Stingray Bay:
where there's sunshine, rain-shower, storm, and calm;
green mangrove, pine-tree, she-oak, coconut palm.
There's mud-crab, sand-crab, shark, and crocodile;
and mudflat, sandbank. A reef runs out a mile
to sea in Stingray Bay. On any old day here,
the sandflies will prove even giants fear;
and, if you choose to wade in Stingray Bay,
there's poisonous stonefish, cone-shells, so they say.
And yet it is a place where children play
and swim and paddle, much to the dismay
of the occasional tourist who comes here, astray,
misguided by the map to Stingray Bay.

CRAB

Shellfish and octopus, and all the insane
Thinking of the undersea, to us is lost.
At most is food, in our higher plane.
But, what of this submarine ghost—
Life, without its meddling monkey? Can
The crab regenerate into prototype merman?
Sea, of nightmare pressure and mask—
Green faces in the gloom—what is your task
In creation; or is it over? Has space
Such aquariums of planets trapped? Was
Eden thus? Oh, pressures which the lace
Sponge of the brain survives. What has
The life of the sea of my ignorance,
But such creatures; much of this wild-shaped chance!

SEA-LEVEL

Over this flat-pan sea, this mud haven,
this shelf of the sea-floor, sea-birds paddle
and the red mud raddles the sea.
You are on creation's level. Proven
your lowly origin, where, in one puddle,
sea-snails and your toes agree—
the same spasms and rhythms. Stub
on a rock, or a sharp stab of a beak;
they draw in. Pain is the one language
spoken to them. You, in the sky, snub
your feet. Impediments! But can you take
your brain's cloud and drift, disengage
those 'body's worms'? Try: disconnect
the thought from their feeling, and soon the soul is wrecked.

THE SHARK

There, in the first breaker, was the shark's shape
trailing the pilchards black in their escape;
so tightly packed, they blacked out the sea
just as a storm cloud does the blue sky.
But, ignorantly, the immigrant waded right in.

'Get out! Get out, you fool!' some bawled above the din
and train-noise of the rolling surf.

Unheard of, in Poland, any danger from a wolf
in the water. Why were they crying, trying to divert
the surfer from his pleasure? In a sea-girt
country he was living now. No warring Prussia,
no fear, ancient fear, of old steam-roller Russia.

In a sea-girt country he was living without fear,
and now they must tell him death loiters near.

THE CORAL REEF

In the baroque style of coral, India,
Java, your conglomerate gods assemble.
Having just walked the reef at low water,
I have a fear of their numbers, a psychic tremble,
a mental numbness at my failure to describe
their Nirvana, their inscrutable jungle of peace
—a peace that is death in stone. As though a rib
were stolen from every mortal, each piece
cemented in place a monument to mankind—a reef?

I walked it—walked on the faces of its gods,
on their many visages . . . on my own belief,
I fear: exhausted my many moods,
my paucity of words—a failure at expression
by this mass of death: unable to follow its vast progression.

DOUGLAS STEWART

—————— ❧ ——————

D OUGLAS STEWART, BORN in 1913 at Eltham, New Zealand, was the son of a lawyer who had emigrated from Melbourne. Stewart, one of Australia's most nationalistic poets, first came to this country in 1933, for a short stay, and then returned to settle in 1938. He felt that his Australian father made him a native of his adopted country.

Stewart came to Sydney to write for the Red Page, the well known literary pages of the *Bulletin*, which published poetry, short stories, reviews and editorial commentary. He was the section's editor from 1940 until 1961, when the magazine was taken over. He then joined Angus and Robertson, the largest, most established Australian publisher, as editor of the prestigious poetry list, and remained there until 1971, when again as the result of a takeover he lost his job. He was married to Margaret Coen, the watercolourist, who had modelled for Norman Lindsay when she was young. He died in 1985.

Stewart was the closest disciple of Lindsay, and the artist responded to the younger poet with equal enthusiasm. Stewart sympathised with Lindsay's anti-modernism, but not his dionysian streak, being genteel to a fault.

Under Stewart's editorship, the Red Page regained its position as the central forum for Australian literature, particularly poetry, but this could not save the rest of the magazine dwindling in relevance.

Stewart championed the young Francis Webb, and regularly published Judith Wright, R.D. FitzGerald, Rosemary Dobson, John Blight, David Campbell, Roland Robinson, and many others. For more than twenty years he encouraged Australian poets to write accessibly, without obscure experiment or academicism, particularly about the country's unique landscape. He preferred poems in fixed form, but was less dogmatic about this than were Hope and McAuley. He and the communist poet John Manifold independently helped revive interest in the bush ballads. He also contributed to a fashion for poem sequences, celebrating the early maritime and outback explorers, which Slessor had begun with 'Five Visions of Captain Cook'.

The poetry Stewart wrote in New Zealand as a young man, such as 'Mending the Bridge', when he may have been looking towards the current thirties English style, uses language which is notably vigorous and contemporary, compared with the language of his later Australian work. In Australia his style became more traditional and closer to the English Georgian poets of earlier in the century.

Stewart wrote six verse plays, some of them enjoying considerable success, but his lyric poetry is his most durable work.

MENDING THE BRIDGE

Burnished with copper light, burnished,
The men are brutal: their bodies jut out square
Massive as rock in the lanterns' stormy glare
Against the devastation of the dark.
Now passionate, as if to gouge the stark
Quarry of baleful light still deeper there
With slow gigantic chopping rhythm they hack,
Beat back and crumple up and spurn the black
Live night, the marsh-black sludgy air.

And clamour the colour of copper light
Swings from their hammering, and speeds, and breaks
Darkness to clots and spattering light, and flakes
Oily, like dazzling snow and storms of oil.
The night that never sleeps, quickens. The soil,
The stones and the grass are alive. The thrush awakes,
Huddles, and finds the leaves gone hard and cool.
The cows in the fields are awake, restless; the bull
Restless. The dogs. A young horse snorts and shakes.

Beneath the square of glaring light
The river still is muttering of flood,
The dark day when thick with ugly mud,
Swirling with logs and swollen beasts (and some
Still alive, drowning) it had come
Snarling, a foul beast chewing living cud,
And grappled with the bridge and tried to rend it,
So now these stronger brutes must sweat to mend it
Labouring in light like orange blood.

Men labour in the city so,
With naked fore-arms singed with copper light
And strangeness on them as with stone they fight,
Each meet for fear, and even the curt drill
Mysterious as trees and a dark hill.
But these are stronger, these oppose their might
To storm and flood and all the land's black power.
Burnished with sweat and lanterns now they tower
Monstrous against the marshes of the night.

Spider-Gums

Where winter's snow and crashing rains
Have forced the snow-gums to their knees,
High in the sky on Kelly's Plains
These frail and delicate spider-trees:

As though some pigtailed fossicker here
Now bleached as quartz on Dead Man Range
Had drawn a Chinese sketch on air
To speak for him when all should change;

Or high from where the Murrumbidgee's
Tussocky rapids flash and race
A flying swarm of water-midges
Hangs in a mist of light and lace.

As though through summer's huge hot noon
Lost drifts of winter linger still
And twenty flakes of snow are blown
All dark against the granite hill;

Or light winds silvery with frost
Have breathed upon the sky's blue glass
To make a tree that seems half ghost
And melts into the russet grass.

As though in earth's deep dream of stone
Some leafy thought was taking form
And fled before the dream was done,
Half-finished out to sun and storm;

Or some tall tree not there at all
Has flecked the sunlight with its shadow
And shadows' shadows glide and fall
Dark green upon air's crystal hollow;

As though, as though—but now I see
The white clouds covering the blue,
A chill breeze beating on the tree
That hardly shakes as it goes through,

And know how earth took deepest thought
In this cold kingdom of the winter
To make some shape of grace to float
On high while snow-gums crack and splinter,

And made this phantom tree at last,
A thing more air than leaf or bough,
That slips clean through the killing blast
And dances clear from all the snow.

THE SILKWORMS

All their lives in a box! What generations,
What centuries of masters, not meaning to be cruel
But needing their labour, taught these creatures such patience
That now though sunlight strikes on the eye's dark jewel
Or moonlight breathes on the wing they do not stir
But like the ghosts of moths crouch silent there.

Look it's a child's toy! There is no lid even,
They can climb, they can fly, and the whole world's their tree;
But hush, they say in themselves, we are in prison.
There is no word to tell them that they are free,
And they are not; ancestral voices bind them
In dream too deep for wind or word to find them.

Even in the young, each like a little dragon
Ramping and green upon his mulberry leaf,
So full of life, it seems the voice has spoken:
They hide where there is food, where they are safe,
And the voice whispers, 'Spin the cocoon,
Sleep, sleep, you shall be wrapped in me soon.'

Now is their hour, when they wake from that long swoon;
Their pale curved wings are marked in a pattern of leaves,
Shadowy for trees, white for the dance of the moon;
And when on summer nights the buddleia gives
Its nectar like lilac wine for insects mating
They drink its fragrance and shiver, impatient with waiting,

They stir, they think they will go. Then they remember
It was forbidden, forbidden, ever to go out;
The Hands are on guard outside like claps of thunder,
The ancestral voice says Don't, and they do not.
Still the night calls them to unimaginable bliss
But there is terror around them, the vast, the abyss,

And here is the tribe that they know, in their known place,
They are gentle and kind together, they are safe for ever,
And all shall be answered at last when they embrace.
White moth moves closer to moth, lover to lover.
There is that pang of joy on the edge of dying—
Their soft wings whirr, they dream that they are flying.

B FLAT

Sing softly, Muse, the Reverend Henry White
Who floats through time as lightly as a feather
Yet left one solitary gleam of light
Because he was the Selborne naturalist's brother

And told him once how on warm summer eves
When moonlight filled all Fyfield to the brim
And yearning owls were hooting to their loves
On church and barn and oak-tree's leafy limb

He took a common half-a-crown pitch-pipe
Such as the masters used for harpsichords
And through the village trod with silent step
Measuring the notes of those melodious birds

And found that each one sang, or rather hooted,
Precisely in the measure of B flat.
And that is all that history has noted;
We know no more of Henry White than that.

So, softly, Muse, in harmony and conformity
Pipe up for him and all such gentle souls
Thus in the world's enormousness, enormity,
So interested in music and in owls;

For though we cannot claim his crumb of knowledge
Was worth much more than virtually nil
Nor hail him for vast enterprise or courage,
Yet in my mind I see him walking still

With eager ear beneath his clerical hat
Through Fyfield village sleeping dark and blind,
Oh surely as he piped his soft B flat
The most harmless, the most innocent of mankind.

DAVID CAMPBELL

B ORN IN 1915 on the family sheep station in the rolling Monaro country beyond Canberra, David Campbell was educated at The King's School, in Sydney, and at Cambridge University. He was an outstanding sportsman in his youth: at King's, captain of the rugby and rowing teams; at Cambridge, winner of a rugby blue against Oxford in 1936, and of two international caps for England in 1937.

John Manifold, who was at Cambridge with him, remembered Campbell striding late into an examination room, then clasping his head theatrically as he read the paper. With every eye now upon him, he drew from his pocket a bottle of whisky, which he drank straight off, before proceeding to work, the room left floundering behind him. Only Manifold later found that the bottle had contained cold tea.

From boyhood, Campbell knew the works of 'Banjo' Paterson and other bush balladists; at Cambridge he discovered the Elizabethan lyricists, and saw a way of creating something of his own in combining these two styles. He wrote his first poems at university, and was surprised at the praise his efforts received, having seen himself until then as 'a pretty dumb footballer'. At Cambridge he also read, most importantly, the poetry of W.B. Yeats.

Campbell graduated on the outbreak of war, returned to Australia to join the Royal Australian Air Force, and married. He flew in New Guinea against the Japanese, becoming a Squadron Leader, and later

Wing Commander. In 1942, while on reconnaisance over Rabaul, he and his co-pilot and gunner were attacked, in a twin-engined Hudson, by two Japanese fighters. Despite receiving more than 250 bullet holes in his plane, having his crew badly wounded, and being shot through the left hand and wrist himself, Campbell eluded the attackers and flew back 500 miles through bad weather, 'the instrument panel falling apart', to land in Port Moresby on one engine and with one tyre shot away. He was awarded the DFC. Later he received the decoration a second time, after bombing raids and supply drops he made in Timor.

Following the war, Campbell took up sheep farming on a property his father had owned near Canberra, and wrote poetry in whatever time he could find from 'hard work and harsh seasons'. In the 1970s, divorced and remarried, and on another, smaller 'run', he began to write in free verse, while still producing characteristically brief and short-lined poems. His ideal was always that poetry should have the clarity and economy of a theorem. He suggested that his change in style, and in subject, as he now ranged beyond pastoral and love poems into politics, fantasy, classical myth and family history, had much to do with the disruptive effects on him of the Vietnam War, to which he was actively opposed.

Campbell's poetry, when read at length, is slighter than a good selection might suggest it would be. He does have, though, a recurring theme: his feeling that the robust appearance of things, which he enjoys so much, is really an illusion. He responded to this intuition positively. Ideas about the cosmos being ultimately only a dance of energy preoccupied him, particularly in his later work. 'What's matter but a hardening of the light?' he wrote, and from this concluded that 'Matter is thought', although in what sense such a totalising conception is to be understood is not defined. What is profound about Campbell's work is not its occasional elusive philosophising but its appetite for life. His poetry has also great warmth and charm.

Campbell maintained as the motto of his work Rilke's words (which echo Nietzsche), 'I praise'. With his friend Douglas Stewart he consciously makes a second generation of the Vitalist school.

Campbell's flamboyance, broken-nosed good looks, enjoyment of drink, and of the company of women and artists, made him an attractive figure. He died at what seemed the surprisingly early age for him of sixty-four, from lung cancer.

HOGAN'S DAUGHTER

Clancy saddles his narrow mare
For frosts have come before the rain,
And he's away with Conroy's sheep
To drove them on the western plain.

He whistles an old dog to the lead,
A roan kelpie to crowd the rear;
And whistles a song to suit himself
As rose-hips dance on the winter brier.

And they string along a drover's mile
And dust is ringing from the shale
When lightning skins the bony ridge
And green as opal falls the hail.

And they string along a drover's mile
When granite heights stand up on air;
The lightning lights on Hogan's pub
And a long girl knitting behind the bar.

'O what is the web you weave, girl?
What is the net you knit so thin
That blows with the lamp and your yellow hair?'
'It's a web to catch a drover in.

'The winds are loose in the mountain sky
And tear the fleece from the fleeing storm;
Tether your mare or ride on by,
Here's a fire to wrap your spirit warm.'

His mare is hitched to the veranda rail;
In long green paddocks stray the sheep,
The dogs are barking in the hall—
And he has kissed her underlip.

'Is it mirage-water brims your eye
Or a spring where a man may drink his fill?'
The lightning clove the cliffs of sky;
He stood alone upon the hill.

Then good-bye to his dark lank wife
And his shack and his shears and his family;
And drought or the devil take Conroy's sheep
And the hips that dance on the brier-tree.

For he rolled a swag of his saddle-cloth
And called his kelpie dogs to heel,
Fixed his eye on the glinting storm;
And he has gone across the hill.

Spring Hares

There is a stranger on the stock route.
See his red beard and eyes of flame!
The sky's his swag; the magpies shout
Across the continent his name:
It is the sun! It is the dawn!—
Bless the day that I was born.

There are two boxers through the gum-trees;
Their shadows spar on the far hill,
Counter and close. What giants are these?
Surprised, a pair of hares stand still.
It's a fine thing at your front gate
To see such angry lovers mate.

Bill is out on the red stallion;
His piebald mob crops blades of fire.
Trees burn, leaves melt; in conflagration
The big buck hare has his desire
Where the red ridge meets the spring sky,
Locked in the sun's irradiant eye.

THE AUSTRALIAN DREAM

The doorbell buzzed. It was past three o'clock.
The steeple-of-Saint-Andrew's weathercock
Cried silently to darkness, and my head
Was bronze with claret as I rolled from bed
To ricochet from furniture. Light! Light
Blinded the stairs, the hatstand sprang upright,
I fumbled with the lock, and on the porch
Stood the Royal Family with a wavering torch.

'We hope,' the Queen said, 'we do not intrude.
The pubs were full, most of our subjects rude.
We came before our time. It seems the Queen's
Command brings only, "Tell the dead marines!"
We've come to you.' I must admit I'd half
Expected just this visit. With a laugh
That put them at their ease, I bowed my head.
'Your Majesty is most welcome here,' I said.
'My home is yours. There is a little bed
Downstairs, a boiler-room, might suit the Duke.'
He thanked me gravely for it and he took
Himself off with a wave. 'Then the Queen Mother?
She'd best bed down with you. There is no other
But my wide bed. I'll curl up in a chair.'
The Queen looked thoughtful. She brushed out her hair
And folded up *The Garter* on a pouf.
'Distress was the first commoner, and as proof
That queens bow to the times,' she said, 'we three
Shall share the double bed. Please follow me.'

I waited for the ladies to undress—
A sense of fitness, even in distress,
Is always with me. They had tucked away
Their state robes in the lowboy; gold crowns lay
Upon the bedside tables; ropes of pearls
Lassoed the plastic lampshade; their soft curls

Were spread out on the pillows and they smiled.
'Hop in,' said the Queen Mother. In I piled
Between them to lie like a stick of wood.
I couldn't find a thing to say. My blood
Beat, but like rollers at the ebb of tide.
'I hope your Majesties sleep well,' I lied.
A hand touched mine and the Queen said, 'I am
Most grateful to you, Jock. Please call me Ma'am.'

TO THE ART OF EDGAR DEGAS

Beachcomber on the shores of tears
Limning the gestures of defeat
In dancers, whores and opera-stars—
The lonely, lighted, various street

You sauntered through, oblique, perverse,
In your home territory a spy,
Accosted you and with a curse
You froze it with your Gorgon's eye.

With what tense patience you refine
The everyness of everyday
And with free colour and a line
Make mysteries of flaccid clay!

By what strange enterprise you live!
Edgy, insatiably alone,
You choose your tenderness to give
To showgirls whom you turn to stone—

But stone that moves, tired stone that leans
To ease involuntarily the toe
Of ballet-girls like watering-cans
(Those arguers at the bar) as though

In their brief pause you found relief
From posed dilemmas of the mind—
Your grudging aristocratic grief,
The wildcat cares of going blind.

Well, walk your evening streets and look
Each last eleven at the show:
The darkening pleasures you forsook
Look back like burning windows now.

MOTHERS AND DAUGHTERS

The cruel girls we loved
Are over forty,
Their subtle daughters
Have stolen their beauty;

And with a blue stare
Of cool surprise,
They mock their anxious mothers
With their mothers' eyes.

ON FROSTY DAYS

On frosty days, when I was young,
I rode out early with the men
And mustered cattle till their long
Blue shadows covered half the plain;

And when we turned our horses round,
Only the homestead's point of light,
Men's voices, and the bridles' sound,
Were left in the enormous night.

And now again the sun has set
All yellow and a greening sky
Sucks up the colour from the wheat—
And here's my horse, my dog and I.

PALLID CUCKOO

Alone the pallid cuckoo now
Fills his clear bottles in the dew:
Four five six seven—climb with him!
And eight brings morning to the brim.

Then from green hills in single file
My ewes and lambs come down the scale:
Four three two one—the matrons pass
And fill their bellies up with grass.

But in the evening light the lambs
Forget their hillward-munching dams;
To cuckoo pipes their dances start
And fill and overflow the heart.

Two Songs with Spanish Burdens

I
A Grey Singlet

I was washing my lover's grey shearing singlet
When a squatter drew rein beside our quince tree
On a red impatient horse, with me at the copper:
And 'How much do you want for that stinking shirt?' says he.

Though his singlet is grey, his skin is a lily.

'A semi-trailer load of trade wethers would not buy it,
Nor a pen of prime lambs sappy from their mothers,
Nor a yarding of vealers with a leg in each corner,
Nor a mob of springing heifers with the dew on their nostrils.'

Though his singlet is grey, his skin is a lily.

'Not for a white homestead with a verandah all around it
And in vine-shade a waterbag of cool well water,
Thyme crushed on stone paths and bruised plums in the orchard,
Would I sell my lover's singlet to a show-off on horseback.'

Though his singlet is grey, his skin is a lily.

II
Spring Lambs

Winter blows itself out with quick cloud and white sunshine;
Crows go down the wind like crepe torn from a funeral
And their cry the tearing. You ride home in the evening
With a flame in one cheek and a lamb on your pommel.

If you feed my lambs, I shall kiss you;
Otherwise I'll feed them and you may kiss me.

Frost feathers the grass and furs the fence wires;
There's ice in the bucket and a moon in the morning
Over the paddocks where shadows are frozen
And you vanish in mist while I stand gazing.

If you feed my lambs, I shall kiss you;
Otherwise I'll feed them and you may kiss me.

White lambs leap up under the quince trees;
They suck blue milk from a dented bucket,
Tugging at my fingers and at my heart strings.
Thoughts follow your hoof tracks like a shy blue heeler.

If you feed my lambs, I shall kiss you;
Otherwise I'll feed them and you may kiss me.

THE LITTLE GREBE

When moved in age to share a varied life
With his unworldly son
My father backed a horse between the shafts
Of an old gig—'Whoa back!'—and off we spun.

He reined beside the rushes of a dam
But his eyes travelled on
Beyond the misted city to the range.
Late snow lay on Franklin.

And while he yarned, I watched the little grebe
Appear and disappear.
The dam filled up with clouds, and when the bird
Bobbed there again, the sky and dam were clear.

So I half-listened to my father's life,
Considering the grebe
And how it fed its feathers to its young
On rafts amongst the reeds.

Those floating incubators hatched the eggs.
Father, I did not know
Your shapely tales would wake in me in age
And fill my mind with distances and sorrow.

DUCHESSES

A mob of dressing-tables is grazing
The pile of the plain
Under paper blue mountains.

Now and then one will pause
And raise its mirror
Reflecting the white sunlight.

Little cupboards
Hop in and out of the drawers
And suck at the crockery knobs.

The only sounds are the snip, snip,
Of grazing furniture
And the rattle of wooden droppings.

A truck is hurrying over the plain.
The mob raises its mirrors,
Little cupboards hop back in the drawers.

The dressing-tables head for the paper hills,
But the truck is upon them.
Pom pom! Corks fly from swivel guns.

Pomeranians snap
At the heels of wheeling dressing-tables.
They snarl in mirrors, savaging the doilies.

The furniture is surrounded.
Men rope the younger pieces
And load them squealing onto the truck.

Now solitary in bedrooms
Dressing-tables look back at women
Who question them with rouge lips.

Sometimes through windows
They glimpse the paper blue mountains,
And the tears of the women fall on the doilies.

THE SECRET LIFE OF A LEADER

I was born in a wire house
They wrapped me in the wind's blanket
My mother's breasts were cans

On my birthday they gave me a rifle
My first love was a dead man's thought
Colours drained to black and white

My first duty was to my parents
They were shuffled away
                    For my second lesson
I shot a close friend and the music master
They looked younger in death

My third task was at peak hour
                              Percussion
Hammered the subway
                              The gutters
Ran with a red ketchup

They said I was ready
My vision spread like a virus
A crippled man blessed me

The city was gay with white flags
                              Skeletons
Cheered from the sidewalks
A schoolgirl presented a sheaf
Of spring flowers and fainted

When they unveiled the statue
I lost all movement in my right side
At my guarded chateau
Resting
          the trees kept rustling
They lopped the branches

I fished in a red river
And caught a beer can
At a farmhouse I rested

The farmer's wife curtsied
                              It was my mother
I picked up a hen egg
                              It blew my hand off
In the yellow nursery
                    I said I'd begin again

Mother tucked me in
And blew out the candle
Shh! she said
              What dreams you have!

JOHN MANIFOLD

—————— ❧ ——————

JOHN MANIFOLD WAS born in Melbourne in 1915 to a
wealthy pastoralist family from the Western District of Victoria.
He was educated at Geelong Grammar and then at Cambridge,
where he joined the Communist party. In 1939 he enlisted in the
British army and served in Europe and West Africa in intelligence.
A *Selected Verse* was published in England and the United States
before he returned to Australia in 1949. Family disapproval of his
politics caused him to settle in Queensland, and for many years he
lived in the Brisbane suburb of Wynnum in a spacious old weather-
board house on stilts, where he held weekly music nights. He was
active in collecting and recording bush songs and ballads, and edited
books about Australian folk songs, as well as writing two classic
scholarly works on Elizabethan music. He died in 1985.

Manifold was an impressive and handsome man, who spoke with
an upper class English accent, his conversation interspersed with
words like 'dinkum' (his ultimate cachet of approval). He was a
faithful Stalinist to the end of his life, as witnessed by his sequence
'Red Rosary: Twelve Commemorative Sonnets' which includes an
elegy for Stalin. For much of his life he was funded by the Soviet
government.

The politically dogmatic position adopted in his poetry is echoed
by his simple and somewhat heavy verse form and rhymes. But de-
spite this, his work is always good-humoured, lucid and civilised.
He remained the gentleman scholar and amateur man of letters, his
verse shapely and never careless, written with pungency and panache.

THE TOMB OF LT. JOHN LEARMONTH, A.I.F.

*'At the end on Crete he took to the hills, and said he'ld fight it out
with only a revolver. He was a great soldier.'*
—One of his men in a letter.

This is not sorrow, this is work: I build
A cairn of words over a silent man,
My friend John Learmonth whom the Germans killed.

There was no word of hero in his plan;
Verse should have been his love and peace his trade,
But history turned him to a partisan.

Far from the battle as his bones are laid
Crete will remember him. Remember well,
Mountains of Crete, the Second Field Brigade!

Say Crete, and there is little more to tell
Of muddle tall as treachery, despair
And black defeat resounding like a bell;

But bring the magnifying focus near
And in contempt of muddle and defeat
The old heroic virtues still appear.

Australian blood where hot and icy meet
(James Hogg and Lermontov were of his kin)
Lie still and fertilise the fields of Crete.

O

Schoolboy, I watched his ballading begin:
Billy and bullocky and billabong,
Our properties of childhood, all were in.

I heard the air though not the undersong,
The fierceness and resolve; but all the same
They're the tradition, and tradition's strong.

Swagman and bushranger die hard, die game,
Die fighting, like that wild colonial boy—
Jack Dowling, says the ballad, was his name.

He also spun his pistol like a toy,
Turned to the hills like wolf or kangaroo,
And faced destruction with a bitter joy.

His freedom gave him nothing else to do
But set his back against his family tree
And fight the better for the fact he knew

He was as good as dead. Because the sea
Was closed and the air dark and the land lost,
'They'll never capture me alive,' said he.

O

That's courage chemically pure, uncrossed
With sacrifice or duty or career,
Which counts and pays in ready coin the cost

Of holding course. Armies are not its sphere
Where all's contrived to achieve its counterfeit;
It swears with discipline, it's volunteer.

I could as hardly make a moral fit
Around it as around a lightning flash.
There is no moral, that's the point of it,

No moral. But I'm glad of this panache
That sparkles, as from flint, from us and steel,
True to no crown nor presidential sash

Nor flag nor fame. Let others mourn and feel
He died for nothing: nothings have their place.
While thus the kind and civilised conceal

This spring of unsuspected inward grace
And look on death as equals, I am filled
With queer affection for the human race.

JUDITH WRIGHT

J UDITH WRIGHT, BORN in 1915, came from a prominent pastoralist family which was granted land in the 1820s. She grew up on the family property near Armidale, New South Wales, and was educated at first by correspondence and then at New England Girls' School and the University of Sydney. Her father, the person in her family to whom she was closest, helped found the University of New England, and the family house of her childhood is now the administrative building there.

On graduating from university, Wright travelled in Europe. After working as a stenographer in Sydney, she returned home to 'Wallamumbi' at the outbreak of World War II, to help run the property. At this time she began writing her first mature poems. From 1944 to 1948 she worked at the University of Queensland, and while there met and married J.P. (Jack) McKinney, twenty-four years older than herself, a farmer, drover, shearer, writer and self-taught, serious philosopher, whose neo-Kantian *The Structure of Modern Thought* appeared posthumously in 1971. McKinney's philosophy, which sees humans as structuring an unknowable 'manifold' according to inherent, archetypal principles, significantly influenced Wright's work. Their marriage was close, but caused Wright to be rejected by her own family for a long period. She and McKinney had one child, a daughter. They lived for many years at Mt Tambourine, out of Brisbane, on a small property that, with its hens and vegetables, was largely self-sufficient. After her husband's death in the mid-sixties, Wright seems to have felt an increasing sense of despair over public events in Australia and the rest of the world. She moved to another small property, outside Canberra, and made it a wildlife sanctuary, where she lives alone.

Wright has been a pioneering and militant conservationist, and is one of the most persistent white voices supporting the Aboriginal campaign for the return of tribal land.

Judith Wright's earliest volumes of verse, *The Moving Image* and *Woman to Man* (the first published when she was thirty-one) were received with vast enthusiasm by Australian critics and fellow writers, and placed her at the forefront of Australian poets. But considerable reservations have developed about her later work, much of which is seen as, at first, portentously mythical, and as then becoming hectoring, drab and impatient with poetry in its concern for its message. Donald Davie, the English poet and critic, her pre-eminent supporter, has all these reservations but concludes that, taking her work as a whole, she remains among the best contemporary poets in the language.

THE UNBORN

I know no sleep you do not stand beside.
You footless darkness following where I go,
you lipless drinker at my drowsy breast—
yet whom I must deny I have denied.
The unpossessing is the unpossessed.

Slight is the foothold from the well of night,
the stair is broken and the keys are lost,
and you whom I have wrecked are wrecked indeed;
and yet you stand upon the edge of sight,
and I have known no path you have not crossed.

The shadow wakeful on my sleeping arm
stares from the hidden depths far under birth.
How like a diamond looks the far-off day,
that crystal that reflects your darkened dream,
that bubble of sunlight broken and blown away.
O gift ungiven. O uncreated earth.

WOMAN TO MAN

The eyeless labourer in the night,
the selfless, shapeless seed I hold,
builds for its resurrection day—
silent and swift and deep from sight
foresees the unimagined light.

This is no child with a child's face;
this has no name to name it by:
yet you and I have known it well.
This is our hunter and our chase,
the third who lay in our embrace.

This is the strength that your arm knows,
the arc of flesh that is my breast,
the precise crystals of our eyes.
This is the blood's wild tree that grows
the intricate and folded rose.

This is the maker and the made;
this is the question and reply;
the blind head butting at the dark,
the blaze of light along the blade.
Oh hold me, for I am afraid.

THE OLD PRISON

The rows of cells are unroofed,
a flute for the wind's mouth,
who comes with a breath of ice
from the blue caves of the south.

O dark and fierce day:
the wind like an angry bee
hunts for the black honey
in the pits of the hollow sea.

Waves of shadow wash
the empty shell bone-bare,
and like a bone it sings
a bitter song of air.

Who built and laboured here?
The wind and the sea say
—Their cold nest is broken
and they are blown away.

They did not breed nor love.
Each in his cell alone
cried as the wind now cries
through this flute of stone.

TRAIN JOURNEY

Glassed with cold sleep and dazzled by the moon,
out of the confused hammering dark of the train
I looked and saw under the moon's cold sheet
your delicate dry breasts, country that built my heart;

and the small trees on their uncoloured slope
like poetry moved, articulate and sharp
and purposeful under the great dry flight of air,
under the crosswise currents of wind and star.

Clench down your strength, box-tree and ironbark.
Break with your violent root the virgin rock.
Draw from the flying dark its breath of dew
till the unliving come to life in you.

Be over the blind rock a skin of sense,
under the barren height a slender dance . . .

I woke and saw the dark small trees that burn
suddenly into flowers more lovely than the white moon.

FLOOD YEAR

Walking up the driftwood beach at day's end
I saw it, thrust up out of a hillock of sand—
a frail bleached clench of fingers dried by wind—
the dead child's hand.

And they are mourning there still, though I forget,
the year of flood, the scoured ruined land,
the herds gone down the current, the farms drowned,
and the child never found.

When I was there the thick hurling waters
had gone back to the river, the farms were almost drained.
Banished half-dead cattle searched the dunes; it rained;
river and sea met with a wild sound.

Oh with a wild sound water flung into air
where sea met river; all the country round
no heart was quiet. I walked on the driftwood sand
and saw the pale crab crouched, and came to a stand
thinking, A child's hand. The child's hand.

FLAME-TREE IN A QUARRY

From the broken bone of the hill
stripped and left for dead,
like a wrecked skull,
leaps out this bush of blood.

Out of the torn earth's mouth
comes the old cry of praise.
Still is the song made flesh
though the singer dies—

flesh of the world's delight,
voice of the world's desire,
I drink you with my sight
and I am filled with fire.

Out of the very wound
springs up this scarlet breath—
this fountain of hot joy,
this living ghost of death.

AT COOLOOLA

The blue crane fishing in Cooloola's twilight
has fished there longer than our centuries.
He is the certain heir of lake and evening,
and he will wear their colour till he dies,

but I'm a stranger, come of a conquering people.
I cannot share his calm, who watch his lake,
being unloved by all my eyes delight in,
and made uneasy, for an old murder's sake.

Those dark-skinned people who once named Cooloola
knew that no land is lost or won by wars,
for earth is spirit: the invader's feet will tangle
in nets there and his blood be thinned by fears.

Riding at noon and ninety years ago,
my grandfather was beckoned by a ghost—
a black accoutred warrior armed for fighting,
who sank into bare plain, as now into time past.

White shores of sand, plumed reed and paperbark,
clear heavenly levels frequented by crane and swan—
I know that we are justified only by love,
but oppressed by arrogant guilt, have room for none.

And walking on clean sand among the prints
of bird and animal, I am challenged by a driftwood spear
thrust from the water; and, like my grandfather,
must quiet a heart accused by its own fear.

REQUEST TO A YEAR

If the year is meditating a suitable gift,
I should like it to be the attitude
of my great-great-grandmother,
legendary devotee of the arts,

who, having had eight children
and little opportunity for painting pictures,
sat one day on a high rock
beside a river in Switzerland

and from a difficult distance viewed
her second son, balanced on a small ice-floe,
drift down the current towards a waterfall
that struck rock-bottom eighty feet below,

while her second daughter, impeded,
no doubt, by the petticoats of the day,
stretched out a last-hope alpenstock
(which luckily later caught him on his way).

Nothing, it was evident, could be done;
and with the artist's isolating eye
my great-great-grandmother hastily sketched the scene.
The sketch survives to prove the story by.

Year, if you have no Mother's day present planned;
reach back and bring me the firmness of her hand.

For One Dying

Come now; the angel leads.
All human lives betray,
all human love erodes
under time's laser ray;

the innocent animals
within us and without
die in corrupted hells
made out of human thought.

Green places and pure springs
are poisoned and laid bare—
even the hawk's high wings
ride on a fatal air.

But come; the angel calls.
Deep in the dreamer's cave
the one pure source upwells
its single luminous wave;

and there, Recorder, Seer,
you wait within your cell.
I bring, in love and fear,
the world I know too well

into your hands. Receive
these fractured days I yield.
Renew the life we grieve
by day to know and hold.

Renew the central dream
in blazing purity,
and let my rags confirm
and robe eternity.

For still the angel leads.
Ruined yet pure we go
with all our days and deeds
into that flame, that snow.

FINALE

The cruellest thing they did
was to send home his teeth from the hospital.
What could she do with those,
arriving as they did days after the funeral?

Wrapped them in one of his clean handkerchiefs
she'd laundered and taken down.
All she could do was cradle them in her hands;
they looked so strange, alone—

utterly jawless in a constant smile
not in the least like his. She could cry no more.
At midnight she took heart and aim and threw
them out of the kitchen-door.

It rocketed out, that finally-parted smile,
into the gully? the scrub? the neighbour's land?
And she went back and fell into stupid sleep,
knowing him dead at last, and by her hand.

SMALLTOWN DANCE

Two women find the square-root of a sheet.
That is an ancient dance:
arms wide: together: again: two forward steps: hands meet
your partner's once and twice.
That white expanse
reduces to a neat
compression fitting in the smallest space
a sheet can pack in on a cupboard shelf.

High scented walls there were of flapping white
when I was small, myself.
I walked between them, playing Out of Sight.
Simpler than arms, they wrapped and comforted—
clean corridors of hiding, roofed with blue—
saying, Your sins too are made Monday-new;
and see, ahead
that glimpse of unobstructed waiting green.
Run, run before you're seen.

But women know the scale of possibility,
the limit of opportunity,
the fence,
how little chance
there is of getting out. The sheets that tug
sometimes struggle from the peg,
don't travel far. Might symbolise
something. Knowing where danger lies
you have to keep things orderly.
The household budget will not stretch to more.

And they can demonstrate it in a dance.
First pull those wallowing white dreamers down,
spread arms: then close them. Fold
those beckoning roads to some impossible world,
put them away and close the cupboard door.

HAROLD STEWART

———— ✂ ————

HAROLD STEWART, BORN at Drummoyne, Sydney, in 1916, attended Fort Street School while James McAuley was a pupil there. Their friendship continued at Sydney University and in the army during World War II, when they were in the same research and civil affairs unit. In 1944, before either had published a book, they concocted the famous 'Ern Malley' poems, as a hoax on the *avant garde* literary magazine *Angry Penguins*. They did this out of the conviction that modernist poetry of the irrational, obscurantist type arose from empty self-aggrandising and was culturally destructive. The success of the hoax was written up world-wide, in *Time* magazine and the London *Times*, and Stewart has always taken great pride in it. Stewart seems to have been the junior partner in the project, with McAuley holding the pen and contributing much of the tone of voice in the poems. The affair has made the perpetrators' names anathema in some circles to this day.

After the war, Stewart worked in a bookshop in Melbourne for fifteen years. His first book of poetry, *Phoenix Wings* (1948), shows him deeply involved in Buddhist and Taoist culture. From the early 1950s, Stewart organised Friday night discussion groups on comparative religion at his workplace. He took lessons in Japanese and in 1960 published *A Net of Fireflies*, the first of his books of rhyming translations from the haiku poets. It continues to sell in many countries and has never been out of print.

Stewart made a trip to Japan in 1962, financed by a patron. He was greatly disappointed with it, but decided to 'obliterate modern Japan from his consciousness' and settle there, which he did, again with assistance, in 1966. Determined to attach himself to the Pure Land school of Buddhism, he simply turned up at the gate of a temple in Kyoto. He was taken in, rather uncertainly, put through a course of study, and ordained as a priest. He is still living in that city, in a small room which is lined with books.

In 1969 Stewart published a second book of haiku translations, *A Chime of Wind-bells*, and then in 1979 a 4,350 line poem, *By the Old Walls of Kyoto*, describing significant Buddhist sites in Kyoto and the philosophy embodied in them, with 300 pages of erudite prose commentary. Stewart has become known in his adopted country as an expert on the culture of old Kyoto and on Japanese Buddhist art.

Stewart's haiku translations are usually criticised by others interested in the form. It is argued that his heroic couplets have a prose explicitness and a sense of closure that destroys the most important feature of haiku, particularly from the Zen viewpoint, which is their suggestion of experience beyond words. Stewart defends the heroic couplet for English-language haiku as being a minimal form indigenous to the Western tradition in which the aural properties of the Japanese poem can be conveyed. Japanese poems do not rhyme but are richly alliterative and onomatopoeic, and Stewart regrets there is no approximation of this in the usual syllabic style of translation. Stewart's translations have a literary excellence of their own, just as 'The Rubaiyat of Omar Khayyam' can be appreciated as a personalised version of its original, and he provides pleasures not inferior to those in FitzGerald.

30 Haiku

Spring

NOBODY
The long spring day: before and after reach
The footprints left along the sandy beach.
—*Shiki*

FROM A HILLSIDE
The rice-fields spread their flooded terracing
Of mirrors: segments in a beetle's wing.
—*Hô-ô*

SOWN WITH GOLD
How far these fields of flowering mustard run:
East to the moonrise, west to the setting sun!
—*Buson*

TRANSMIGRATION
Lighting one candle with another's flame
At dusk in spring—the same, yet not the same.
—*Buson*

THE BOOK-BROWSER
An open shop with picture-books in rows,
On each a paperweight: the spring wind blows.
—*Kitô*

AT THE CHINESE WINDOW
The pear-tree blossoming in the moonlit night,
A lady reads her letter by its light.
—*Buson*

THE SPRING SEA
All day, with gently undulating swell,
The spring sea rose and fell, and rose and fell . . .
—*Buson*

AND SO
And so the spring buds burst, and so I gaze,
And so the blossoms fall, and so my days . . .
—*Onitsura*

SUMMER

THE NOON CONVOLVULUS
Ah! It will never wash its face of blue
In dew of morning or in evening dew.
                              — *Yayu*

AFTER THE HEAT
A moonlit evening: here beside the pool,
Stripped to the waist, a snail enjoys the cool.
                              — *Issa*

A CHANGE OF SERVANTS
Umbrella in hand, the housemaid due to leave
Stands gazing out: a rainy summer's eve.
                              — *Kyoroku*

WIND, STEAM, AND SPEED
As wind-waves race across the rice field's sea,
Steam sweeps over my bowl of clear green tea.
                              — *Hô-ô*

NOCTURNE
Where is the moon? Engulfed in clouds once more.
The bell lies sunken on the deep sea-floor.
                              — *Bashô*

MORNING SERVICE
While nuns intone within the upstairs hall,
Through tall bamboo outside the raindrops fall.
                              — *Hô-ô*

THE HOUR-GLASS
The colts with frisky vigour scour the plain,
Whose sandstone cliff is crumbling, grain by grain.
                              — *Tôhô*

INTERIOR VISTAS
Hot-spring hotel: down every corridor,
Mountains in summer green abruptly soar.
                              — *Shiki*

THE OLD FOLLY
The octopus, while summer moonshine streams
Into the trap, enjoys its fleeting dreams.
                              — *Bashô*

AUTUMN

SQUARE, TRIANGLE, AND CIRCLE
Beneath the bed's mosquito-net, I tie
One corner up: the harvest moon is high.
                                        —*Chiyo*

ON THE DEATH OF THE POET ISSHÔ
Shake, O desolate grave-mound, shake! My wail
Of mourning is the autumn's headlong gale!
                                        —*Bashô*

CHAIN-MAIL
A chestnut dropped in. A goldfish rose to drink.
Their widening rings of water interlink.
                                        —*Kijiro*

LAST POEM
Though on a journey I have fallen ill,
My dreams on withered moorland wander still . . .
                                        —*Bashô*

COLD MEMENTO
A chill runs through the bedroom where I roam,
Treading by chance upon my dead wife's comb.
                                        —*Buson*

A DELICIOUS NASHI
Peeling a woody pear, sweet drops run down
The knife that cuts the skin of oil-spot brown.
                                        —*Shiki*

THE TOMBS AT MUKDEN
The imperial tombs are cold. Through middle air
The sun and moon at one another stare.
                                        —*Seishi*

WINTER

MONOCHROME AT NIGHTFALL
Only one monk, one woman, left to row
Over the ferry through the falling snow.
—*Meisetsu*

WHAT THE EAGLE SAW
Snowflakes falling, through the air for miles
Above Shisaku's bay of pine-clad isles.
—*Hô-ô*

SELF–ABSORBED
Chanting, beating the bowl, from place to place,
I drink the raindrops running down my face.
—*Raizen*

MORNING RELIEF
How round and straight the hole is that I bore
By leaking in the snow outside my door!
—*Issa*

UNBIDDEN DUTY
Our simple honest servant: every day
From next door, too, he sweeps the snow away.
—*Issa*

ON THE NIGHT BEFORE BASHÔ'S DEATH
Tugging from side to side the quilt we share,
Wryly we smile—in spite of our despair.
—*Izen*

JAMES McAULEY

———— ❧ ————

J AMES McAULEY WAS born in 1917 and grew up in Home-
bush, a working class Sydney suburb. His father was a builder
who speculated in renovating houses. McAuley went to the selective
Fort Street High School, and then to Sydney University where he
took a Master's degree in English and studied philosophy and
German. He became known at university as a poet and jazz pianist.
One of his lecturers, the outstanding philosopher John Anderson,
influenced McAuley towards classicism in art and anti-communism
in politics, but failed to persuade him about a materialist ontology—
McAuley was already set on the course which would make him a
Catholic convert.

'The Incarnation of Sirius', from his first book, *Under Alderbaran*,
expresses his rejection of what he called 'the Magian heresy', in
which individuals propose a world-view and millenarian solutions
based on personal emotion and intuition. His book, appearing in
1946, demonstrates an ambivalence towards this heresy: many of
the poems, although classical in form, are influenced by German
Romanticism, French Symbolism, Blake and Christopher Brennan
—all of them infected by a Magian impulse. The heightened excite-
ment of language present in this volume is largely and deliberately
missing from his second book of verse, *A Vision of Ceremony* (1956),
and from subsequent collections. His acceptance of the self-restraint
imposed by classical formalism and by his puritan view of Catholi-
cism had become complete.

During World War II McAuley served in the Australian Army's Directorate of Research and Civil Affairs, helping train the personnel who would re-establish civil administration in New Guinea. Later he was a lecturer at the School of Pacific Administration. In 1956, he became, part-time, the first editor of *Quadrant*, a right wing intellectual journal published by the Congress for Cultural Freedom, which still flourishes. In 1961 McAuley accepted an appointment as reader in poetry at the University of Tasmania, where he was later professor of English, a position held until his death in 1976.

The 'Ern Malley' hoax poems, co-authored with Harold Stewart and published in 1944 when McAuley was twenty-four, were foisted upon Max Harris, the editor of *Angry Penguins*, a magazine promoting surrealism in an Australian setting. McAuley and Stewart concocted in one afternoon, at their army barracks in Melbourne, sixteen poems supposedly written by a garage mechanic, who had died at the Keatsian age of twenty-five. Malley's poems were 'discovered' by his sister Ethel, who sent them to Harris, and who appears now in her correspondence as a slyly comic creation worthy of Barry Humphries. *Angry Penguins* was detested by the hoaxers because of the free-associational rhetoric and meaninglessness of the work it promoted. In playing their trick on the magazine, McAuley and Stewart made use of a dictionary, a collected Shakespeare, a rhyming manual, a book of quotations, and a report on the control of mosquitoes by draining swamps, from which they took lines and words at random. So as to be sure that the hoax worked, the Malley poems contain some obviously striking lines, but they are for the most part hyperbole and deliberate bathos. Each author was careful to interrupt the other's stream of consciousness, to be sure that no unintended 'profundity' could be attributed to them, and all of the poems are ultimately absurd. None of them have a formal wholeness or are works of art. Still, ever since the hoax was so crushingly revealed, there have been those who have claimed the Malley opus is really that of a genuine modernist poet. It is regularly lamented that modern poetry in Australia was held up to ridicule and set back by this affair.

Late in his life McAuley's emotions opened up again, and his orthodoxy relaxed to a degree, perhaps as the result of an experience of cancer, of which he was apparently cured, but which was to claim him some years afterwards. Although more spontaneous, and more personal, these later poems did not recapture the striking language of his earliest book.

Probably more than any other Australian poet, McAuley had a formally argued philosophical position, which informed his poetry, and religious and political views that he proselytised as poet, critic and editor. Later in his life he seems to have become more sceptical about his search for a tradition that was independent of personal feeling.

TERRA AUSTRALIS

Voyage within you, on the fabled ocean,
And you will find that Southern Continent,
Quiros' vision—his hidalgo heart
And mythical Australia, where reside
All things in their imagined counterpart.

It is your land of similes: the wattle
Scatters its pollen on the doubting heart;
The flowers are wide-awake; the air gives ease.
There you come home; the magpies call you Jack
And whistle like larrikins at you from the trees.

There too the angophora preaches on the hillsides
With the gestures of Moses; and the white cockatoo,
Perched on his limbs, screams with demoniac pain;
And who shall say on what errand the insolent emu
Walks between morning and night on the edge of the plain?

But northward in valleys of the fiery Goat
Where the sun like a centaur vertically shoots
His raging arrows with unerring aim,
Stand the ecstatic solitary pyres
Of unknown lovers, featureless with flame.

THE INCARNATION OF SIRIUS

In that age, the great anagram of God
Had bayed the planets from the rounds they trod,
And gathered the fixed stars in a shining nation
Like restless birds that flock before migration.

For the millennial instinct of new flight
Resolved the antimony that fixed their light;
And, echoing in the troubled soul of Earth,
Quickened a virgin's womb, to bring to birth

What scarce was human: a rude avatar
That glistened with the enclosed wrath of a star
The woman died in pangs, before she had kissed
The monstrous form of God's antagonist.

But at its showing forth, the poets cried
In a strange tongue; hot mouths prophesied
The coolness of the bloody vintage-drops:
'Let us be drunk at least, when the world stops!'

Anubis-headed, the heresiarch
Sprang to a height, fire-sinewed in the dark,
And his ten fingers, bracketed on high,
Were a blazing candelabrum in the sky.

The desert lion antiphonally roared;
The tiger's sinews quivered like a chord;
Man smelt the blood beneath his brother's skin
And in a loving hate the sword went in.

And then the vision sank, bloody and aborted.
The stars that with rebellion had consorted
Fled back in silence to their former stations.
Over the giant face of dreaming nations

The centuries-thick coverlet was drawn.
Upon the huddled breast Aldebaran
Still glittered with its sad alternate fire:
Blue as of memory, red as of desire.

CHORUS III OF *PROMETHEUS*

from The Hero and the Hydra

In spring the air breaks with a splintering cry
Of lust and rage; bright feathers stain; red blood
Flows from the bull's flank; insects pierce and die;
And all would perish in that wrathful mood
I thought, until in vision once I saw
The goddess Ceremony giving law

To creatures of the wild air and the wood;
Excitement changed to dance and courtesy.
Far out upon a seaward rock she stood
And watched the wheeling gulls, the parquetry
Of fish that slide within the tranquil wave;
I saw the inborn rituals that can save

From self-destructive fear the angry droves
Of cattle and the labyrinths of the ant;
For Ceremony blessed their anxious loves
And made the swarming darkness jubilant.
Also I marked how wisely she prescribes
Tradition to the uninstinctive tribes

Of men; to live in a concentric maze
Of custom while the big flute and the drum
Proclaim the dance, and well-tuned voices raise
A shield of sound to ward off what may come.
But now that men are cast out from the sleep
Of ancient order, they no longer keep

The ratios of the planets. Once they knew
A natural tuning of their love and hate
By ritual enactment and taboo;
But though they try again it is too late:
The myths are void, their patterns wear away
To markings on the streets where children play.

Then as the bee deserts the blackened comb
That hived the honey of forgotten springs,
Or as the ant, beneath her pebbled dome,
Abandons after patient harvestings
Her sunken riddle, Ceremony fled
And left her former works untenanted.

In a foreboding anguish then I cried
Upon the goddess, who departing said:
'If I return it shall be as the bride
Of one that here in exile droops his head,
Whom now triumphant eagles tear at will.'
But at her words earth sullened and grew still.

ONE TUESDAY IN SUMMER

That sultry afternoon the world went strange.
Under a violet and leaden bruise
The air was filled with sinister yellow light;
Trees, houses, grass took on unnatural hues.

Thunder rolled near. The intensity grew and grew
Like doom itself with lightnings on its face.
And Mr Pitt, the grocer's order-man,
Who made his call on Tuesdays at our place,

Said to my mother, looking at the sky,
'You'd think the ending of the world had come.'
A leathern little man, with bicycle-clips
Around his ankles, doing our weekly sum,

He too looked strange in that uncanny light;
As in the Bible ordinary men
Turn out to be angelic messengers,
Pronouncing the Lord's judgments why and when.

I watched the scurry of the small black ants
That sensed the storm. What Mr Pitt had said
I didn't quite believe, or disbelieve;
But still the words had got into my head,

For nothing less seemed worthy of the scene.
The darkening imminence hung on and on,
Till suddenly, with lightning-stroke and rain,
Apocalypse exploded, and was gone.

By nightfall things had their familiar look.
But I had seen the world stand in dismay
Under the aspect of another meaning
That rain or time would hardly wash away.

Because

My father and my mother never quarrelled.
They were united in a kind of love
As daily as the *Sydney Morning Herald*,
Rather than like the eagle or the dove.

I never saw them casually touch,
Or show a moment's joy in one another.
Why should this matter to me now so much?
I think it bore more hardly on my mother,

Who had more generous feeling to express.
My father had dammed up his Irish blood
Against all drinking praying fecklessness,
And stiffened into stone and creaking wood.

His lips would make a switching sound, as though
Spontaneous impulse must be kept at bay.
That it was mainly weakness I see now,
But then my feelings curled back in dismay.

Small things can pit the memory like a cyst:
Having seen other fathers greet their sons,
I put my childish face up to be kissed
After an absence. The rebuff still stuns

My blood. The poor man's curt embarrassment
At such a delicate proffer of affection
Cut like a saw. But home the lesson went:
My tenderness thenceforth escaped detection.

My mother sang *Because*, and *Annie Laurie*,
White Wings, and other songs; her voice was sweet.
I never gave enough, and I am sorry;
But we were all closed in the same defeat.

People do what they can; they were good people,
They cared for us and loved us. Once they stood
Tall in my childhood as the school, the steeple.
How can I judge without ingratitude?

Judgment is simply trying to reject
A part of what we are because it hurts.
The living cannot call the dead collect:
They won't accept the charge, and it reverts.

It's my own judgment day that I draw near,
Descending in the past, without a clue,
Down to that central deadness: the despair
Older than any hope I ever knew.

Parish Church

We used to sing at Easter in the choir
With trumpet and harmonium and drums,
Feeling within our hearts new-kindled fire.
Now I'm the only one that ever comes.

I bring with me my griefs, my sins, my death,
And sink in silence as I try to pray.
Though in this calm no impulse stirs my breath,
At least there's nothing that I would unsay.

ROSEMARY DOBSON

———— ❧ ————

ROSEMARY DOBSON, BORN in Sydney in 1920, was edu-
cated as a boarder at the Frensham Girls' School, near Mitta-
gong, on the southern tablelands of New South Wales. Her mother
was widowed early; her father was the son of Austin Dobson, the
English poet. After leaving school, she studied art, and was taught to
draw by Thea Proctor, one of the first post-impressionists in Aus-
tralia. In her early twenties she joined the editorial department of the
publisher Angus and Robertson, and worked there with the legendary
editor Beatrice Davis, and with Nan McDonald, the latter becoming
a close friend. Her first collection of poetry was published when she
was twenty-four.

Dobson married Alec Bolton, who became, from 1966 to 1971,
the London editor for Angus and Robertson. During this period she
travelled in Europe, deepening her appreciation of Western art, par-
ticularly that of the Renaissance (both Northern and Italian), which
has been important to much of her work as a poet. In 1972 her hus-
band was appointed publisher to the National Library of Australia in
Canberra, where they have since lived. They have three children.

Rosemary Dobson has published six collections of poetry, and
several editions of her selected poems. At different periods her writ-
ing has shown an admiration for the work of certain of her Austral-
ian contemporaries: in some earlier poems, Kenneth Slessor; in later
poems, Judith Wright and David Campbell. These influences have
been more and more absorbed into her own voice. Decoration has
given way to existential disquiet, although her work has always dis-
played an attractive gratitude towards experience.

from THE CONTINUANCE OF POETRY: TWELVE POEMS FOR DAVID CAMPBELL

AT THE COAST

The high wind has stripped the bark from the gum-trees,
Smooth-boled they follow each other down to the water.

From rented houses the daughters of professors
Emerge smooth-limbed in this light summer season.

They step from behind the trees at the edge of the water
As smooth as ochre and as cool as lemon.

And which are girls and which are smooth-limbed saplings?
The light is trembling on them from the water.

They glow and flicker in and out of shadow
Like poetry behind the print on pages.

POEMS OF THE RIVER WANG

Two poets walking together
May pause suddenly and say,
Will this be your poem, or mine?

May offer courteously,
Please take it. No, you first.
Wang Wei and P'ei Ti

Made twenty poems each of the Wang River,
Apricot Wood House, South Hill, the Pepper Garden.
Later Wang Wei wrote to his friend,

Could you join me once more?
Out walking now I see blond grass,
Wild orchids, black cattle, and the daylight moon.

COCK CROW

Wanting to be myself, alone,
Between the lit house and the town
I took the road, and at the bridge
Turned back and walked the way I'd come.

Three times I took that lonely stretch,
Three times the dark trees closed me round,
The night absolved me of my bonds
Only my footsteps held the ground.

My mother and my daughter slept,
One life behind and one before,
And I that stood between denied
Their needs in shutting-to the door.

And walking up and down the road
Knew myself, separate and alone,
Cut off from human cries, from pain,
And love that grows about the bone.

Too brief illusion! Thrice for me
I heard the cock crow on the hill,
And turned the handle of the door
Thinking I knew his meaning well.

WHO?

Who, then, was 'Auntie Molly'? No-one now
Can tell me who she was: or how it was
She and my Mother shared a rented house
One summer for a fortnight—we took a train
And from the station trudged a country road.
I know she worked year-long and lived alone
Somewhere with a strange name, like Rooty Hill.

Postoffice-Store-in-one sold bread and milk.
Returning to our house we scuffed along
Cloth-hatted, sandalled, kicking at the stones.
Mother and Auntie Molly walked ahead
And suddenly Mother stopped, threw back her head
And laughed and laughed there in the dusty road.
We were amazed to hear our Mother laugh.

The fowl-yard fence sagged with ripe passion-fruit,
We bought cream in a jug. At night we sat
Around the lamp-lit table, colouring in.
In bed, near sleep, we'd hear the rise and fall
Of their grave voices—hers, and Auntie Molly's,
Whom no-one now would know; who made my Mother
Laugh joyfully in the middle of the road.

GWEN HARWOOD

GWEN HARWOOD (NEE FOSTER), born 1920, was raised in Brisbane in a family devoted to music. She studied piano and composition, taught piano and was a church organist. In 1945 she married William Harwood, a linguist, and settled in Tasmania. They have had five children.

Harwood began writing poetry in the late 1950s, but her first book was not published until 1963. In the early sixties she was made briefly notorious by newspapers as the 'Tas. housewife' who had hoaxed the *Bulletin* magazine. It had printed a sonnet of hers that read acrostically 'Fuck all editors', and when this was discovered the proprieter recalled all unsold copies. 'It was just a piece of natural mischief,' Harwood explained.

Harwood says that she has loved domestic life and raising her children, and that her sonnets about women's domestic *angst* do not refer to her own experience. Her earlier poems show the influence of A.D. Hope. Harwood was not herself an academic, nor was she closely linked to the Melbourne campus poets of the sixties and seventies who espoused and practised a cerebral, academic style of poetry, but her work, particularly her earlier books, have elements of that style, and with her greater vitality, she can be seen as this movement's leading exemplar in Australia.

She has written libretti for well-known musicians who are friends, and her interests also include German language and culture, gardening and domestic animals. She has found the Tasmanian landscape melancholy and chilling, but thinks her poetry may have benefited from this. Her poetry has an elusively intellectual surface, and flourishes the name of Wittgenstein. That philosopher, however, has been open to widely different interpretations, and nowhere does she define her understanding of him. Wittgenstein's walk-on appearances in the blue-stocking brightness of Harwood's set-pieces seem curiously wilful. Despite her air of intellectual assurance, her real strengths are in reminiscence and the expression of personal emotion.

The adoption of loosened forms in Harwood's later work has freed her own voice, and her most recent book *Bone Scan* is widely regarded as her best collection.

NEW MUSIC

to Larry Sitsky

Who can grasp for the first time
these notes hurled into empty space?
Suddenly a tormenting nerve
affronts the fellowship of cells.
Who can tell for the first time
if it is love or pain he feels,
violence or tenderness that calls
plain objects by outrageous names

and strikes new sound from the old names?
At the service of a human vision,
not symbols, but strange presences
defining a transparent void,
these notes beckon the mind to move
out of the smiling context of
what's known; and what can guide it is
neither wisdom nor power, but love.

Who but a fool would enter these
regions of being with no name?
Secure among their towering junk
the wise and powerful congregate
fitting old shapes to old ideas,
rocked by their classical harmonies
in living sleep. The beggars' stumps
bang on the stones. Nothing will change.

Unless, wakeful with questioning,
some mind beats on necessity,
and being unanswered learns to bear
emptiness like a wound that no
word but its own can mend; and finds
a new imperative to summon
a world out of unmeasured darkness
pierced by a brilliant nerve of sound.

AN IMPROMPTU FOR ANN JENNINGS

Sing, memory, sing those seasons in the freezing
   suburb of Fern Tree, a rock-shaded place
with tree ferns, gullies, snowfalls and eye-pleasing
   prospects from paths along the mountain-face.

Nursing our babies by huge fires of wattle,
   or pushing them in prams when it was fine,
exchanging views on diet, or Aristotle,
   discussing Dr Spock or Wittgenstein,

cleaning up infants and the floors they muddied,
   bandaging, making ends and tempers meet—
sometimes I'd mind your children while you studied,
   or you'd take mine when I felt near defeat;

keeping our balance somehow through the squalling
   disorder, or with anguish running wild
when sickness, a sick joke from some appalling
   orifice of the nightwatch, touched a child;

think of it, woman: each of us gave birth to
   four children, our new lords whose beautiful
tyrannic kingdom might restore the earth to
   that fullness we thought lost beyond recall

when, in the midst of life, we could not name it,
   when spirit cried in darkness, '*I will have . . .*'
but what? have what? There was no word to frame it,
   though spirit beat at flesh as in a grave

from which it could not rise. But we have risen.
   Caesar's we were, and wild, though we seemed tame.
Now we move where we will. Age is no prison
   to hinder those whose joy has found its name.

We are our own. All Caesar's debts are rendered
    in full to Caesar. Time has given again
a hundredfold those lives that we surrendered,
    the love, the fruitfulness; but not the pain.

Before the last great fires we two went climbing
    like gods or blessed spirits in summer light
with the quiet pulse of mountain water chiming
    as if twenty years were one long dreaming night,

above the leafy dazzle of the streams
    to fractured rock, where water had its birth,
and stood in silence, at the roots of dreams,
    content to know: our children walk the earth.

NIGHT THOUGHTS: BABY & DEMON

Baby I'm sick. I need
nursing. Give me your breast.
My orifices bleed.
I cannot sleep. My chest
shakes like a window. Light
guts me. My head's not right.

Demon, we're old, old chap.
Born under the same sign
after some classic rape.
Gemini. Yours is mine.
Sickness and health. We'll share
the end of this affair.

Baby, I'm sick to death.
But I can't die. You do
the songs, you've got the breath.

Give them the old soft shoe.
Put on a lovely show.
Put on your wig, and go.

The service station flags, denticulate
plastic, snap in the wind. Hunched seabirds wait

for light to quench the unmeaning lights of town.
This day will bring the fabulous summer down.

Weather no memory can match will fade
to memory, leaf-drift in the pines' thick shade.

All night salt water stroked and shaped the sand.
All night I heard it. Your bravura hand

chimed me to shores beyond time's rocking swell.
The last cars leave the shabby beach motel.

Lovers and drunks unroofed in sobering air
disperse, ghost-coloured in the streetlight-glare.

> Rock-a-bye Baby
>   in the motel
> Baby will kiss
>   and Demon will tell.

One candle lights us. Night's cool airs begin
to lick the luminous edges of our skin.

> When the bough bends
>   the apple will fall
> Baby knows nothing
>   Demon knows all.

Draw up the voluptuously crumpled sheet.
In rose-dark silence gentle tongues repeat
the body's triumph through its grand eclipse.
I feel your pulsebeat through my fingertips.

Baby's a rocker
    lost on the shore.
Demon's a mocker.
    Baby's a whore.

World of the happy, innocent and whole:
the body's the best picture of the soul
couched like an animal in savage grace.
Ghost after ghost obscures your sleeping face.

My baby's like a bird of day
    that flutters from my side,
my baby's like an empty beach
    that's ravished by the tide.

So fair are you, my bonny lass,
    so sick and strange am I,
that I must lie with all your loves
    and suck your sweetness dry.

And drink your juices dry, my dear,
    and grind your bones to sand,
then I will walk the empty shore
    and sift you through my hand.

And sift you through my hand, my dear,
    and find you grain by grain,
and build your body bone by bone
    and flesh those bones again,

with flesh from all your loves, my love,
    while tides and seasons stream,
until you wake by candle-light
    from your midsummer dream,

and like some gentle creature meet
    the huntsman's murderous eye,
and know you never shall escape
    however fast you fly.

Unhoused I'll shout my drunken songs
   and through the streets I'll go
compelling all I meet to toast
   the bride they do not know.

Till all your tears are dry, my love,
   and your ghosts fade in the sun.
Be sure I'll have your heart, my love,
   when all your loving's done.

Naked Vision

I was sent to fetch an eye
promised for a fresh corneal graft.
At the doctor's rooms nurse gave me
a common paper bag;
in that, a sterile jar;
in that, the disembodied eye.

I sat in Davey Street
on a low brick garden wall
and looked. The eye looked back.
It gazed, lucid and whole,
from its colourless solution.
The window of whose soul?

Trees in St David's Park
refreshed the lunchtime lovers:
riesling gold, claret dark;
late flowers flaunted all colours.
But my friend and I had eyes
only for one another.

In flawless solitude
it stared, blue as the sky.
Nothing seemed out of range
of our crystalline exchange.
The longing in that eye
will haunt me till I die.

A MUSIC LESSON

Kröte's not well. His mood is bloody.
A pupil he can hardly stand
attacks a transcendental study.
—Lord, send me one real pianist.
Soul of a horse! He shapes her hand
and breathes apologies to Liszt.

'Reflect: in order to create
we must know how to. Think about
the balance between height and weight,
shoulder to fingertip; a hanging
bridge, resilient, reaching out
with firm supports. Let's have no banging!

'Playing begins inside your brain.
Music's much more than flesh and bone.
Relax, and listen. If you strain
your muscles *here* and *here* contract.
You get a stiff, unlovely tone.'
His pupil says, 'Is that a fact?'

She plays the passage louder, faster;
indeed deliberately tries
to infuriate her music master.
'The year that Liszt was born, a comet
blazed over European skies.'
'Am I to draw conclusions from it?

'And, if so, what?' the tyro sneers.
—Cold heart, stiff hands. How to explain?
'When a new genius appears
it's like that fiery head of light
drawing us in its golden train.
Now, shall we try to get it right?

'Does it give you no pride to say
"My teacher's teacher learned from Liszt?"
Feel in your hands, before you play,
the body's marvellous architecture:
the muscles between hand and wrist
kept flexible; now try to picture

the finger forming, from the point
where it rests on the key, an arc
curving through every finger-joint,
supporting the whole arm's free weight.
Now the least effort makes its mark.
The instrument can sing.'
                                        'I'm late,'

the pupil whines. The lesson's over.
The teacher pours himself a gin,
pats the piano like a lover
(—Dear mistress, we're alone once more).
Liszt, with his upper lip gone in,
beams from the cover of a score.

Abbé, forsooth! A toast to you,
old friend, old fiend in monkish dress.
I know you had your off days too.
At Schumann's, Clara said, you played
his work so badly once (confess!)
that only her good manners made

her sit in silence in that room.
—Have mercy on all pianists,
Architect of the world, of whom
I ask that I may live to see
Halley's Comet.
                    If God exists
then music is his love for me.

THE SECRET LIFE OF FROGS

Mr Gabriel Fur, my Siamese,
brings to the hearth a Common Toadlet,
Crinia tasmaniensis.
Mice are permitted, frogs forbidden.
It will live. I carry it outside.
Its heartbeat troubles my warm hand
and as I set it down I see
two small girls in a warmer land.

My friend Alice and I would sit
cradling our frogs behind the tankstand.
Other fathers would talk about
the Great War. Mine would only say,
'I used to be a stretcher-bearer.'
Not seen, not heard, in childhood's earshot
of the women on the back veranda,
we knew about atrocities.
Some syllables we used as charms:
Passchendaele   Mons   Gallipoli.
We knew about Poor George, who cried
if any woman touched her hair.
He'd been inside a brothel when

the Jerries came and started shooting.
(We thought a brothel was a French
hotel that served hot broth to diggers.)
The girl that he'd been with was scalped.
Every Frog in the house was killed.

Well, that was life for frogs. At school
the big boys blew them up and spiked them.
One bully had the very knife
with which his father killed ten Germans—
twenty—a hundred—numbers blossomed.
Dad the Impaler! making work
for the more humble stretcher-bearers.

In safety by the dripping tankstand
our frogs with matchstick hands as pale
as the violet stems they lived among
cuddled their vulnerable bellies
in hands that would not do them wrong.

THE TWINS

Three years old when their mother died
in what my grandmother called
accouchement, my father labour,
they heard the neighbours intone
'A mercy the child went with her.'

Their father raised them somehow.
No one could tell them apart.
At seven they sat in school
in their rightful place, at the top
of the class, the first to respond
with raised arm and finger-flick.

When one gave the answer, her sister
repeated it under her breath.
An inspector accused them of cheating,
but later, in front of the class,
declared himself sorry, and taught us
a marvellous word: *telepathic*.

On Fridays, the story went,
they slept in the shed, barred in
from their father's rage as he drank
his dead wife back to his house.
For the rest of the week he was sober
and proud. My grandmother gave them
a basket of fruit. He returned it.
'We manage. We don't need help.'

They could wash their own hair, skin rabbits,
milk the cow, make porridge, clean boots.

Unlike most of the class I had shoes,
clean handkerchiefs, ribbons, a toothbrush.
We all shared the schoolsores and nits
and the language I learned to forget
at the gate of my welcoming home.

One day as I sat on the fence
my pinafore goffered, my hair
still crisp from the curlers, the twins
came by. I scuttled away
so I should not have to share
my Saturday sweets. My mother
saw me, and slapped me, and offered
the bag to the twins, who replied
one aloud and one sotto voce,
'No thank you. We don't like lollies.'

They lied in their greenish teeth
as they knew, and we knew.
                              Good angel
give me that morning again
and let me share, and spare me
the shame of my parents' rebuke.

If there are multiple worlds
then let there be one with an ending
quite other than theirs: leaving school
too early and coming to grief.

Or if this is our one life sentence,
hold them in innocence, writing
Our Father which art in Heaven
in copperplate, or drawing
(their work being done) the same picture
on the backs of their slates: a foursquare
house where a smiling woman
winged like an angel welcomes
two children home from school.

NIGHT AND DREAMS

I

'I come to you in a dream of ages
past', sings Crab. He swirls his velvet-
seaweed cloak. 'When first we met,
and last, you will recall, I was
imprisoned in your father's house.'

Sea colours on his carapace,
wave-hiss, tide-rustle in his voice.
'Some fiend had tied my fearful claws—'
—Yes, I recall. I must have been
a skinny child of eight or nine

that night my father brought you home—
'No, let *me* tell', says Crab, 'this is
my aria, *my* party piece.
Grandmother, mother, father, brother
and you, went to the local theatre

leaving me bound in parching darkness.
I prayed: Redeemer Crab, release me
by your own sidelong righteousness
from these straightforward evildoers.
Take me where my transparent children

float in their manifold sea vision.
Silence. Mouse-whisper, cockroach-scuffle.
I felt, not far, the Brisbane River
ebbing to salt creek, mangrove swamp,
and burst my bonds, O yes I did!

and raged through your dark house, and hid.
That night you dared not go to bed
finding me gone when you returned.
Splintered pencils and toys proclaimed
my ocean strength. How soon forgotten

what Stan and Olly did and said!
Time, time. I felt the tide returning
far off. O Salt Redeemer, come
(I prayed) let navies drown to feed me
with rotten stump, decaying belly,

or if I am to die, allow me
one crunchbone tender-balancing foot.'
—My father caught you. 'Ah, he did.
"We'll cook the brute tonight", he said.
"Bring me the hatpin." Someone put

a diamond eye on a steel stalk
into your father's hand to stab
my stalked eyes. O the blaze of pain

eclipsing light's immense mandala!
Sea green, sea blue, I raged to red.

Boiling, Crab died. I became Crab.'

II

Crab is dressed for the feast: on lettuce shredded
to seaweed ribbons, cracked claws reassembled,
he lies among parsley curls and radish roses.
Our starchy Sunday-snowy cloth is set
with what remains of Greatgrandmother's china,
translucent white, rimmed with a deepsea blue.
On his great serving dish Crab's at the centre
of a splendid colour wheel: cucumber slices,
tomato, celery, carrot, egg: my work,
duly admired. My grandmother says grace.
'Where would you eat like this', my father asks,
passing the homemade bread, 'except in Queensland?'
A lovely room. Windows give on the garden,
rose and green panes of bubble-glass enchanting
the dullest day. The sideboard mirror offers
more light. Such light, restoring, recomposing
many who dined here. Most of them are dead.

III

'That's enough of pentameters',
says Crab, returning to my dream.
—What shall I write, I ask. He writes,
so I won't miss his fearful joke:
THE DIRE BELLY VARIATIONS!

Making himself a cairn of stones
he says, 'This is my own rock group.
O I'm the original punk rocker
with a hatpin through my brain, my brain,
with a diamond hatpin through my brain.'

—Your jokes are awful. 'I know worse.'
—Impossible. 'Shall I rehearse
the names of those who've died from cancer?
O I'm the original merry prankster,
a diamond hatpin's all my eye.

Tell me, where are those who ate
my claws, my tender body meat?
Laurel and Hardy fans, long gone!
You cracked my hardware, ate my software.
Now I'm programmed in your brain.'

IV

More and more of the great questions,
such as: what am I doing here
in gumboots and a summer nightdress
in a moonlit garden chasing sheep?

The sheep are out. It's not a dream.
I'll mend the broken fence tomorrow.
What's left of night? Enough to dream in.
What dreams will come? Who else but Crab.

I ate him sixty years ago.
Ocean of memory, transposing
feaster and feast. He beckons, wearing
seaweed clothes, with sidelong charm.

'Shall we go to a pirate movie?'
—You like the sea? 'I like the bodies,
and "Take the lady below and make
her comfortable", that's what I like.

I can't be bothered with the love scenes.
I've opened hearts. I know what's in them.'
At interval he buys refreshments,
'Two seafood sticks. One without crab.

Come live with me and be my supper
where colours have no boundaries,
where every word is writ in water,
I'll put my arm around your waist.

I'll put my armour round your waist.
Shell after shell my soft self waxes.
Seek help! Sea kelp for drowning sailors.
Great questions all have wavering answers.'

Ghosts crowd to hear. O my lost loves.
Waking to hard–edge sunlit colours,
sharp birdsong, lamb-bleat, I recall
myself among the moonlit sheep

questioning—what? Why should I care
how long ago my death began?
Am I a ghost dreaming I'm human
with herbs to plant, a fence to mend?

CROW-CALL

'He lives eternally who lives in the present'
—Tractatus 6.4311

Let this be eternal life:
light ebbing, my dinghy drifting
on watershine, dead centre
of cloud and cloud-reflection—
high vapour, mind's illusion.

And for music, Baron Corvo,
my half tame forest raven
with his bad leg unretracted
beating for home, lamenting
or, possibly, rejoicing
that he saw the world at all.

Space of a crow-call, enclosing
the self and all it remembers.
Heart-beat, wing-beat, a moment.
My line jerks taut. The cod
are biting. This too is eternal:
the death of cod at twilight.
And this: food on my table
keeping a tang of ocean.

So many, in raven darkness.
Why give death fancy names?

Corvo, where have you settled
your crippled leg for the night?

LEX BANNING

L EX BANNING WAS born in 1921. Afflicted from birth with cerebral palsy, he spoke and moved with difficulty. He grew up with his mother at Punchbowl in the outer suburbs of Sydney, and went to local schools. Vocational counsellors advised him to drop out of high school and to work at shoe repairs. After two years of this, during which he continued to read widely, he applied for, and was granted, entry to the University of Sydney. He graduated in arts, and became a librarian and freelance journalist. Banning's intelligence was incisive and dandified, with affinities to Slessor, but lacking Slessor's inventive genius with language. Well-known in Sydney's bohemia, appreciated as a wit, he was attractive to women, and was married for a time to a doctor. He had a cult following among a small coterie of friends, which continues to this day. A user of amphetamines and an enthusiastic drinker, Banning's health failed rapidly and he was dead at the age of forty-four. He distilled a painful existence in lapidary epigrams.

FIVE

Truly to set in words,
five things are my despair;
the flower of the poinciana,
the scent of a woman's hair,

the burst of a cigarette-end
flung hard against a stone,
the arc of water falling,
the longing in the bone.

NAN McDONALD

———— ❧ ————

NAN McDONALD WAS born in 1921 in the Sydney suburb of Eastwood. After graduating from Sydney University in arts, she worked for the publishing firm Angus and Robertson as an editor during one of its most interesting periods. McDonald never married, lived always with members of her family, and died when she was fifty-two of cancer.

Hal Porter has described her in *The Extra*, one of his volumes of autobiography: 'She looks [the way] one expects a poetess to look: pale, stilled, as tall and serene as a Parmigianino Madonna. She matches her poems ... [and yet] within the seeming temperance of her poetry ... stir darkness, world-weariness, despair, civilized anguish.' Porter comments that though he saw McDonald shortly before her death, and corresponded with her, she never gave any indication to him of her illness.

Nan McDonald's poetry can remind one of Emily Brontë's, though the Englishwoman is more passionate: there is a similar exultation in cold, inhuman places; a style similarly plain, muted, and austere; and in both an undertone of stoic Protestant religion. McDonald's relatively early death, too, was evidently long anticipated and accepted.

PHOTOGRAPH OF AN ACTRESS, c. 1860

Long schoolroom days, drowsy with chanting voices
And heat from the iron roof, and on the wall,
Flesh drought-devoured and eyes set on despair,
The explorers come to their last camp. Recall
That picture when you look on this, for there—
In the pack in the foreground? In the leader's rags?—
This small flat case lay hidden. When night came
He drew it out and kissed, late and alone,
Her young round throat, smooth cheek, and curled dark hair. . .
Then, being mortal, may have known love's flame
Dying within him by the dying fire;
Merely to live became his heart's desire.

As for her, her heart broke, but was joined once more
And served her well enough in later years
(Her talent was too slight for tragedy)
Yet a flawed heart reflects a different light,
At times a double scene. So on nights long after
When the rain murmured like remembered tears
On the high theatre roof, she still might see
The desert sun strike downward, hot and white,
Blinding the gaslight, showing the crack in the gilt,
Moth-graze in plush, melting the paint she wore—
See players mime and mouth like phantoms then
Against the rock-hewn figures of doomed men.

No doubt the applause of London crowds was sweet
But it would have an undertone for ears
That had learnt first in Melbourne how the walls
May reel to wave on bursting wave of cheers
Bearing the rider on down the long street
(His eyes still seeking hers); how the sound falls
Away so soon, and faintly out of silence
Comes to the few who listen the northward tread
Of horses and of camels, then human feet
Stumbling in dust, and last the tiny whisper
Of running ants over dry sand, dry skin,
And in the sockets where those eyes had been.

She died of fever in New Orleans, still young,
Far indeed from the land of her Irish hero's sleeping.
How should her light foot print so harsh a ground,
Her smile find place in that grim tableau hung
On schoolroom walls? Yet it may be when sickness
Had burned her body gaunt as his, and dried
Her lips enough to take the poor kiss given
Her pictured face so long ago, she found
His camp at last, and there, too great for weeping,
Held to her breast the adder of that country,
Felt the fangs bite, the intricate knot untied,
Set her crown straight, and lay down at his side.

THE BARREN GROUND

I think of it, that high, bare place in the mountains,
Always under a cool grey blowing sky
Where the eagle hangs black and alone—clean wind whistling
Through tussock and long low swell of scrub, and through
Hollows the rainy centuries have worn
In the huge ruinous heaps of silent stone,
I trace on the map the way from the blue-edged coast
Across green, where the rich farms lie, through the deepening brown
That marks the rising ground, till the clear road fades
And a broken track goes climbing on to that space
Empty of all but the three words standing plain,
And I think I could lie down there, and be at peace.

It was not named for a blue dog, a dead horse,
Nor for some dark tribe's thought that haunts the ear
And still eludes the brain; no bold explorer
Made record of his desperate journey there;
No settler left his name to cry when the bush
Has flowed back across the furrows and the cold hearth,
When the fruit-trees have gone wild and the children are scattered,

'By sorrow and sweat I was conqueror of this earth.'
No, it was not named for glory or possession,
The foolish dreams of man, whose stiffening hand
Lets the bright coin drop and follows it down to dust,
But simply for itself—The Barren Ground.

How lovely its fall on the ear bewildered with words,
On the mind sick with the eddies of thought, for at last
The eyes are filled with the glitter of light on the leaves,
With the million-petalled flowers, and can only thirst—
Turning from life grown rank and smelling of death—
With a great thirst for the truth of barrenness.
For what is life, or what is death, who knows?
But all men know that peace is only peace.

Yet it may not be as I dream—three words on the map
Are all my knowledge, and that I have seen as well
Through a gap in the hills, rising far and strange in the evening,
The darkening ramparts of its eastern wall.
But the heart has its own routes and its journeys' ends,
And sooner or later strikes, though travelling blind,
The rocky track where the long road gives out
And comes on a grey day to its Barren Ground.

ERIC ROLLS

—————— ✦ ——————

ERIC ROLLS WAS born at Grenfell, in western New South
Wales in 1923, and went from Fort Street School in Sydney
straight into the army, during World War II. On his discharge, after
serving in New Guinea and Bougainville, he took up a Soldiers'
Settlement property near Narrabri in the New South Wales wheat
belt. He is married with a grown-up family.

Rolls' output of verse has been small, ranging from 'folk song' to
satire, from bawdy and macabre pieces in *Sheaf Tosser* to free verse
recollections of wartime New Guinea in *The Green Mosaic*. He is best
known for his acclaimed non-fiction prose: works such as *They All
Ran Wild*, about rabbits and other pests introduced into Australia,
and *A Million Wild Acres*, an ecological history of the Pilliga forest
near his home. He has commented that his feeling for poetry has
perhaps found its truest fulfillment in these factual books, which
freely display his eye for striking and sensuous detail and his exuber-
ant interest in life.

MEG'S SONG AND DAVIE'S SONG

Meg.   Yesterday I was a maid
And timidly down the paddock strayed
With one wild bluebell at my breast
That pricked me so I could not rest
To where young Davie stooked the hay.
O he was strong as the spring day.
In the shade of a stook in a hay-sweet haze
I sat and slacked my trembling knees
And laughed with Davie standing there
As I fitted wheat ears in my hair.

Davie. Corn plump and corn crisp
Meg has a waist to clasp
And breasts that were never kissed
And loins that had never sung
To vibrant pluck of hand and tongue:
Burning naked as the sky
We sang together Meg and I.
I speared her like a sheaf of hay
And tossed her maidenhead away.

Meg.   Now today I try to work
But my arms are heavy as I sweep
And every little while I look
To Davie down amongst the hay
And through the open door I keep
Asking quietly if I may
Come to him again today
And will that he may hear, may see
And turn about and beckon me.
O quickly then I'll gladly run
And naked in the glorious sun
Kiss for love and kiss for fun
And when at last he breaks my thighs
My mother's love I will despise.

Davie. Corn crisp and corn plump
        Meg rolls upon her rump
        Like a sheaf of hay unbound
        Wind teased about the ground
        And darling darling are her cries
        As I take her by the thighs.

FRANCIS WEBB

—————— ❧ ——————

F RANCIS WEBB WAS born in Adelaide in 1925, and, following
the death of his mother when he was two years old, grew up
with his paternal grandparents in the comfortable North Shore area
of Sydney. He was educated by the Christian brothers, and learned
from his grandfather a love of classical music and sailing. During
World War II he joined the Royal Australian Air Force, training in
Canada, but was not involved in combat. In England in 1949 he
suffered his first breakdown. His schizophrenia, as it was diagnosed,
gradually worsened and he was to spend almost the entire second
half of his life in mental asylums, at first in England, and later in
Australia.

In the early sixties he lived for a few months in Sydney, in lodg-
ings that a priest arranged for him with two young women. One of
these, Mary Sharah, remembers that he went every day to surf, and
came back each time disturbed by the sight of the young people on
the beach, and by his own ageing. He would go to confession twice
a day, and to Mass every day and several times on Sunday. At his
own request he was returned to institutional care. At first this was
in Melbourne, near his married sister, about whose child he wrote
the poem 'Five Days Old', then later in Sydney. Sir Herbert Read,
the English poet and critic, visited him, and wrote that he was one of
the major poets of the century, to be ranked with Eliot, Rilke and
Pasternak.

In the last years of his life Webb's standing as a poet contrasted savagely with his personal circumstances. For a period when he was institutionalised at Sydney's Callan Park, he was disfigured by psoriasis and was so heavily sedated that he was incapable of maintaining a coherent conversation when visited by other writers. Piety and fear of communism obsessed him but his personal dignity and courtesy survived this ordeal. His medication was later reduced; his coherence returned, his psoriasis went and he was allowed to go on walks with visitors through the grounds. Not long afterwards, in 1973, aged forty-eight, he died.

Critical opinion is divided on Webb's poetry. Some have inclined towards Read's assessment—Douglas Stewart believed Webb had created 'a new language'; David Campbell (who corresponded with him) decided that he 'went higher' than any other Australian poet. Others have found his work turbid.

Webb's poetry shows the influence of the heavily metred and rhymed early poetry of Robert Lowell, and an attraction to a similar vehemence and strain in R.D. FitzGerald. The subject matter of his early 'explorer' poems, like 'A Drum for Ben Boyd' and 'Eyre All Alone', is modelled on Slessor. But it was most of all Slessor's subjective imagery and personification (used by Slessor sparingly), which seem to have been taken up by Webb, and turned to something looming and distorted.

A knowledge of Webb's references will clarify many of his apparent obscurities. An example is 'Morgan's Country', which refers to a bushranger, and Webb here intentionally conveys the feeling of madness, with a real *frisson* and controlled power. Webb often used historical settings, but his most moving poems arose from his experiences in hospitals. The closest parallel to his poetry, with its intensity and lofty architecture, is perhaps the music of Bruckner, his favourite composer.

MORGAN'S COUNTRY

This is Morgan's country: now steady, Bill.
(Stunted and grey, hunted and murderous.)
Squeeze for the first pressure. Shoot to kill.

Five: a star dozing in its cold cavern.
Six: first shuffle of boards in the cold house.
And the sun lagging on seven.

The grey wolf at his breakfast. He cannot think
Why he must make haste, unless because their eyes
Are poison at every well where he might drink.

Unless because their gabbling voices force
The doors of his grandeur—first terror, then only hate.
Now terror again. Dust swarms under the doors.

Ashes drift on the dead-sea shadow of his plate.
Why should he heed them? What to do but kill
When his angel howls, when the sounds reverberate

In the last grey pipe of his brain? At the window sill
A blowfly strums on two strings of air:
Ambush and slaughter tingle against the lull.

But the Cave, his mother, is close beside his chair,
Her sunless face scribbled with cobwebs, bones
Rattling in her throat when she speaks. And there

The stone Look-out, his towering father, leans
Like a splinter from the seamed palm of the plain.
Their counsel of thunder arms him. A threat of rain.

Seven: and a blaze fiercer than the sun.
The wind struggles in the arms of the starved tree,
The temple breaks on a threadbare mat of glass.

Eight: even under the sun's trajectory
This country looks grey, hunted and murderous.

THE GUNNER

When the gunner spoke in his sleep the hut was still,
Uneasily strapped to the reckless wheel of his will;
Silence, humble, directionless as fog,
Lifted, and minutes were rhythmical on the log;

While slipstream plucked at a wafer of glass and steel,
Engines sliced and scooped at the air's thin wall,
And those dim spars dislodged from the moon became
Red thongs of tracer whipping boards aflame.

Listening, you crouched in the turret, watchful and taut
—*Bogey two thousand, skipper, corkscrew to port*—
Marvellous, the voice: driving electric fires
Through the panel of sleep, the black plugs, trailing wires.

The world spoke through its dream, being deaf and blind,
Its words were those of the dream, yet you might find
Forgotten genius, control, alive in this deep
Instinctive resistance to the perils of sleep.

FIVE DAYS OLD

for Christopher John

Christmas is in the air.
You are given into my hands
Out of quietest, loneliest lands.
My trembling is all my prayer.
To blown straw was given
All the fullness of Heaven.

The tiny, not the immense,
Will teach our groping eyes.
So the absorbed skies
Bleed stars of innocence.
So cloud-voice in war and trouble
Is at last Christ in the stable.

Now wonderingly engrossed
In your fearless delicacies,
I am launched upon sacred seas,
Humbly and utterly lost
In the mystery of creation,
Bells, bells of ocean.

Too pure for my tongue to praise,
That sober, exquisite yawn
Or the gradual, generous dawn
At an eyelid, maker of days:
To shrive my thought for perfection
I must breathe old tempests of action

For the snowflake and face of love.
Windfall and word of truth.
Honour close to death.
O eternal truthfulness, Dove,
Tell me what I hold—
Myrrh? Frankincense? Gold?

If this is man, then the danger
And fear are as lights of the inn,
Faint and remote as sin
Out here by the manger.
In the sleeping, weeping weather
We shall all kneel down together.

A Death at Winson Green

There is a green spell stolen from Birmingham;
Your peering omnibus overlooks the fence,
Or the grey, bobbing lifelines of a tram.
Here, through the small hours, sings our innocence.
Joists, apathetic pillars plot this ward,
Tired timbers wheeze and settle into dust,
We labour, labour: for the treacherous lord
Of time, the dazed historic sunlight, must
Be wheeled in a seizure towards one gaping bed,
Quake like foam on the lip, or lie still as the dead.

Visitors' Day: the graven perpetual smile,
String-bags agape, and pity's laundered glove.
The last of the heathens shuffles down the aisle,
Dark glass to a beauty which we hate and love.
Our empires rouse against this ancient fear,
Longsufferings, anecdotes, levelled at our doom;
Mine-tracks of old allegiance, prying here,
Perplex the sick man raving in his room.
Outside, a shunting engine hales from bed
The reminiscent feast-day, long since dead.

Noon reddens, trader birds deal cannily
With Winson Green, and the slouch-hatted sun
Gapes at windows netted in wire, and we
Like early kings with book and word cast down
Realities from our squared electric shore.
Two orderlies are whistling-in the spring;
Doors slam; and a man is dying at the core
Of triumph won. As a tattered, powerful wing
The screen bears out his face against the bed,
Silver, derelict, rapt, and almost dead.

Evening gropes out of colour; yet we work
To cleanse our shore from limpet histories;
Traffic and factory-whistle turn berserk;
Inviolate, faithful as a saint he lies.
Twilight itself breaks up, the venal ship,
Upon the silver integrity of his face.
No bread shall tempt that fine, tormented lip.
Let shadow switch to light—he holds his place.
Unmarked, unmoving, from the gaping bed
Towards birth he labours, honour, almost dead.

The wiry cricket moiling at his loom
Debates a themeless project with dour night,
The sick man raves beside me in his room;
I sleep as a child, rouse up as a child might.
I cannot pray; that fine lip prays for me
With every gasp at breath; his burden grows
Heavier as all earth lightens, and all sea.
Time crouches, watching, near his face of snows.
He is all life, thrown on the gaping bed,
Blind, silent, in a trance, and shortly, dead.

HOSPITAL NIGHT

The side-room has sweated years and patience, rolls its one eye
Skyward, nightward; hours beyond sleep I lie;
And the fists of some ardent Plimsoll have laboured this wall
Clear of its plaster beside my chosen head.
Someone murmurs a little, dithers in bed.
Against that frail call
Are imminent the siege-works of a huge nightfall.

Trees, drawn up, rustle forward in the steep time of gloaming;
Crude green labours, gathers itself to a darkness, dreaming
Of perished ice-world summers, birds few, unwieldy, tame.
Darkness is astir, pondering, touching
Kinship with the first Dark in a trunk's crouching.
Darkness lays claim
To that vague breath-labour of a century, my name.

Someone calls again in his sleep, and my thought is pain,
Pain, till chanticleer will carol truce again
To the faceless joustings of green and green by an old cell,
With time roundabout, and labouring shapes of sin;
To the knotted fists of lightning, or tilting rain;
To the wind's lapse and swell
—Old die-hards of whom the birds shiver to tell.

Sleep is a labour amid the dilatory elder light;
But now a star is uttered in the long night,
Pitched beyond altercations of tree and storm;
For these, isled upon time, are murmuring, murmuring ever
Of good or evil becoming a darkness; but never
Darkens that star,
Housed in a glory, yet always a wanderer.

It is pain, truth, it is you, my father, beloved friend,
Come to me in the guile and darkness of a day's end,
As a frail intense blue burning, near nor far.
Old hands were stripped from the keyboard of time, they favour
White notes nor black, but they glitter and glitter of a lover,
As out of war
I labour, breathing deeply, and tremble towards your star.

LEGIONARY ANTS

The world, the tranquil punctual gyroscope,
Is more or less at peace after her fashion,
Broad bowels work, creatures rejoice or mope,
There is clash of interests in all dogged creation,
When silence comes as at noiseless thwack of a drum,
And look! the warriors come.

First shudder away the birds, all flaking, wheeling
Out of range and all forgetful of their young,
Crying at the ominous shadowy floor stealing
Over their earth; and then not giving tongue.
Now all things hold silent, and the surf
Breaks on beleaguered turf.

They come. And whose ear can divine the awful waves,
Signals of command suspired by what demagogue?
They tumble in orgies of commitment, these black slaves,
All activity, but insensible as rotted log.
Their mad absorbed unity of hunger and mirth
Is the belly-heave of earth.

The wounded mammal whimpers and butts and runs,
Glazing, eaten alive. The three-days' chick
Shrills fear, and like a paradigm of guns
Anarchy gorges itself and life is sick.
Look close for a second, stranger, you will find
Blear paradigm also of our mind.

For this is our mind for today—never creation
But all nakedness. Odours and colours blent
And sounds and shapes, swivel throughout that ration
Of basic nerves, like darkness imminent;
But sometimes in moments of withdrawal one sees, feels
Certain subterranean wheels.

As their cloud progresses it may assume strange shapes:
Of devouring lover and organ, it may weep
Like mandibles of rain and whatever rapes
The fruit and flesh of life in very sleep.
Sleep is ever the enemy, it seems,
To all who dream these dreams.

But punctilious night now sweeps away all lust
On wheels, and another, a blessed, silence broods
Over many bones left twinkling in the dust.
Earth debates bitterly in these solitudes
Whether she dare replace, below, above,
The singings, ramblings of love.

PNEUMO–ENCEPHALOGRAPH

Tight scrimmage of blankets in the dark;
Nerve-fluxions, flints coupling for the spark;
Today's guilt and tomorrow's blent;
Passion and peace trussed together, impotent;
Dilute potage of light
Dripping through glass to the desk where you sit and write;
Hour stalking lame hour. . . .
May my every bone and vessel confess the power
To loathe suffering in you
As in myself, that arcane simmering brew.

Only come to this cabin of art:
Crack hardy, take off clothes, and play your part.
Contraband enters your brain;
Puckered guerilla faces patrol the vein;
The spore of oxygen passes
Skidding over old inclines and crevasses,
Hunting an ancient sore,
Foxhole of impulse in a minute cosmic war.
Concordat of nature and desire
Was revoked in you; but fire clashes with fire.

Let me ask, while you are still,
What in you marshalled this improbable will:
Instruments supple as the flute,
Vigilant eyes, mouths that are almost mute,
X-rays scintillant as a flower,
Tossed in a corner the plumes of falsehood, power?
Only your suffering.
Of pain's amalgam with gold let some man sing
While, pale and fluent and rare
As the Holy Spirit, travels the bubble of air.

HARRY

It's the day for writing that letter, if one is able,
And so the striped institutional shirt is wedged
Between this holy holy chair and table.
He has purloined paper, he has begged and cadged
The bent institutional pen,
The ink. And our droll old men
Are darting constantly where he weaves his sacrament.

Sacrifice? Propitiation? All are blent
In the moron's painstaking fingers—so painstaking.
His vestments our giddy yarns of the firmament,
Women, gods, electric trains, and our remaking
Of all known worlds—but not yet
Has our giddy alphabet
Perplexed his priestcraft and spilled the cruet of innocence.

We have been plucked from the world of commonsense,
Fondling between our hands some shining loot,
Wife, mother, beach, fisticuffs, eloquence,
As the lank tree cherishes every distorted shoot.
What queer shards we could steal
Shaped him, realer than the Real:
But it is no goddess of ours guiding the fingers and the thumb.

She cries: *Ab aeterno ordinata sum.*
He writes to the woman, this lad who will never marry.
One vowel and the thousand laborious serifs will come
To this pudgy Christ, and the old shape of Mary.
Before seasonal pelts and the thin
Soft tactile underskin
Of air were stretched across earth, they have sported and are one.

Was it then at this altar-stone the mind was begun?
The image besieges our Troy. Consider the sick
Convulsions of movement, and the featureless baldy sun
Insensible—sparing that compulsive nervous tic.
Before life, the fantastic succession,
An imbecile makes his confession,
Is filled with the Word unwritten, has almost genuflected.

Because the wise world has for ever and ever rejected
Him and because your children would scream at the sight
Of his mongol mouth stained with food, he has resurrected
The spontaneous though retarded and infantile Light.
Transfigured with him we stand
Among walls of the no-man's-land
While he licks the soiled envelope with lover's caress

Directing it to the House of no known address.

WILD HONEY

Saboteur autumn has riddled the pampered folds
Of the sun; gum and willow whisper seditious things;
Servile leaves now kick and toss in revolution,
Wave bunting, die in operatic reds and golds;
And we, the drones, fated for the hundred stings,
Grope among chilly combs of self-contemplation
While the sun, on sufferance, from his palanquin
Offers creation one niggling lukewarm grin.

But today is Sports Day, not a shadow of doubt:
Scampering at the actual frosty feet
Of winter, under shavings of the pensioned blue,
We are the Spring. True, rain is about:
You mark old diggings along the arterial street
Of the temples, the stuttering eyeball, the residue
Of days spent nursing some drugged comatose pain,
Summer, autumn, winter the single sheet of rain.

And the sun is carted off; and a sudden shower:
Lines of lightning patrol the temples of the skies;
Drum, thunder, silence sing as one this day;
Our faces return to the one face of the flower
Sodden and harried by diehard disconsolate flies.
All seasons are crammed into pockets of the grey.
Joy, pain, desire, a moment ago set free,
Sag in pavilions of the grey finality.

Under rain, in atrophy, dare I watch this girl
Combing her hair before the grey broken mirror,
The golden sweetness trickling? Her eyes show
Awareness of my grey stare beyond the swirl
Of golden fronds: it is her due. And terror,
Rainlike, is all involved in the golden glow,
Playing diminuendo its dwarfish rôle
Between self-conscious fingers of the naked soul.

Down with the mind a moment, and let Eden
Be fullness without the prompted unnatural hunger,
Without the doomed shapely ersatz thought: see faith
As all such essential gestures, unforbidden,
Persisting through Fall and landslip; and see, stranger,
The overcoated concierge of death
As a toy for her gesture. See her hands like bees
Store golden combs among certified hollow trees.

Have the gates of death scrape open. Shall we meet
(Beyond the platoons of rainfall) a loftier hill
Hung with such delicate husbandries? Shall ascent
Be a travelling homeward, past the blue frosty feet
Of winter, past childhood, past the grey snake, the will?
Are gestures stars in sacred dishevelment,
The tiny, the pitiable, meaningless and rare
As a girl beleaguered by rain, and her yellow hair?

PETER PORTER

ᢟ

PETER PORTER WAS born in Brisbane in 1929. His mother died when he was nine years old, and he was sent to boarding schools, which he hated, particularly for the sport. His father, a warehouseman in the Manchester trade, was withdrawn and had little rapport with his only child. After leaving high school, Porter tried cadet journalism, but felt out of place with Australians—a cavedweller among the beach-goers—and left by ship for England in 1951. He lived in London on a clerk's wage in unheated bedsitters, read almost continuously from public libraries, learned about classical music with Australian friends, and continued, as he had done since high school, to write hundreds of poems. Later he was introduced into 'The Group', a circle of poets who met regularly in London during the early sixties to analyse and discuss each other's work. Porter greatly benefited from this contact, and began to publish prolifically and to win acceptance among the English poetry establishment.

Porter married and had two daughters, and worked for some years in advertising, though he was without ambition there. In his forties he began working as a full-time freelance writer. In 1974 his wife Jannice, who had been an alcoholic, committed suicide. Porter's seventh book, *The Cost of Seriousness*, is preoccupied with her death, and is uncharacteristically emotive and direct in many of its poems. He has brought up his two young daughters alone. Since a visit in 1974, Porter has regularly returned to Australia.

Porter's poetry is known for its intellectuality: in his work every experience is mediated through the intellect, copious allusions attaching to it in the process. At the same time, his poetry is about a sceptical and satirical denial of all intellectual systems—political, literary, philosophical—on behalf of rationality and critical thinking. But while rejecting monistic solutions and seeing only 'a jumble of contrivances . . ./ the dirt-caked misery of the way the world survives', he is not a facile sceptic but a defender of liberal humanist attitudes. A great admirer of Auden and Wallace Stevens, his work has an expressionistic fervour, an *angst*, at its best, which is quite unlike anything in his examplars. Since the *Collected Poems* (1983) he has become more than ever cerebral, aphoristic, and disjunctive— 'philosophising' (though always brilliantly) in fleeting 'captions'. The language and an extraordinarily well-stocked mind freely associate together, in this recent work, producing at times the most original and incisive satire in contemporary poetry.

THE GREAT POET COMES HERE IN WINTER

Frau Antonia is a cabbage:
If I were a grub I'd eat a hole in her.
Here they deliver the milk up a private path
Slippery as spit—her goddess' hands
Turn it to milk puddings. Blow, little wind,
Steer in off this cardboard sea,
You are acclimatized like these vines
Warring on an inch of topsoil
You are agent of the Golden Republic,
So still blow for me—our flowers look one way,
If I were a good poet I would walk on the sea.

The sea is actually made of eyes.
Whether of drowned fishermen or of peasants
Accustomed to the hard bargains of the saints
I cannot say. Whether there will be
Any mail from Paris or even broccoli
For dinner is in doubt. My hat blew off the planet,
I knelt by the infinite sand of the stars
And prayed for all men. Being German, I have a lot of soul.
Nevertheless, why am I crying in this garden?
I refuse to die till fashion comes back to spats.

From this turret the Adriatic
Burns down the galley lanes to starved Ragusa,
How strange it can wash up condoms.
The world is coming unstitched at the seams.
All yesterday the weather was a taste
In my mouth, I saw the notes of Beethoven
Lying on the ground, from the horn
Of a gramophone I heard Crivelli's cucumbers
Crying out for paint. In the eyes of a stray bitch
Ribbed with hunger, heavy with young,
I saw the peneplain of all imagined
Misery, horizontal and wider than the world.

I gave her my unwrapped sugar. We said Mass
Together, she licking my fingers and me
Knowing how she would die, not glad to have lived.
She took her need away, I thought her selfish
But stronger than God and more beautiful company.

A CONSUMER'S REPORT

The name of the product I tested is *Life*,
I have completed the form you sent me
and understand that my answers are confidential.

I had it as a gift,
I didn't feel much while using it,
in fact I think I'd have liked to be more excited.
It seemed gentle on the hands
but left an embarrassing deposit behind.
It was not economical
and I have used much more than I thought
(I suppose I have about half left
but it's difficult to tell)—
although the instructions are fairly large
there are so many of them
I don't know which to follow, especially
as they seem to contradict each other.
I'm not sure such a thing
should be put in the way of children—
It's difficult to think of a purpose
for it. One of my friends says
it's just to keep its maker in a job.
Also the price is much too high.
Things are piling up so fast,
after all, the world got by
for a thousand million years
without this, do we need it now?
(Incidentally, please ask your man

to stop calling me 'the respondent',
I don't like the sound of it.)
There seems to be a lot of different labels,
sizes and colours should be uniform,
the shape is awkward, it's waterproof
but not heat resistant, it doesn't keep
yet it's very difficult to get rid of:
whenever they make it cheaper they seem
to put less in—if you say you don't
want it, then it's delivered anyway.
I'd agree it's a popular product,
it's got into the language; people
even say they're on the side of it.
Personally I think it's overdone,
a small thing people are ready
to behave badly about. I think
we should take it for granted. If its
experts are called philosophers or market
researchers or historians, we shouldn't
care. We are the consumers and the last
law makers. So finally, I'd buy it.
But the question of a 'best buy'
I'd like to leave until I get
the competitive product you said you'd send.

AFFAIR OF THE HEART

I have been having an affair
with a beautiful strawberry blonde.

At first she was willing to do anything,
she would suck and pump and keep on going.

She never tired me out and she flung
fireworks down the stairs to me.

What a girl I said over the telephone
as I worked her up to a red riot.

You are everywhere, you are the goddess
of tassels shining at my finger ends.

You set the alarm clock to remind us
to do it before leaving for the office.

You are classic like Roman gluttony,
priapic like St Tropez' lights.

She put up with a lot: I forgot about her
and went on the booze—I didn't eat or ring.

I borrowed from her in indigence.
I was frightened and fell back on her.

An experienced friend told me in his flat
among the press cuttings: they've got to play the field!

Of course, I said, but I knew where that was—
down my left arm, my left side, my windy stomach.

She was sometimes late and when alone
hammered me on the bed springs like a bell.

She was greedy as a herring gull and screamed
when my dreams were of Arcadian fellating.

I woke in her sweat; I had to do something,
so called in Dr Rhinegold and his machine.

Meanwhile, the paradigm was obvious:
it's me that's in you said a polar couple—

me, the love of hopeless meetings, the odd biter;
no, me, the wife by the rotary drier

with the ready hand. Dr Rhinegold moved
mountains for me and said the electric hearse

might not run. But you're sick, man, sick,
like the world itself waiting in Out Patients.

I know how the affair will end—
but not yet, Lord, not yet. It isn't hope,

it's being with her where the scenery's good,
going to concerts with her, eating Stravinsky.

It's something more. I haven't finished explaining
why I won't write my autobiography.

These poems are my reason. She knows
she can't leave me when the act's improving.

She could imagine our old age: a black-
fronted house in a Victorian Terrace

or a cat-piss Square. Working on Modernism
while the stark grey thistles push to the door.

She can't let me go with my meannesses intact,
I'll write her such letters she'll think it's

Flann O'Brien trapped in a windmill. I'll
say her the tropes of tenebrae (or Tannochbrae).

I'll squeal in fear at her feet—Oh, stay with me
I'll plead—look, the twentieth century

is darkening like a window; love is toneless
on the telephone with someone else to see—

only memory is like your tunnelling tongue,
only your fingers tinkering tell me I'm alive.

On the Train between Wellington and Shrewsbury

The process starts—
on the rails pigs' blood,
lambs' blood in the trees

With a red tail
through the slab-white sky
the blood bird flies

This man beside me
is offering friendly
sandwiches of speech:
he's slaughtered twenty pigs
this morning—
                    he takes away
the sins of the word

I can smell his jacket,
it's tripe-coloured,
old tripe,
drained-out, veteran tripe
that has digested the world

I shut my eyes on
his lullaby of tripe
and the blood goes back to bed

(Someone's got to do it
and I'm grateful
and my neighbour's grateful
and we say so,
but thank God it's only
fourteen minutes to Shrewsbury)

Fourteen minutes to consider
the girl reading Scott Fitzgerald—
she has a red cashmere top
bright as a butcher's window

Shut out the sun and the cameras—
I want to talk to a doctor
about Circe's magic circle—
'you see, it was on the woman herself
the bristles sprang
and the truffle-hunting tongue'

What is it makes my penis
presentable?
hot blood—
enough of it, in the right place

With such red cheeks
my interlocutor from the abbatoirs
must have hypertension

On his knees he has
a lumpish parcel, well-knotted
with white string—
it makes all the difference
when you know it's really fresh

At one time our species
always had it fresh;
one time there were no cashmere tops
or butcher's shops

It consoles me that poems
bring nothing about,
it hurts me that poems
do so little

I was born after
man invented meat
and a shepherd invented poetry

At a time when there are only
fourteen killing minutes
between Wellington and Shrewsbury.

ON FIRST LOOKING INTO CHAPMAN'S HESIOD

For 5p at a village fête I bought
Old Homer-Lucan who popped Keats's eyes,
Print smaller than the Book of Common Prayer
But Swinburne at the front, whose judgement is
Always immaculate. I'll never read a tenth
Of it in what life I have left to me
But I did look at *The Georgics*, as he calls
The Works and Days, and there I saw, not quite
The view from Darien but something strange
And balking—Australia, my own country
And its edgy managers—in the picture of
Euboeaen husbandry, terse family feuds
And the minds of gods tangential to the earth.

Like a Taree smallholder splitting logs
And philosophizing on his dangling billies,
The poet mixes hard agrarian instances
With sour sucks to his brother. Chapman, too,
That perpetual motion poetry machine,
Grinds up the classics like bone meal from
The abbatoirs. And the same blunt patriotism,
A long-winded, emphatic, kelpie yapping
About our land, our time, our fate, our strange

And singular way of moons and showers, lakes
Filling oddly—yes, Australians are Boeotians,
Hard as headlands, and, to be fair, with days
As robust as the Scythian wind on stone.

To teach your grandmother to suck eggs
Is a textbook possibility in New South Wales
Or outside Ascra. And such a genealogy too!
The Age of Iron is here, but oh the memories
Of Gold—pioneers preaching to the stringybarks,
Boring the land to death with verses and with
Mental Homes, 'Care-flying ease' and 'Gift-
devouring kings' become the Sonata of the Shotgun
And Europe's Entropy; for 'the axle-tree, the quern,
The hard, fate-fostered man' you choose among
The hand castrator, kerosene in honey tins
And mystic cattlemen: the Land of City States
Greets Australia in a farmer's gods.

Hesiod's father, caught in a miserable village,
Not helped by magic names like Helicon,
Sailed to improve his fortunes, and so did
All our fathers—in turn, their descendants
Lacked initiative, other than the doctors' daughters
Who tripped to England. Rough-nosed Hesiod
Was sure of his property to a slip-rail—
Had there been grants, he'd have farmed all
Summer and spent winter in Corinth
At the Creative Writing Class. Chapman, too,
Would vie with Steiner for the Pentecostal
Silver Tongue. Some of us feel at home nowhere,
Others in one generation fuse with the land.

I salute him then, the blunt old Greek whose way
Of life was as cunning as organic. His poet
Followers still make me feel déraciné
Within myself. One day they're on the campus,
The next in wide hats at a branding or

Sheep drenching, not actually performing
But looking the part and getting instances
For odes that bruise the blood. And history,
So interior a science it almost seems
Like true religion—who would have thought
Australia was the point of all that craft
Of politics in Europe? The apogee, it seems,
Is where your audience and its aspirations are.

'The colt, and mule, and horn-retorted steer'—
A good iambic line to paraphrase.
Long storms have blanched the million bones
Of the Aegean, and as many hurricanes
Will abrade the headstones of my native land:
Sparrows acclimatize but I still seek
The permanently upright city where
Speech is nature and plants conceive in pots,
Where one escapes from what one is and who
One was, where home is just a postmark
And country wisdom clings to calendars,
The opposite of a sunburned truth-teller's
World, haunted by precepts and the Pleiades.

AN EXEQUY

In wet May, in the months of change,
In a country you wouldn't visit, strange
Dreams pursue me in my sleep,
Black creatures of the upper deep—
Though you are five months dead, I see
You in guilt's iconography,
Dear Wife, lost beast, beleaguered child,
The stranded monster with the mild
Appearance, whom small waves tease,
(Andromeda upon her knees
In orthodox deliverance)
And you alone of pure substance,
The unformed form of life, the earth
Which Piero's brushes brought to birth
For all to greet as myth, a thing
Out of the box of imagining.

This introduction serves to sing
Your mortal death as Bishop King
Once hymned in tetrametric rhyme
His young wife, lost before her time;
Though he lived on for many years
His poem each day fed new tears
To that unreaching spot, her grave,
His lines a baroque architrave
The Sunday poor with bottled flowers
Would by-pass in their mourning hours,
Esteeming ragged natural life
('Most dearly loved, most gentle wife'),
Yet, looking back when at the gate
And seeing grief in formal state
Upon a sculpted angel group,
Were glad that men of god could stoop
To give the dead a public stance
And freeze them in their mortal dance.

The words and faces proper to
My misery are private—you
Would never share your heart with those
Whose only talent's to suppose,
Nor from your final childish bed
Raise a remote confessing head—
The channels of our lives are blocked,
The hand is stopped upon the clock,
No-one can say why hearts will break
And marriages are all opaque:
A map of loss, some posted cards,
The living house reduced to shards,
The abstract hell of memory,
The pointlessness of poetry—
These are the instances which tell
Of something which I know full well,
I owe a death to you—one day
The time will come for me to pay
When your slim shape from photographs
Stands at my door and gently asks
If I have any work to do
Or will I come to bed with you.
O scala enigmatica,
I'll climb up to that attic where
The curtain of your life was drawn
Some time between despair and dawn—
I'll never know with what halt steps
You mounted to this plain eclipse
But each stair now will station me
A black responsibility
And point me to that shut-down room,
'This be your due appointed tomb.'

I think of us in Italy:
Gin-and-chianti-fuelled, we
Move in a trance through Paradise,
Feeding at last our starving eyes,
Two people of the English blindness

Doing each masterpiece the kindness
Of discovering it—from Baldovinetti
To Venice's most obscure jetty.
A true unfortunate traveller, I
Depend upon your nurse's eye
To pick the altars where no Grinner
Puts us off our tourists' dinner
And in hotels to bandy words
With Genevan girls and talking birds,
To wear your feet out following me
To night's end and true amity,
And call my rational fear of flying
A paradigm of Holy Dying—
And, oh my love, I wish you were
Once more with me, at night somewhere
In narrow streets applauding wines,
The moon above the Apennines
As large as logic and the stars,
Most middle-aged of avatars,
As bright as when they shone for truth
Upon untried and avid youth.

The rooms and days we wandered through
Shrink in my mind to one—there you
Lie quite absorbed by peace—the calm
Which life could not provide is balm
In death. Unseen by me, you look
Past bed and stairs and half-read book
Eternally upon your home,
The end of pain, the left alone.
I have no friend, or intercessor,
No psychopomp or true confessor
But only you who know my heart
In every cramped and devious part—
Then take my hand and lead me out,
The sky is overcast by doubt,
The time has come, I listen for
Your words of comfort at the door,
O guide me through the shoals of fear—
'Fürchte dich nicht, ich bin bei dir.'

WHAT I HAVE WRITTEN I HAVE WRITTEN

It is the little stone of unhappiness
which I keep with me. I had it as a child
and put it in a drawer. There came
a heap of paper to put beside it,
letters, poems, a brittle dust
of affection, sallowed by memory.
Aphorisms came. Not evil, but
the competition of two goods
brings you to the darkened room.
I gave the stone to a woman
and it glowed. I set my mind
to hydraulic work, lifting words
from their swamp. In the light from the stone
her face was bloated. When she died
the stone returned to me, a present
from reality. The two goods
were still contending. From wading pools
the children grew to darken
gardens with their shadows. Duty
is better than love, it suffers no betrayal.

Beginning again, I notice
I have less breath but the joining
is more golden. There is a long way to go,
among gardens and alarms,
after-dinner sleeps peopled by toads
and all the cries of childhood.
Someone comes to say my name
has been removed from the Honourable
Company of Scribes. Books in the room
turn their backs on me.

Old age will be the stone and me together.
I have become used to its weight
in my pocket and my brain.
To move it from lining to lining
like Beckett's tramp,
to modulate it to the major

or throw it at the public—
all is of no avail. But I'll add
to the songs of the stone. These words
I take from my religious instruction,
complete responsibility—
let them be entered in the record,
What I have written I have written.

ALCESTIS AND THE POET

As the little blue-tongued lizard runs across
The floor and clambers on the cushions, so I
Have spent my life in your service. I have
Risen from beds of my own melancholy to grant
Your distress an audience, heard the chorus of self
Desert its lord to swell your tragedy. It wasn't
Self-effacement but a bonding-up of time. We
Start with bodies from our wounded parents, not knowing
That the early flesh is useless, that its greyness
Towards death is what we love in it. So,
As young Shakespearean gestures, we glow among our feelings
And are pointless. Then, as the shades of madness
Intervene, we become important. Voices singing German ask
'Watchman, what of the night?'; geniuses ever upward tell
Of willing death, of lining tombs for study, Chattertons
Who persist in books. The soft arrival counts. Now,
When the rake of afternoon has laid the shadows,
We are ready to do each other service. Can
I march tongue-tied to the end; will you
Find the inexplicable, the out-of-reach-of-art
Intensity you mourn for outside Hades? I took
Your place and watched the stories grow. But it
Was no more than giving up a good position
In the queue—we are all for darkness. Death
Is in the small print, as Stevie Smith showed,
Ringing the word in galleys on her final bed—

Thus the loving woman does her duty and is
Woven into legend. The king sits in his kitchen,
Not certain if the world knows of her sacrifice,
Though don't his cats despise him? Are you there
Where each new disappointment makes you think that life
Is geared to reparation? And this time who is
Hercules? The joy of giving up, of saying sweetly,
'It could never have worked—real love must be
Thrown away or it will burn us.' The rest
Is timing. On the moon, they say, we find
The things we've sacrificed, pristine and waxing. Such dreams
Are cheats. Sited in great art, but tearful still,
The creatures that we are make little gestures, then
Go to nothing. The wind urges the trees to sigh
For us: it is not a small thing to die,
But looking back I see only the disappointed man
Casting words upon the page. Was it for this
I stepped out upon the stairs of death obediently?

BRUCE DAWE

B RUCE DAWE WAS born in Geelong, Victoria, in 1930 and left high school at the age of sixteen, an educational 'drop-out'. He held a variety of menial jobs, and tells of how one day, while working on a building site at a university, he watched the students arrive and remarked to a fellow worker, 'What lucky bastards, I wish I was one of them.' He decided to complete his matriculation, went to night school, and then in 1954 began an arts degree at Melbourne University. While there, his interest in writing poetry was stimulated by a group of poets on the academic staff: Vincent Buckley, Chris Wallace-Crabbe and Philip Martin. He also became a Catholic at this time and the influence of a humanist Catholicism remains fundamental to his work. In 1959 he joined the Royal Australian Air Force, as a clerk, and continued with it until 1969, having by then married, published two books of poetry, and completed a degree from the University of Queensland. After working as a teacher in Toowoomba, Queensland, his wife's home town, he was appointed to a lectureship at the Darling Downs Institute of Advanced Education. He now holds a PhD.

Dawe is a public poet who takes up social causes in his work: homelessness, unemployment, opposition to capital punishment and to the Vietnam War. He is not a propagandist for a political programme; his stance is a more basically humane one. A watchful critic of totalitarianism, he has rejected sweeping social prescriptions.

Nor does he try to idealise the victims, the 'lost people' he speaks for, in his work. Their weaknesses are portrayed with affectionate irony, or exasperation at the seemingly intractable condition of their lives. A widely felt change of heart throughout society would seem to be what he relies upon.

Dawe's use of colloquial speech, and his feeling for the details of suburban life, are unsurpassed by any Australian poet. He is a compelling reader of his own work and has become Australia's largest-selling poet.

DRIFTERS

One day soon he'll tell her it's time to start packing,
and the kids will yell 'Truly?' and get wildly excited for no reason,
and the brown kelpie pup will start dashing about, tripping everyone
    up,
and she'll go out to the vegetable-patch and pick all the green
    tomatoes from the vines,
and notice how the oldest girl is close to tears because she was happy
    here,
and how the youngest girl is beaming because she wasn't.
And the first thing she'll put on the trailer will be the bottling-set she
    never unpacked from Grovedale,
and when the loaded ute bumps down the drive past the blackberry-
    canes with their last shrivelled fruit,
she won't even ask why they're leaving this time, or where they're
    heading for
—she'll only remember how, when they came here,
she held out her hands bright with berries,
the first of the season, and said:
'Make a wish, Tom, make a wish.'

HOMECOMING

All day, day after day, they're bringing them home,
they're picking them up, those they can find, and bringing them
    home,
they're bringing them in, piled on the hulls of Grants, in trucks, in
    convoys,
they're zipping them up in green plastic bags,
they're tagging them now in Saigon, in the mortuary coolness
they're giving them names, they're rolling them out of
the deep-freeze lockers—on the tarmac at Tan Son Nhut
the noble jets are whining like hounds,
they are bringing them home

—curly-heads, kinky-hairs, crew-cuts, balding non-coms
—they're high, now, high and higher, over the land, the steaming
    chow mein,
their shadows are tracing the blue curve of the Pacific
with sorrowful quick fingers, heading south, heading east,
home, home, home—and the coasts swing upward, the old
    ridiculous curvatures
of earth, the knuckled hills, the mangrove-swamps, the desert
    emptiness . . .
in their sterile housing they tilt towards these like skiers
—taxiing in, on the long runways, the howl of their homecoming
    rises
surrounding them like their last moments (the mash, the splendour)
then fading at length as they move
on to small towns where dogs in the frozen sunset
raise muzzles in mute salute,
and on to cities in whose wide web of suburbs
telegrams tremble like leaves from a wintering tree
and the spider grief swings in his bitter geometry
—they're bringing them home, now, too late, too early.

THE ROCK-THROWER

Out in the suburbs I hear
trains rocketing to impossible destinations
cry out against the intolerable waste,
at 3.40 in the morning hear the dog-frost
bark over the dark back-yards with their young trees
and tubular-steel swings where tomorrow's children
laughingly dangle their stockinged feet already
and the moon coats with white primer
the youthful lawns, the thirtyish expectations.

Midway between the hills and the sea
our house rocks quietly in the flow of time, each morning
we descend to sandy loam, the birds

pipe us ashore, on the rimed grass
someone has left four sets of footprints
as a sign to us that we are not alone
but likely to be visited
at some unearthly hour by a dear friend
who bears a love for us, wax-wrapped and sealed,
sliced, white, starch-reduced . . .

Sometimes I wake at night, thinking:
Even now he may be at work,
the rock-thrower in the neighbouring suburb, turning
the particular street of his choice
back to an earlier settlement—the men armed,
mounting guard, eyeing the mysterious skies,
tasting the salt of siege, the cleansing sacrament
of bombardment, talking in whispers, breaking humbly
the bread of their small fame,
as the planes going north and south
wink conspiratorially overhead
and the stones rain down . . .
And sometimes, too, dieselling homewards
when the bruised blue look of evening
prompts speculations upon the reasons for existence
and sets the apprehensive traveller to fingering thoughtfully
his weekly ticket, when the sun draws its bloody
knuckles back from the teeth of roof-tops
and the wounded commuter limps finally up the cement path
—I think of the rock-thrower, the glazier's benefactor,
raining down meaning from beyond the subdivisions,
proclaiming the everlasting evangel of vulnerability
—and the suburbs of men shrink to one short street
where voices are calling now from point to point:
'Is that you, Frank?'
                        'Is that you, Les?'
                                        'Is that you, Harry?'
'See anything?'
                'Nup . . .'
                        'Nup . . .'
                                'Nup . . .'

KATRINA

Katrina, now you are suspended between earth and sky.
Tubes feed you glucose intravenously. Naked you lie
In your special room in Ward Fifteen. Is your life
Opening again or closing finally? We do not know, but fear
The telephone call from a nurse whose distant sympathy
Will be the measure of our helplessness. Your twin brother's
Two-month-old vigour hurts us, remembering
Thin straws of sunlight on your bowed legs kicking
In defiance of your sickness, your body's wasting.
Against the black velvet of death threatening
Your life shines like a jewel, each relapse a flash of light
The more endearing. Your mother grieves already, so do I.
Miracles do not tempt us. We are getting in early,
Although we know there is no conditioning process which can
        counter
The karate-blow when it comes,
No way we can arrange the date-pad to conceal
The page torn-off, crumpled, thrown away.
Katrina, I had in mind a prayer, but only this came,
And you are still naked between earth and sky.
Transfusion-wounds in your heels, your dummy taped in your
        mouth.

WOOD-EYE

No nursing-sister ever walked
into our ward but Wood-eye cocked an eye
(the good one, still unbandaged)
in our direction, lay there like a lamb
thinking his lion's thoughts. Calm fingers took
like a professional sneak-thief his stirred pulse.
I've never seen a man whose libido's red-light
as steadily burned in that last street

whose name nobody knows. In Wood-eye's world
all roads led to Gomorrah where he practised
as a sort of resident specialist on call
24 hours a day. No instrument
but had its phallic relevance: thermometer,
spatula, syringe were sign-posts on the way
to a consummation devoutly to be wished . . .
'Would I?' he murmured, writhing on the rack
of unrealizable possibilities as some cool
sister exited: 'Oh Jesus, would I, what!'

So we called him 'Wood-eye'. Something in his look
suggested that that eye-ball swivelling
in its carven socket, and that unseen eye
under the gauze-pad were like wooden things
intent on meaning more than just themselves
—totems, you might say, to which we looked
for meaning while we hunched around the ward
or lay like anchorites on sheets that smelled
as clean as bakers' aprons. Wood-eye's wit
flapped like a pennon on a distant hill. He was the ravaged,
he was mystery, the figure slouching off into the night,
into the gun-fire crackling like leaves,
coming back at dawn and saying nothing
or nothing with his lips that could drown out
the heavy music of his silences.

And if now I could know
his cancer cured, the bandages dispersed,
the hospital a fleering memory,
the knives not feared, the sexy sisters gone
from his mind's racing rink,
the need to grin upon a leaden fate,
all passed away, all passed,
                                  would I rejoice
until this sober skin
burst open like a grape from which might be stamped out
the final wine of love, would I rejoice, then,
would I, _would_ I what!

AT SHAGGER'S FUNERAL

At Shagger's funeral there wasn't much to say
That could be said
In front of his old mum—she frightened us, the way
She shook when the Reverend read
About the resurrection and the life, as if
The words meant something to her, shook, recoiled,
And sat there, stony, stiff
As Shagger, while the rest of us, well-oiled,
Tried hard to knuckle down to solemn facts,
Like the polished box in the chapel aisle
And the clasped professional sorrow, but the acts
Were locked inside us like a guilty smile
That caught up with us later, especially when
We went round to pick up his reclaimed Ford,
The old shag-wagon, and beat out the dust
From tetron cushions, poured
Oil in the hungry sump, flicked the forsaken
Kewpie doll on the dash-board,
Kicked hub-caps tubercular with rust.

The service closed with a prayer, and silence beat
Like a tongue in a closed mouth.
Of all the girls he'd loved or knocked or both,
Only Bev Whiteside showed—out in the street
She gripped her hand-bag, said, 'This is as far
As I'm going, boys, or any girl will go,
From now on.'
                              Later, standing about
The windy grave, hearing the currawongs shout
In the camphor-laurels, and his old lady cry
As if he'd really been a son and a half,
What could any of us say that wasn't a lie
Or that didn't end up in a laugh
At his expense—caught with his britches down
By death, whom he'd imagined out of town?

VIVIAN SMITH

─────── ❧ ───────

VIVIAN SMITH HAD a working class childhood in Hobart, Tasmania, where he was born in 1933. As a boy he sold newspapers in the streets, and used his wage to buy books. He is a graduate of the University of Tasmania, and lectured there in French; his doctorate was from Sydney University, where he is now Reader in English. His wife also lectured in languages at the University of Tasmania and is the daughter of Viennese parents who settled in Australia.

Smith's literary influences and affinities include Rilke, of the *Neue Gedichte*, James McAuley, Shaw Neilson and Philip Larkin. His poetry is essentially lyrical, relying on quatrains and other verse forms to achieve musical effects. Although his metrics are strict, and his meaning and imagery lucid, the overall mood of his poetry is one of uncertainty; there is a closely underlying fear of mortality. His earlier poems about Tasmania evoke a chill, bony, almost empty and sometimes punishing landscape. Later poems, after his move to Sydney, celebrate subtropical light and colour, but psychological ease still remains just out of reach. Smith has published four books of poetry, some critical studies, and translations from the German, particularly that of Paul Celan.

AT AN EXHIBITION
OF HISTORICAL PAINTINGS, HOBART

The sadness in the human visage stares
out of these frames, out of these distant eyes;
the static bodies painted without love
that only lack of talent could disguise.

Those bland receding hills are too remote
where the quaint natives squat with awkward calm.
One carries a kangaroo like a worn toy,
his axe alert with emphasized alarm.

Those nearer woollen hills are now all streets;
even the water in the harbour's changed.
Much is alike and yet a slight precise
disparity seems intended and arranged—

as in that late pink terrace's façade.
How neat the houses look. How clean each brick.
One cannot say they look much older now,
but somehow more themselves, less accurate.

And see the pride in this expansive view:
churches, houses, farms, a prison tower;
a grand gesture like wide-open arms
showing the artist's trust, his clumsy power.

And this much later vision, grander still:
the main street sedate carriages unroll
towards the inappropriate, tentative mountain:
a flow of lines the artist can't control—

the foreground nearly breaks out of its frame
the streets end so abruptly in the water. . . .
But how some themes return. A whaling ship.
The last natives. Here that silent slaughter

is really not prefigured or avoided.
One merely sees a profile, a full face,
a body sitting stiffly in a chair:
the soon-forgotten absence of a race. . . .

Album pieces: bowls of brown glazed fruit. . . .
I'm drawn back yet again to those few studies
of native women whose long floral dresses
made them first aware of their own bodies.

History has made artists of all these
painters who lack energy and feature.
But how some gazes cling. Around the hall
the pathos of the past, the human creature.

TASMANIA

Watercolour country. Here the hills
rot like rugs beneath enormous skies
and all day long the shadows of the clouds
stain the paddocks with their running dyes.

In the small valleys and along the coast,
the land untamed between the scattered farms,
deconsecrated churches lose their paint
and failing pubs their fading coats of arms.

Beyond the beach the pine trees creak and moan,
in the long valley poplars in a row,
the hills breathing like a horse's flank
with grasses combed and clean of the last snow.

THE MAN FERN NEAR THE BUS STOP

The man fern near the bus stop waves at me
one scaly feather swaying out of the dark,
slightly drunk with rain and freckled with old spores
it touches me with its slow question mark.

Something in the shadows catches at the throat,
smelling like old slippers, drying like a skin,
scraped like an emu or a gumboot stuck with fur,
straining all the time to take me in.

Cellophane crinkles in the fern's pineapple heart.
The fur parts slowly showing a crumpled horn.
A ruffled seahorse stands in swaying weed,
and held in cotton wool, a mouse unborn.

I look down at it now, a tiny toe, a crook,
remembering voices and growth without choice—
the buds of fingers breaking into power
and long fibres breaking in the voice.

BARRY HUMPHRIES

———— ⅜ ————

BARRY HUMPHRIES, AUSTRALIA'S best-known satirist, was born in Melbourne in 1934 and educated at the University of Melbourne. He began his lifelong involvement with the theatre in university reviews. There are many stories of his dada activities during his student years: of his secreting sliced ham amongst lingerie displays in department stores; being served an elaborate breakfast on a suburban train, each course brought on at a different station; and holding an art exhibition featuring such objects as 'Pus in Boots', which made use of custard. After graduating, Humphries worked as an actor and as a revue performer, and in 1959 moved to London to work in theatre and television. In 1962 he toured Australia with *A Nice Night's Entertainment*, his first full-scale, one-man show, in which he plays various *kitsch* characters. Since then he has become famous in English-speaking countries for satirising the philistinism of the Australian middle class. His most famous creation is Edna Everage, who has evolved from a tasteless, pretentious housewife and mum into Dame Edna, international megastar. A celebration of vitality underlies Dame Edna's vulgarity, as in 'Edna's Hymn', which balances between mockery and affectionate nostalgia.

In his 'private life' Humphries has artistically-flopping hair, wears bow ties and large hats, collects art, and has a reticent, charming manner. He has been married several times and has four children. A selection of his light verse and some serious poems was published in 1991.

EDNA'S HYMN

Recitative:

When I get home from a day's shopping in a city street,
I pop on the kettle, though I'm nearly dropping on my feet—
Make a nice cup of tea.
Then I switch on my favourite channel,
It's the best time for me as I flick off my flyaway panel.
When I get home from a treat at a flesh-and-blood theatre—
If you call it a treat peering up and down each street for a meter—
I think of old songs and the memories they bring back,
While my thoughtful Norm helps me off with my left and right
        sling-back.
And I think of old songs from old shows as I powder my nose,
And I think of a dear old hymn that time will never dim for me
Before I met my Norm it was the only hymn for me.

Chorus:

All things bright and beautiful, all creatures great and small,
All things wise and wonderful, Australia has them all:
Our famous ballerinas, Joan Sutherland their star,
Our Hoover vacuum cleaners, our Cadbury's chocolate bar,
A cloth all Persil snowy for Austral picnic spread,
Where hums the humble blowie and beetroot stains the bread.

All things bright and beautiful—Pavlovas that we bake,
All things wise and wonderful—Australia takes the cake.
Our great big smiling beaches, the smell of thick Kwik Tan,
Our lovely juicy peaches that never blow the can,
Our gorgeous modern cities so famed throughout the earth,
The Paris end of Collins Street, the Melbourne end of Perth.

All things bright and beautiful—though cynics sneer and plot,
All things wise and wonderful—Australia's got the lot!
The Farex that we scrape off those wee Australian chins,
The phenol that we sprinkle inside our rubbish bins,
Our plate-glass picture windows, venetians open wide—
In the land where nothing happens, there's nothing much to hide.

All things bright and beautiful—
Our wonderful wealth of natural mineral resources.
All things wise and wonderful—
And our even more wonderful wealth of different brands of tomato
    sauces.

Coda:
Australia is a Saturday with races on the trannie;
Australia is the talcy smell of someone else's granny;
Australia is a kiddie with zinc cream on its nose;
Australia's voice is Melba's voice—it's also Normie Rowe's;
Australia's famous postage stamps are stuffed with flowers and
    fauna;
Australia is the Little Man who's open round the corner.
Australia is a sunburnt land of sand and surf and snow;
All ye who do not love her—ye know where ye can go.

CHRIS WALLACE-CRABBE

———— ✺ ————

C HRIS WALLACE-CRABBE WAS born in Melbourne in
1934 and grew up there, becoming a cadet metallurgist. He
then went to the University of Melbourne and graduated in English,
where he was appointed to the staff and now holds a personal chair
in the English department. He has published ten volumes of poetry,
a selection from his work, three collections of essays and a novel.

Wallace-Crabbe seems to us the most distinguished of the Mel-
bourne school of academic poets, which includes Vincent Buckley,
Philip Martin, Peter Steele, Evan Jones and Jennifer Strauss. His
poetry is urbane, restrained, often ironic and is always concerned to
demarcate limits and draw intellectual conclusions. It is quintessen-
tially academic, in that it is detached from its subjects, which seem to
have been intellectually well-handled and cooled before the reader
encounters them.

In Light and Darkness

To the noonday eye, light seems an ethical agent,
Straight from the shoulder, predictable, terribly quick, though
It climbs in a curve to space's unlikely limit,
        Thus posing a problem for mathematicians and God,
Whatever He turns out to be and wherever His dwelling.
Rich is the clotting of gold in the late afternoon or
Turning to twilight, one last blaze of watery colour
        Where man can project his false dreams in figures of light,
Pretending that all his environment loyally loves him,
Seas of ice and burning plains.
                                        Too easy
Bending nature before us, but light is defiant
        Coming by night from dead stars with terrible speed.
So is our planet rebuked, and we meet in mirrors
Desperate masks, eyes of imprisoned strangers
And lips that open to say, 'We are only mirages',
        While the lawns outside are green and the roses real.

You dub the sun a realist? Then it will plague you,
Wading with stork-legs into the green water,
Lending the oak-bole moss its leopard shadows
        Or streaking paddocks darkly with sunset sheep
Fifty feet long.
                                Nothing is quite so rococo
As dawnlight caught on a fishscale formation of cirrus,
Nor quite so romantic as one gilded westering biplane.
        We just don't live in a hard intellectual glare.

No one, of course, endures darkness or daylight entirely:
Cyclic change betrays our terrestrial journey
And what looked like trees at dawn turn out to be crosses,
        Suddenly black as the florid sun goes down,
And maybe at midnight resemble gallows or statues
As we slip past, childlike, alone.

No wonder
Sly poets admiringly use, but will not warm to
     The subtle machines that teach our world to spin.
These are too steady for reverence: gods must be changeable
Since worship is saved for what we cannot govern;
Gods push up grass, channel the dense sap through pine-boughs
     And amass the pewter cloudbanks of summer storm.

Once I awoke, a child in a chill mountain morning,
To see the small town—undreamed transfiguration—
Mantled in white, its slate and stone and timber
     Bright with that foreign cloak of innocence.
And I walked into old-world beauty; the gilt sun rising
Fell in a garden where time itself was congealing
As we shaped wonderful igloos under the stringybarks
     And took no account of thaw. But noon came on.
Something was lost in the brown receding slush there
Which has not returned, something other than childhood:
A notion, rather, of clear crystalline standards
     Freezing life to one shape, like a photograph.

Yet this is the point:
                              a photograph leaves out living
For Eton crops, old blazers, baptismal lace or
Some late-Victorian smile turned stiff and waxy,
     All arabesques, but never the heart of the thing,
Which is neither good nor bad, but one maze of motion
Through which we dance, into and out of the darkness
To tireless music: motes in the curled winds' breathing
     And more than motes, faced with the corners of choice.
And so at night below all the brilliant clusters
Of lamps in the sky, the living, dead and dying
Poised in their dance, I cling to the crust here stolidly
     And pray for a perfect day.

                    Out in the cold
Of hoarfrost and starlight, we fear for tomorrow's choosing
And cherish dreams made in meticulous patterns;
But come to norrow, we will neither be Christ nor Gandhi
        But will breathe this common air and rejoice with the birds.

All that I ask is that myriad lights, ever changing,
Continue to play on this great rind of ranges and gullies,
Flooding the vision of dreaming dwellers in cities
        Who walk out in summer pursuing something to praise:
        We will neither be simple nor clear till the end of our days.

A WINTRY MANIFESTO

It was the death of Satan first of all,
The knowledge that earth holds though kingdoms fall,
        Inured us to a stoic resignation,
        To making the most of a shrunken neighbourhood;

And what we drew on was not gold or fire,
No cross, not cloven hoof about the pyre,
        But painful, plain, contracted observations:
        The gesture of a hand, dip of a bough

Or seven stubborn words drawn close together
As a hewn charm against the shifting weather.
        Our singing was intolerably sober
        Mistrusting every trill of artifice.

Whatever danced on needle-points, we knew
That we had forged the world we stumbled through
        And, if a stripped wind howled through sighing alleys,
        Built our own refuge in a flush of pride

Knowing that all our gifts were for construction—
Timber to timber groined in every section—
    And knowing, too, purged of the sense of evil,
    These were the walls our folly would destroy.

We dreamed, woke, doubted, wept for fading stars
And then projected brave new avatars,
    Triumphs of reason. Yet a whole dimension
    Had vanished from the chambers of the mind,

And paramount among the victims fled,
Shrunken and pale, the grim king of the dead;
    Withdrawn to caverns safely beyond our sounding
    He waits as a Pretender for his call,

Which those who crave him can no longer give.
Men are the arbiters of how they live,
    And, stooped by millstones of authority,
    They welcome tyrants in with open arms.

Now in the shadows of unfriendly trees
We number leaves, discern faint similes
    And learn to praise whatever is imperfect
    As the true breeding-ground for honesty,

Finding our heroism in rejection
Of bland Utopias and of thieves' affection:
    Our greatest joy to mark an outline truly
    And know the piece of earth on which we stand.

RANDOLPH STOW

——— 〄 ———

RANDOLPH STOW WAS born in 1935 in Geraldton, a coastal town of Western Australia. His father was a lawyer and his mother came from a long-established pastoralist family, among the earliest pioneers of the state. Stow grew up on the dynastic property with the workmen—the Kevs and Harrys and Jabulmaras of one of his poems—and throughout his life he has found a close affinity with working and tribal people. By the time he graduated from the University of Western Australia in Arts, he had already published a volume of poetry and two novels.

Stow went to work as a storeman on an isolated mission station in the Kimberley Ranges, before being invited to the University of Adelaide as a tutor. Missing the outback, he decided the way to return was to train to be an anthropologist, a course he took up at Sydney University. Short of money after two years there, he became in 1959 a cadet patrol officer and assistant to the Government Anthropologist in New Guinea. However, while leading his first patrol, in the Trobriand Islands, he contracted a severe form of malaria and was invalided home with suicidal depression. From 1960 he spent three years in London as an outpatient of a hospital for tropical diseases. He later lived in a number of countries before returning to England to settle in East Anglia, from where his forebears had emigrated in 1830. There, in 1969, he began *Visitants*, which is widely regarded as the best of his nine novels and is set in the Trobriand Islands, but he was unable to finish it until ten years later. This writing block he attributes to an addiction to the drug mandrax, prescribed after a car accident. During his years of creative inactivity Stow lived in obscurity in a rented farm cottage, on a trickle of royalties. For much of this period he worked as a barman in a village pub, unpaid except for his drinks. His writing of *The Girl Green as Elderflower*, long researched but actually produced in one month in 1979, helped him complete *Visitants* in the same year. Stow has now settled in Suffolk in a small terrace house in Old Harwich, by the docks.

The main influences on his poetry, he says, have been Whitman, Rimbaud and St John Perse, who loosened the line of his extremely precocious juvenilia and gave his work the associative daring of its imagery. Stow's verse has a uniquely high-pitched emotionality. He is the only Australian poet whose novels and poetry are equally accomplished. A theme of his work in both forms is isolation: a sense of 'otherness' within nature and society. Despite the subjectivity of the imagery in his poems, what he says of his novels is also true of his verse: 'I always was a quite fanatical realist, always attempting to be more exact about things . . .'

Stow's output of poetry is small, even though it is his preferred medium: he has published two volumes, a slim selected edition, *A Counterfeit Silence* (1969), and nine new poems in an anthology of his work, *Randolph Stow* (1990).

RUINS OF THE CITY OF HAY

The wind has scattered my city to the sheep.
Capeweed and lovely lupins choke the street
where the wind wanders in great gaunt chimneys of hay
and straws cry out like keyholes.

Our yellow Petra of the fields: alas!
I walk the ruins of forum and capitol,
through quiet squares, by the temples of tranquillity.
Wisps of the metropolis brush my hair.
I become invisible in tears.

This was no ratbags' Eden: these were true haystacks.
Golden, but functional, our mansions sprang from dreams
of architects in love (*O my meadow queen!*).
No need for fires to be lit on the yellow hearthstones;
our walls were warmer than flesh, more sure than igloos.
On winter nights we squatted naked as Esquimaux,
chanting our sagas of innocent chauvinism.

In the street no vehicle passed. No telephone,
doorbell or till was heard in the canyons of hay.
No stir, no sound, but the sickle and the loom,
and the comments of emus begging by kitchen doors
in the moonlike silence of morning.

Though the neighbour states (said Lao Tse) lie in sight of the city
and their cocks wake and their watchdogs warn the inhabitants
the men of the city of hay will never go there
all the days of their lives.

But the wind of the world descended on lovely Petra
and the spires of the towers and the statues and belfries fell.
The bones of my brothers broke in the breaking columns.
The bones of my sisters, clasping their broken children,
cracked on the hearthstones, under the rooftrees of hay.

I alone mourn in the temples, by broken altars
bowered in black nightshade and mauve salvation-jane.

And the cocks of the neighbour nations scratch in the straw.
And their dogs rejoice in the bones of all my brethren.

ENDYMION

My love, you are no goddess: the bards were mistaken;
no lily maiden, no huntress in silver glades.

You are lovelier still by far, for you are an island;
a continent of the sky, and all virgin, sleeping.

And I, who plant my shack in your mould-grey gullies,
am come to claim you: my orchard, my garden, of ash.

To annex your still mountains with patriotic ballads,
to establish between your breasts my colonial hearth.

And forgetting all trees, winds, oceans and open grasslands,
and forgetting the day for as long as the night shall last,

to slumber becalmed and lulled in your hollowed hands,
to wither within to your likeness, and lie still.

Let your small dust fall, let it tick on my roof like crickets.
I shall open my heart, knowing nothing can come in.

THE EMBARKATION

En el puerto
los mástiles están llenos de nidos
y el viento
gime entre las alas de los pájaros
LAS OLAS MECEN EL NAVÍO MUERTO
—Vicente Huidobro

Winds in the harbour hiss
through wings of birds. Weeds drip
down from the fretted chain.
This is the gulls' domain,
not mine. How should I hope
again to put out, in this?

Rock on the waves, dead ship

Sunflowers stab to the sky
through salt-white ribs of boats
beached on the sand. The quay
crumbles; and though the sea
billow at dawn like wheat,
thirsts for horizons die.

The masts are full of nests

My house is a ruined cell
embattled; crowned and bound
with bougainvillaea, torn
by flowering branch and thorn
whose purple burns at noon
harshly against the swell.

Through wings, through wings, the wind

What should the white sand yield
but hungry, angry things?
A chestnut sun goes down.
The weak must dare to drown,
and harvest as they can
the salt, enormous field.

The harbour sighs with wings

Parent or kinsman, wake,
come to the sea's dark lip,
cry me farewell: who glide
white arm into black tide
and strike, for life or sleep
(that sleep for living's sake)

through waves, to the dead ship

THE LAND'S MEANING

for Sidney Nolan

The love of man is a weed of the waste places,
One may think of it as the spinifex of dry souls.

I have not, it is true, made the trek to the difficult country
where it is said to grow; but signs come back,
reports come back, of continuing exploration
in that terrain. And certain of our young men,
who turned in despair from the bar, upsetting a glass,
and swore: 'No more' (for the tin rooms stank of flyspray)
are sending word that the mastery of silence
alone is empire. What is God, they say,
but a man unwounded in his loneliness?

And the question (applauded, derided) falls like dust
on veranda and bar; and in pauses, when thinking ceases,
the footprints of the recently departed
march to the mind's horizons, and endure.

And often enough as we turn again, and laugh,
cloud, hide away the tracks with an acid word,
there is one or more gone past the door to stand
(wondering, debating) in the iron street,
and toss a coin, and pass, to the township's end,
where one-eyed 'Mat, eternal dealer in camels,
grins in the dusty yard like a split fruit.

But one who has returned, his eyes blurred maps
of landscapes still unmapped, gives this account:

'The third day, cockatoos dropped dead in the air.
Then the crows turned back, the camels knelt down and stayed
       there,
and a skin-coloured surf of sandhills jumped the horizon
and swamped me. I was bushed for forty years.

'And I came to a bloke all alone like a kurrajong tree.
And I said to him: "Mate—I don't need to know your name—
Let me camp in your shade, let me sleep, till the sun goes down."'

CONVALESCENCE

Who is this who has come to my homestead with strains of Sibelius
and the smell of heath to undo me, using my sickness
as warrant to seize on my lands, and the loves of childhood
and memories of health to make swift my capture?

You, mover—you. I am weak; let it be no other.

And whose is this, the white-petalled ship at the headlands
beating me back from the reef? It is some pirate
covets the coral-gashed hulk and the rotted rigging;
a frigate-bird writes his cipher above the masthead.

You, mover—you. I am weak; let it be no other.

Is it you indeed, who I thought lay bleeding and dying
long, long ago? Ah brother, our house is deserted,
and I cannot tell whose terrible footsteps it echoes,
nor the names of the derelict moons that darken the sky.

THE SINGING BONES

'Out where the dead men lie.'—Barcroft Boake

Out there, beyond the boundary fence, beyond
the scrub-dark flat horizon that the crows
returned from, evenings, days of rusty wind
raised from the bones a stiff lament, whose sound
netted my childhood round, and even here still blows.

My country's heart is ash in the market-place,
is aftermath of martyrdom. Out there
its sand-enshrined lay saints lie piece by piece,
Leichhardt by Gibson, stealing the wind's voice,
and Lawson's tramps, by choice made mummia and air.

No pilgrims leave, no holy-days are kept
for these who died of landscape. Who can find,
even, the camp-sites where the saints last slept?
Out there their place is, where the charts are gapped,
unreachable, unmapped, and mainly in the mind.

They were all poets, so the poets said,
who kept their end in mind in all they wrote
and hymned their bones, and joined them. Gordon died
happy, one surf-loud dawn, shot through the head,
and Boake astonished, dead, his stockwhip round his throat.

Time, time and time again, when the inland wind
beats over myall from the dunes, I hear
the singing bones, their glum Victorian strain.
A ritual manliness, embracing pain
to know; to taste terrain their heirs need not draw near.

FROST PARROTS

Hunted south-east, the Cape unglimpsed, from Tristan,
we met a coast not known till then, a stone
unwieldy country, fringed with trees in flower,
which flowers all at once blew towards us, crying.

Parrots—but vast; and death-chill, lovely things.
For in their glinting feathers was the blue
of broken glaciers and the talc of rime
and all the shades of ice: as lilac, rose,
the greens of clefts and flame of midday sunsets.
As for their trees, without them those were bare
and black as frosted charcoal, branched like coral.

Their cry was like the creak of snow you ache through
or chink of ice-spikes in a bough long martyred
or locked streams breaking up. And colder things;
jangling bedsprings in contemptuous attics,
and bottles rolled down alleys we forgot.

Their eyes were frost-stars. In their look was death.
To something. Something needed, till that day.

LES MURRAY

❧

LES MURRAY COMES from Bunyah, a farming district long settled by the Murray clan, near Taree on the north coast of New South Wales. He was born in 1938 and grew up on the dairy farm that his father rented from his father. Murray's mother died suddenly when he was twelve; he was an only child, and father and son were both emotionally devastated. Two years at Taree High School added to the misery of those years, but it was there that his interest in poetry began. He then enrolled at Sydney University.

After some years of self-education in the library, Murray dropped out of university and became a translator of technical and scholarly works at the Australian National University in Canberra. In 1962 he married Valerie Morelli, and in 1964 was baptised into the Catholic Church. His first book, *The Ilex Tree* (shared with Geoffrey Lehmann), was published in 1965. From 1967 Murray and his wife (now with two small children) lived for more than a year, precariously, in England and Europe. Returning to Australia, he resumed his university course and received in 1969 'the least distinguished BA ever awarded by Sydney University' (his words). He then worked for the Commonwealth Public Service in both Canberra and Sydney, before deciding to risk a full-time career as a poet.

Murray has frequently been supported by the Literature Board of the Australia Council; in return he has published nine books of poetry; a verse novel, *The Boys Who Stole The Funeral*; a selected verse, *The Vernacular Republic*, which has been regularly updated; his collected poems; and three collections of essays. He edited *Poetry Australia* magazine from 1973 to 1980, and from 1978 to 1991 was the poetry adviser for the publisher Angus & Robertson. He compiled the *New Oxford Book of Australian Verse* and the *Collins Dove Anthology of Australian Religious Verse*.

The ideal of community is a central preoccupation of Murray's writing, and the main body of his work can be seen as a defence of the values of his local farming community at Bunyah, and of other Bunyahs across Australia. This loyalty may be the outcome of his early loss of family life, and is embodied in his return to live in Bunyah with his wife and children, near his elderly father. His politics have been labelled agrarian populist, and with his Catholicism, and his outspokenness against whatever he sees as totalitarian, have made him controversial, in some quarters. However, he is the first Australian poet to enjoy a high international reputation, and his success abroad marks the end of the colonial era in Australian poetry.

A significant early influence on Murray's work was that of Kenneth Slessor. Slessor's physicality, his richly packed detail, his mimetic use of sound and rhythm, his hobbyist's enthusiasm for arcana were all formative values for the younger poet. Murray's early poetry has a lyrical clarity and precise observation that has continued into some of the later work, but the major line of development has come about through his reactiveness, his sense of embattlement, which has led to an overbearing, brilliantly baroque philosophising, and to an often witty polemic.

Murray has been superficially regarded as a nature poet, but what matters to him most often is people in the landscape, working the land. Technical, natural, linguistic, culinary or social history, grisly and piquant stories, some of them picked up while on the road on his reading tours, popular inventions of speech—all of these feed into the worldplay of his work.

He displays, among poets writing in English at present, a uniquely gifted language.

'The Buladelah-Taree Holiday Song Cycle', in some ways his best achievement, is based on the rhythms of, and takes its structure from, 'The Song Cycle of the Moon Bone', an Aboriginal chant from Arnhem Land, translated by the anthropologist R.M. Berndt. Murray's poem, one imagines, intends to show through this allusion, against Aboriginal land-rights activists like Judith Wright, that white Australians, too, have developed their own deep attachments to this country, mythologising it for themselves, and that this is not to be devalued and overlooked. At the same time, Murray's serious pastiche of an 'Aboriginal' form indicates a respect for that culture, which indeed he has spoken on behalf of, and has long taken an interest in. As always, it is a sense of harmony, of community, free of sophisticated resentments, which is his ideal.

THE PRINCES' LAND

for Valerie, on her birthday

Leaves from the ancient forest gleam
in the meadow brook, and dip, and pass.
Six maidens dance on the level green,
a seventh toys with an hourglass,

letting fine hours sink away,
turning to sift them back again.
An idle prince, with a cembalo,
sings to the golden afternoon.

Two silver knights, met in a wood,
tilt at each other, clash and bow.
Upon a field seme of birds
Tom Bread-and-Cheese sleeps by his plough.

But now a deadly stillness comes
upon the brook, upon the green,
upon the seven dancing maids,
the dented knights are dulled to stone.

The hours in the hourglass
are stilled to fine fear, and the wood
to empty burning. Tom the hind
walks in his sleep in pools of blood.

The page we've reached is grey with pain.
Some will not hear, some run away,
some go to write books of their own,
some few, as the tale grows cruel, sing Hey

but we who have no other book
spell out the gloomy, blazing text,
page by slow page, wild year by year,
our hope refined to what comes next,

and yet attentive to each child
who says he's looked ahead and seen
how the tale will go, or spied
a silver page two pages on,

for, as the themes knit and unfold,
somewhere far on, where all is changed,
beyond all twists of grief and fear,
we look to glimpse that land again:

the brook descends in music through
the meadows of that figured land,
nine maidens from the ageless wood
move in their circles, hand in hand.

Two noble figures, counterchanged,
fence with swift passion, pause and bow.
All in a field impaled with sun
the Prince of Cheese snores by his plough.

Watching bright hours file away,
turning to sift them back again,
the Prince of Bread, with a cembalo
hums to the golden afternoon.

VINDALOO IN MERTHYR TYDFIL

The first night of my second voyage to Wales,
tired as rag from ascending the left cheek of Earth
I nevertheless went to Merthyr in good company
and warm in neckclothing and speech in the butcher's Arms
till Time struck us pintless, and Eddie Rees steamed in brick lanes
and under the dark of the White Tip we repaired shouting

to I think the Bengal. I called for curry, the hottest,
vain of my nation, proud of my hard mouth from childhood,
the kindly brown waiter wringing the hands of dissuasion
O vindaloo, sir! You sure you want vindaloo, sir?
But I cried Yes please, being too far in to go back
the bright bells of Rhymney moreover sang in my brains.

Fair play, it was frightful. I spooned the chicken of Hell
in a sauce of rich yellow brimstone. The valley boys with me
tasting it, croaked to white Jesus. And only pride drove me,
forkful by forkful, observed by hot mangosteen eyes,
by all the carnivorous castes and gurus from Cardiff
my brilliant tears washing the unbelief of the Welsh.

Oh it was a ride on Watneys plunging red barrel
through all the burning ghats of most carnal ambition
and never again will I want such illumination
for three days on end concerning my own mortal coil
but I signed my plate in the end with a licked knife and fork
and green-and-gold spotted, I sang for my pains like the free
before I passed out among all the stars of Cilfynydd.

THE BROAD BEAN SERMON

Beanstalks, in any breeze, are a slack church parade
without belief, saying *trespass against us* in unison,
recruits in mint Air Force dacron, with unbuttoned leaves.

Upright with water like men, square in stem-section
they grow to great lengths, drink rain, keel over all ways,
kink down and grow up afresh, with proffered new greenstuff.

Above the cat-and-mouse floor of a thin bean forest
snails hang rapt in their food, ants hurry through several dimensions,
spiders tense and sag like little black flags in their cordage.

Going out to pick beans with the sun high as fence-tops, you find
plenty, and fetch them. An hour or a cloud later
you find shirtfulls more. At every hour of daylight

appear more that you missed: ripe, knobbly ones, fleshy-sided,
thin-straight, thin-crescent, frown-shaped, bird-shouldered, boat-
    keeled ones,
beans knuckled and single-bulged, minute green dolphins at suck,

beans upright like lecturing, outstretched like blessing fingers
in the incident light, and more still, oblique to your notice
that the noon glare or cloud-light or afternoon slants will uncover

till you ask yourself Could I have overlooked so many, or
do they form in an hour? unfolding into reality
like templates for subtly broad grins, like unique caught expressions,

like edible meanings, each sealed around with a string
and affixed to its moment, an unceasing colloquial assembly,
the portly, the stiff, and those lolling in pointed green slippers. . . .

Wondering who'll take the spare bagfulls, you grin with
    happiness
—it is your health—you vow to pick them all
even the last few, weeks off yet, misshapen as toes.

THE ACTION

We have spoken of the Action,
the believer-in-death, maker of tests and failures.
It is through the Action
that the quiet homes empty, and barrack beds fill up, and cities
that are cover from God.
The Action, continual breakthrough,
cannot abide slow speech. It invented Yokels,
it invented the Proles, who are difficult/noble/raffish,
it invented, in short, brave Us and the awful Others.
The smiling Action
makes all things new: its rites are father-killing,
sketching of pyramid plans, and the dance of Circles.

Turning slowly under trees, footing off the river's linen
to come into shade—some waterhens were subtly
edging away to their kampongs of chomped reeds—
eel-thoughts unwound through me. At a little distance
I heard New Year children slap the causeway.
                                 Floating
in Coolongolook River, there below the junction
of Curreeki Creek,
                      water of the farms upheld me.

We were made by the Action:
the apes who agreed to speech ate those who didn't,
Action people tell us.
Rome of the waterpipes came of the Action, lost it,
and Louis' Versailles, in memory of which we mow grass.
Napoleon and Stalin were, mightily, the Action.
All the Civilizations, so good at royal arts and war
and postal networks—
it is the myriad Action
keeps them successive, prevents the achievement for good
of civilization.

Wash water, cattle water, irrigation-pipe-tang water
and water of the Kyle,
                              the chain-saw forests up there
where the cedar getter walks at night with dangling pockets,
water of the fern-tree gushers' heaping iron,
water of the bloodwoods, water of the Curreeki gold rush,
water of the underbrush sleeping shifts of birds
all sustained me,
                         thankful for great dinners
that had made me a lazy swimmer, marvellous floater,
looking up through oaks
                              to the mountain Coolongolook,
the increase-place of flying fox people, dancers—

Now talk is around of a loosening in republics,
retrievals of subtle water: all the peoples
who call themselves The People,
all the unnoticed cultures,
remnants defined by a tilt in their speech, traditions
that call the stars, say, Great Bluff, Five Hounds of Oscar,
the High and Low Lazies,
spells, moon-phase farming—all these are being canvassed.
The time has come round for republics of the cultures
and for rituals, with sound: the painful washings-clean
of smallpox blankets.
It may save the world,
or be the new Action.

                                                  Leaves
were coming to my lips, and the picnic on the bank
made delicious smoke.
                         Soon, perhaps, I'd be ready
to go and eat steak amongst Grandmother's people,
talk even to children,
                              dipping my face again
I kneaded my muscles, softening the Action.

THE BULADELAH-TAREE HOLIDAY SONG CYCLE

I

The people are eating dinner in that country north of Legge's Lake;
behind flywire and venetians, in the dimmed cool, town people eat
     Lunch.
Plying knives and forks with a peek-in sound, with a tuck-in sound
they are thinking about relatives and inventory, they are talking
     about customers and visitors.
In the country of memorial iron, on the creek-facing hills there,
they are thinking about bean plants, and rings of tank water, of
     growing a pumpkin by Christmas;
rolling a cigarette, they say thoughtfully Yes, and their companion
     nods, considering.
Fresh sheets have been spread and tucked tight, childhood rooms
     have been seen to,
for this is the season when children return with their children
to the place of Bingham's Ghost, of the Old Timber Wharf, of the
     Big Flood That Time,
the country of the rationalized farms, of the day-and-night farms,
     and of the Pitt Street farms,
of the Shire Engineer and many other rumours, of the tractor
     crankcase furred with chaff,
the places of sitting down near ferns, the snake-fear places, the cattle-
     crossing-long-ago places.

II

It is the season of the Long Narrow City; it has crossed the Myall, it
     has entered the North Coast,
that big stunning snake; it is looped through the hills, burning all
     night there.
Hitching and flying on the downgrades, processionally balancing on
     the climbs,
it echoes in O'Sullivan's Gap, in the tight coats of the flooded-gum
     trees;
the tops of palms exclaim at it unmoved, there near Wootton.
Glowing all night behind the hills, with a north-shifting glare,
     burning behind the hills;
through Coolongolook, through Wang Wauk, across the Wallamba,

the booming tarred pipe of the holiday slows and spurts again;
   Nabiac chokes in glassy wind,
the forests on Kiwarrak dwindle in cheap light; Tuncurry and Forster
   swell like cooking oil.
The waiting is buffed, in timber village off the highway, the waiting
   is buffeted:
the fumes of fun hanging above ferns; crime flashes in strange
   windscreens, in the time of the Holiday.
Parasites weave quickly through the long gut that paddocks shine
   into;
powerful makes surging and pouncing: the police, collecting
   Revenue.
The heavy gut winds over the Manning, filling northward, digesting
   the towns, feeding the towns;
they all become the narrow city, they join it;
girls walking close to murder discard, with excitement, their names.
Crossing Australia of the sports, the narrow city, bringing home the
   children.

III

It is good to come out after driving and walk on bare grass;
walking out, looking all around, relearning that country.
Looking out for snakes, and looking out for rabbits as well;
going into the shade of myrtles to try their cupped climate, swinging
   by one hand around them,
in that country of the Holiday . . .
stepping behind trees to the dam, as if you had a gun,
to that place of the Wood Duck,
to that place of the Wood Duck's Nest,
proving you can still do it; looking at the duck who hasn't seen you,
the mother duck who'd run Catch Me (broken wing) I'm Fatter
   (broken wing), having hissed to her children.

IV

The birds saw us wandering along.
Rosellas swept up crying out *we think we think*; they settled farther
   along;
knapping seeds off the grass, under dead trees where their eggs were,
   walking around on their fingers,

flying on into the grass.

The heron lifted up his head and elbows; the magpie stepped aside a
    bit,

angling his chopsticks into pasture, turning things over in his head.

At the place of the Plough Handles, of the Apple Trees Bending
    Over, and of the Cattlecamp,

there the vealers are feeding; they are loosely at work, facing
    everywhere.

They are always out there, and the forest is always on the hills;

around the sun are turning the wedgetail eagle and her mate, that
    dour brushhook-faced family:

they settled on Deer's Hill away back when the sky was opened,

in the bull-oak trees way up there, the place of fur tufted in the grass,
    the place of bone-turds.

V

The Fathers and the Great-Grandfathers, they are out in the
    paddocks all the time, they live out there,

at the place of the Rail Fence, of the Furrows Under Grass, at the
    place of the Slab Chimney.

We tell them that clearing is complete, an outdated attitude, all over;

we preach without a sacrifice, and are ignored; flowering bushes
    grow dull to our eyes.

We begin to go up on the ridge, talking together, looking at the
    kino-coloured ants,

at the yard-wide sore of their nest, that kibbled peak, and the
    workers heaving vast stalks up there,

the brisk compact workers; jointed soldiers pour out then, tense with
    acid; several probe the mouth of a lost gin bottle;

Innuendo, we exclaim, *literal minds!* and go on up the ridge,
    announced by finches;

passing the place of the Dingo Trap, and that farm hand it caught,
    and the place of the Cowbails,

we come to the road and watch heifers,

little unjoined devons, their teats hidden in fur, and the cousin with
    his loose-slung stockwhip driving them.

We talk with him about rivers and the lakes; his polished horse is
    stepping nervously,

printing neat omegas in the gravel, flexing its skin to shake off flies;
his big sidestepping horse that has kept its stones; it recedes
    gradually, bearing him;
we murmur *stone-horse* and *devilry* to the grinners under grass.

VI

Barbecue smoke is rising at Legge's Camp; it is steaming into the
    midday air,
all around the lake shore, at the Broadwater, it is going up among
    the paperbark trees,
a heat-shimmer of sauces, rising from tripods and flat steel, at that
    place of the Coneshells,
at that place of the Seagrass, and the tiny segmented things
    swarming in it, and of the Pelican.
Dogs are running around disjointedly; water escapes from their
    mouths,
confused emotions from their eyes; humans snarl at them Gwanout
    and Hereboy, not varying their tone much;
the impoverished dog people, suddenly sitting down to nuzzle
    themselves; toddlers side with them:
toddlers, running away purposefully at random, among cars, into
    big drownie water (come back, Cheryl-Ann!).
They rise up as charioteers, leaning back on the tow-bar; all their
    attributes bulge at once;
swapping swash shoulder-wings for the white-sheeted shoes that
    bear them,
they are skidding over the flat glitter, stiff with grace, for once not
    travelling to arrive.
From the high dunes over there, the rough blue distance, at length
    they come back behind the boats,
and behind the boats' noise, cartwheeling, or sitting down, into the
    lake's warm chair;
they wade ashore and eat with the families, putting off that
    uprightness, that assertion,
eating with the families who love equipment, and the freedom from
    equipment,
with the fathers who love driving, and lighting a fire between stones.

VII

Shapes of children were moving in the standing corn, in the child-
    labour districts;
coloured flashes of children, between the green and parching stalks,
    appearing and disappearing.
Some places, they are working, racking off each cob like a lever,
    tossing it on the heaps;
other places, they are children of child-age, there playing jungle:
in the tiger-striped shade, they are firing hoehandle machine guns,
    taking cover behind fat pumpkins;
in other cases, it is Sunday and they are lovers.
They rise and walk together in the sibilance, finding single rows
    irksome, hating speech now,
or, full of speech, they swap files and follow defiles, disappearing
    and appearing;
near the rain-grey barns, and the children building cattleyards beside
    them;
the standing corn, gnawed by pouched and rodent mice; generations
    are moving among it,
the parrot-hacked, medicine-tassled corn, ascending all the creek
    flats, the wire-fenced alluvials,
going up in patches through the hills, towards the Steep Country.

VIII

Forests and State Forests, all down off the steeper country;
    mosquitoes are always living in there:
they float about like dust motes and sink down, at the places of the
    Stinging Tree,
and of the Staghorn Fern; the males feed on plant-stem fluid,
    absorbing that watery ichor;
the females meter the air, feeling for the warm-blooded smell,
    needing blood for their eggs.
They find the dingo in his sleeping-place, they find his underbelly
    and his anus;
they find the possum's face, they drift up the ponderous pleats of the
    fig tree, way up into its rigging,
the high camp of the fruit bats; they feed on the membranes and ears
    of bats; tired wings cuff air at them;

their eggs burning inside them, they alight on the muzzles of cattle,
the half-wild bush cattle, there at the place of the Sleeper Dump, at
the place of the Tallowwoods.

The males move about among growth tips; ingesting solutions, they
crouch intently;
the females sing, needing blood to breed their young; their singing is
in the scrub country;
their tune comes to the name-bearing humans, who dance to it and
irritably grin at it.

IX

The warriors are cutting timber with brash chainsaws; they are
trimming hardwood pit-props and loading them;
Is that an order? they hoot at the peremptory lorry driver, who
laughs; he is also a warrior.

They are driving long-nosed tractors, slashing pasture in the
dinnertime sun;
they are fitting tappets and valves, the warriors, or giving finish to a
surfboard.

Addressed on the beach by a pale man, they watch waves break and
are reserved, refusing pleasantry;
they joke only with fellow warriors, chaffing about try-ons and the
police, not slighting women.

Making Timber a word of power, Con-rod a word of power, Sense
a word of power, the Regs. a word of power,
they know belt-fed from spring-fed; they speak of being *stiff*, and
being *history*;
the warriors who have killed, and the warriors who eschewed
killing,
the solemn, the drily spoken, the life peerage of endurance; drinking
water from a tap,
they watch boys who think hard work a test, and boys who think it
is not a test.

X

Now the ibis are flying in, hovering down on the wetlands,
on those swampy paddocks around Darawank, curving down in
ragged dozens,

on the riverside flats along the Wang Wauk, on the Boolambayte
        pasture flats,
and away towards the sea, on the sand moors, at the place of the
        Jabiru Crane,
leaning out of their wings, they step down; they take out their
        implement at once,
out of its straw wrapping, and start work; they dab grasshopper and
        ground-cricket
with nonexistence . . . spiking the ground and puncturing it . . .
        they swallow down the outcry of a frog;
they discover titbits kept for them under cowmanure lids, small slow
        things.
Pronging the earth, they make little socket noises, their
        thoughtfulness jolting down-and-up suddenly;
there at Bunyah, along Firefly Creek, and up through Germany,
the ibis are all at work again, thin-necked ageing men towards
        evening; they are solemnly all back
at Minimbah, and on the Manning, in the rye-and-clover irrigation
        fields;
city storemen and accounts clerks point them out to their wives,
remembering things about themselves, and about the ibis.

XI

Abandoned fruit trees, moss-tufted, spotted with dim lichen paints;
        the fruit trees of the Grandmothers,
they stand along the creekbanks, in the old home paddocks, where
        the houses were;
they are reached through bramble-grown front gates, they creak at
        dawn behind burnt skillions,
at Belbora, at Bucca Wauka, away in at Burrell Creek,
at Telararee of the gold-sluices.
The trees are split and rotten-elbowed; they bear the old-fashioned
        summer fruits,
the annual bygones: china pear, quince, persimmon;
the fruit has the taste of former lives, of sawdust and parlour song,
        the tang of Manners;
children bite it, recklessly,
at what will become for them the place of the Slab Wall, and of the

Coal Oil Lamp,
the place of moss-grit and swallows' nests, the place of the
    Crockery.

XII

Now the sun is an applegreen blindness through the swells, a white
    blast on the sea-face, flaking and shoaling;
now it is burning off the mist, it is emptying the density of trees, it is
    spreading upriver,
hovering above the casuarina needles, there at Old Bar and Manning
    Point;
flooding the island farms, it abolishes the milkers' munching breath
as they walk towards the cowyards; it stings a bucket here, a teacup
    there.
Morning steps into the world by ever more southerly gates; shadows
    weaken their north skew
on Middle Brother, on Cape Hawke, on the dune scrub toward Seal
    Rocks;
steadily the heat is coming on, the butter-water time, the clothes-
    sticking time;
grass covers itself with straw; abandoned things are thronged with
    spirits;
everywhere wood is still with strain; birds hiding down the creek
    galleries, and in the cockspur canes;
the cicada is hanging up her sheets; she takes wing off her music-
    sheets.
Cars pass with a rational zoom, panning quickly towards Wingham,
through the thronged and glittering, the shale-topped ridges, and the
    cattlecamps,
towards Wingham for the cricket, the ball knocked hard in front of
    smoked-glass ranges, and for the drinking.
In the time of heat, the time of flies around the mouth, the time of
    the west verandah;
looking at that umbrage along the ranges, on the New England side;
clouds begin assembling vaguely, a hot soiled heaviness on the sky,
    away there towards Gloucester;
a swelling up of clouds, growing there above Mount George, and
    above Tipperary;

far away and hot with light; sometimes a storm takes root there, and
    fills the heavens rapidly;
darkening, boiling up and swaying on its stalks, pulling this way and
    that, blowing round by Krambach;
coming white on Bulby, it drenches down on the paddocks, and on
    the wire fences;
the paddocks are full of ghosts, and people in cornbag hoods
    approaching;
lights are lit in the house; the storm veers mightily on its stem, above
    the roof; the hills uphold it;
the stony hills guide its dissolution; gullies opening and crumbling
    down, wrenching tussocks and rolling them;
the storm carries a greenish-grey bag; perhaps it will find hail and
    send it down, starring cars, flattening tomatoes,
in the time of the Washaways, of the dead trunks braiding water, and
    of the Hailstone Yarns.

XIII

The stars of the holiday step out all over the sky.
People look up at them, out of their caravan doors and their
    campsites;
people look up from the farms, before going back; they gaze at their
    year's worth of stars.
The Cross hangs head-downward, out there over Markwell;
it turns upon the Still Place, the pivot of the Seasons, with one
    shoulder rising:
'Now I'm beginning to rise, with my Pointers and my Load . . .'
hanging eastwards, it shines on the sawmills and the lakes, on the
    glasses of the Old People.
Looking at the Cross, the galaxy is over our left shoulder, slung up
    highest in the east;
there the Dog is following the Hunter; the Dog Star pulsing there
    above Forster; it shines down on the Bikies,
and on the boat-hire sheds, there at the place of the Oyster; the place
    of the Shark's Eggs and her Hide;
the Pleiades are pinned up high on the darkness, away back above
    the Manning;
they are shining on the Two Blackbutt Trees, on the rotted river
    wharves, and on the towns;

standing there, above the water and the lucerne flats, at the place of
   the Families;
their light sprinkles down on Taree of the Lebanese shops, it mingles
   with the streetlights and their glare.
People recover the starlight, hitching north,
travelling north beyond the seasons, into that country of the
   Communes, and of the banana:
the Flying Horse, the Rescued Girl, and the Bull, burning steadily
   above that country.
Now the New Moon is low down in the west, that remote direction
   of the Cattlemen,
and of the Saleyards, the place of steep clouds, and of the Rodeo;
the New Moon who has poured out her rain, the moon of the
   Planting-times.
People go outside and look at the stars, and at the melon-rind moon,
the Scorpion going down into the mountains, over there towards
   Waukivory, sinking into the tree-line,
in the time of the Rockmelons, and of the Holiday . . .
the Cross is rising on his elbow, above the glow of the horizon;
carrying a small star in his pocket, he reclines there brilliantly,
above the Alum Mountain, and the lakes threaded on the Myall
   River, and above the Holiday.

IMMIGRANT VOYAGE

My wife came out on the *Goya*
in the mid-year of our century.

In the fogs of that winter
many hundred ships were sounding;
the DP camps were being washed to sea.

The bombsites and the ghettoes
were edging out to Israel,
to Brazil, to Africa, America.

The separating ships were bound away
to the cities of refuge
built for the age of progress.

Hull-down and pouring light
the tithe-barns, the cathedrals
were bearing the old castes away.

O

Pattern-bombed out of babyhood,
Hungarians-become-Swiss,
the children heard their parents:
Argentina? Or Australia?
Less politics, in Australia . . .

Dark Germany, iron frost
and the waiting many weeks
then a small converted warship
under the moon, turning south.

Way beyond the first star
and beyond Cap Finisterre
the fishes and the birds
did eat of their heave-offerings.

O

The *Goya* was a barracks:
mess-queue, spotlights, tower,
crossing the Middle Sea.

In the haunted blue light
that burned nightlong in the sleeping-decks
the tiered bunks were restless
with the coughing, demons, territory.

On the Sea of Sweat, the Red Sea,
the flat heat melted even
dulled deference of the injured.
Nordics and Slavonics
paid salt-tax day and night, being
absolved of Europe

but by the Gate of Tears
the barrack was a village
with accordeons and dancing
(Fräulein, kennen Sie meinen Rhythmus?)
approaching the southern stars.

O

Those who said Europe
has fallen to the Proles
and the many who said
we are going for the children,

the nouveau poor
and the cheerful shirtsleeve Proles,
the children, who thought
No Smoking signs meant men
mustn't dress for dinner,

those who had hopes
and those who knew that they
were giving up their lives

were becoming the people
who would say, and sometimes urge,
in the English-speaking years:
we came out on the *Goya*.

O

At last, a low coastline,
old horror of Dutch sail-captains.

Behind it, still unknown,
sunburnt farms, strange trees, family jokes
and all the classes of equality.

As it fell away northwards
there was one last week for songs,
for dreaming at the rail,
for beloved meaningless words.

Standing in to Port Phillip
in the salt-grey summer light
the village dissolved
into strained shapes holding luggage;

now they, like the dour
Australians below them, were facing
encounter with the Foreign
where all subtlety fails.

O

Those who, with effort,
with concealment, with silence, had resisted
the collapsed star Death,
who had clawed their families from it,
those crippled by that gravity

were suddenly, shockingly
being loaded aboard lorries:
They say, another camp—
One did not come for this—

As all the refitted
ships stood, oiling, in the Bay,
spectres, furious and feeble,
accompanied the trucks through Melbourne,

resignation, understandings
that cheerful speed dispelled at length.

That first day, rolling north
across the bright savanna,
not yet people, but numbers.
Population. Forebears.

O

Bonegilla, Nelson Bay,
the dry-land barbed wire ships
from which some would never land.

In these, as their parents
learned the Fresh Start music:
physicians nailing crates,
attorneys cleaning trams,
the children had one last
ambiguous summer holiday.

Ahead of them lay
the Deep End of the schoolyard,
tribal testing, tribal soft-drinks,
and learning English fast,
the Wang-Wang language.

Ahead of them, refinements:
thumbs hooked down hard under belts
to repress gesticulation;

ahead of them, epithets:
wog, reffo, Commo Nazi,
things which can be forgotten
but must first be told.

And farther ahead
in the years of the Coffee Revolution
and the Smallgoods Renaissance,
the early funerals:

the misemployed, the unadaptable,
those marked by the Abyss,

friends who came on the _Goya_
in the mid-year of our century.

THE QUALITY OF SPRAWL

Sprawl is the quality
of the man who cut down his Rolls-Royce
into a farm utility truck, and sprawl
is what the company lacked when it made repeated efforts
to buy the vehicle back and repair its image.

Sprawl is doing your farming by aeroplane, roughly,
or driving a hitchhiker that extra hundred miles home.
It is the rococo of being your own still centre.
It is never lighting cigars with ten-dollar notes:
that's idiot ostentation and murder of starving people.
Nor can it be bought with the ash of million-dollar deeds.

Sprawl lengthens the legs; it trains greyhounds on liver and beer.
Sprawl almost never says Why not? with palms comically raised
nor can it be dressed for, not even in running shoes worn
with mink and a nose ring. That is Society. That's Style.
Sprawl is more like the thirteenth banana in a dozen
or anyway the fourteenth.

Sprawl is Hank Stamper in Never Give an Inch
bisecting an obstructive official's desk with a chain saw.
Not harming the official. Sprawl is never brutal
though it's often intransigent. Sprawl is never Simon de Montfort
at a town-storming: Kill them all! God will know his own.
Knowing the man's name this was said to might be sprawl.

Sprawl occurs in art. The fifteenth to twenty-first
lines in a sonnet, for example. And in certain paintings;
I have sprawl enough to have forgotten which paintings.
Turner's glorious Burning of the Houses of Parliament
comes to mind, a doubling bannered triumph of sprawl—
except, he didn't fire them.

Sprawl gets up the nose of many kinds of people
(every kind that comes in kinds) whose futures don't include it.
Some decry it as criminal presumption, silken-robed Pope Alexander
dividing the new world between Spain and Portugal.
If he smiled *in petto* afterwards, perhaps the thing did have sprawl.

Sprawl is really classless, though. It's John Christopher Frederick
    Murray
asleep in his neighbours' best bed in spurs and oilskins
but not having thrown up:
sprawl is never Calum who, in the loud hallway of our house,
reinvented the Festoon. Rather
it's Beatrice Miles going twelve hundred ditto in a taxi,
No Lewd Advances, No Hitting Animals, No Speeding,
on the proceeds of her two-bob-a-sonnet Shakespeare readings.
An image of my country. And would that it were more so.

No, sprawl is full-gloss murals on a council-house wall.
Sprawl leans on things. It is loose-limbed in its mind.
Reprimanded and dismissed
it listens with a grin and one boot up on the rail
of possibility. It may have to leave the Earth.
Being roughly Christian, it scratches the other cheek
and thinks it unlikely. Though people have been shot for sprawl.

MACHINE PORTRAITS WITH PENDANT SPACEMAN

for Valerie

The bulldozer stands short as a boot on its heel-high ripple soles;
it has toecapped stumps aside all day, scuffed earth and trampled
     rocks
making a hobnailed dyke downstream of raw clay shoals.
Its work will hold water. The man who bounced high on the box
seat, exercising levers, would swear a full frontal orthodox
oath to that. First he shaved off the grizzled scrub
with that front end safety razor supplied by the school of hard
     knocks
then he knuckled down and ground his irons properly; they copped
     many a harsh rub.
At knock-off time, spilling thunder, he surfaced like a sub.

O

Speaking of razors, the workshop amazes with its strop,
its elapsing leather drive belt angled to the slapstick flow
of fast work in the Chaplin age; tightened, it runs like syrup,
streams like a mill-sluice, fiddles like a glazed virtuoso.
With the straitlaced summary cut of Sam Brownes long ago
it is the last of the drawn lash and bullocking muscle
left in engineering. It's where the panther leaping, his swift shadow
and all such free images turned plastic. Here they dwindle, dense
     with oil,
like a skein between tough factory hands, pulley and Diesel.

O

Shaking in slow low flight, with its span of many jets,
the combine seeder at nightfall swimming over flat land
is a style of machinery we'd imagined for the fictional planets:
in the high glassed cabin, above vapour-pencilling floodlights, a
     hand,

gloved against the cold, hunts along the medium-wave band
for company of Earth voices; it crosses speech garble music—
the Brandenburg Conch the Who the Illyrian High Command—
as seed wheat in the hoppers shakes down, being laced into the thick
night-dampening plains soil, and the stars waver out and stick.

O

Flags and a taut fence discipline the mountain pasture
where giant upturned mushrooms gape mildly at the sky
catching otherworld pollen. Poppy-smooth or waffle-ironed, each
    armature
distils wild and white sound. These, Earth's first antennae
tranquilly angled outwards, to a black, not a gold infinity,
swallow the millionfold numbers that print out as a risen
glorious Apollo. They speak control to satellites in high
bursts of algorithm. And some of them are tuned to win
answers to fair questions, viz. What is the Universe in?

O

How many metal-bra and trumpet-flaring film extravaganzas
underlie the progress of the space shuttle's Ground Transporter
    Vehicle
across concrete-surfaced Florida? Atop oncreeping house-high
    panzers,
towering drydock and ocean-liner decks, there perches a gridiron
    football
field in gradual motion; it is the god-platform; it sustains the bridal
skyscraper of liquid Cool, and the rockets borrowed from the
    Superman
and the bricked aeroplane of Bustout-and-return, all vertical,
conjoined and myth-huge, approaching the starred gantry where
    human
lightning will crack, extend, and vanish upwards from this caravan.

O

Gold-masked, the foetal warrior
unslipping on a flawless floor,
I backpack air; my life machine
breathes me head-Earthwards, speaks the Choctaw
of tech-talk that earths our discipline—

but the home world now seems outside-in;
I marvel that here background's so fore
and sheathe my arms in the unseen

a dream in images unrecalled
from any past takes me   I soar
at the heart of fall on a drifting line

this is the nearest I have been
to oneness with the everted world
the unsinking leap   the stone unfurled

O

In a derelict village picture show I will find a projector,
dust-matted, but with film in its drum magazines, and the lens
mysteriously clean. The film will be called *Insensate Violence*,
no plot, no characters, just shoot burn scream beg claw
bayonet trample brains—I will hit the reverse switch then, in
     conscience,
and the thing will run backwards, unlike its coeval the machinegun;
blood will unspill, fighters lift and surge apart; horror will be undone
and I will come out to a large town, bright parrots round the
     saleyard pens
and my people's faces healed of a bitter sophistication.

O

The more I act, the stiller I become;
the less I'm lit, the more spellbound my crowd;
I accept all colours, and with a warming hum
I turn them white and hide them in a cloud.
To give long life is a power I'm allowed
by my servant, Death. I am what you can't sell
at the world's end—and if you're still beetle-browed
try some of my treasures: an adult bird in its shell
or a pink porker in his own gut, Fritz the Abstract Animal.

O

No riddles about a crane. This one drops a black clanger on cars
and the palm of its four-thumbed steel hand is a raptor of wrecked
        tubing;
the ones up the highway hoist porridgy concrete, long spars
and the local skyline; whether raising aloft on a string
bizarre workaday angels, or letting down a rotating
man on a sphere, these machines are inclined to maintain
a peace like world war, in which we turn over everything
to provide unceasing victories. Now the fluent lines stop, and strain
engrosses this tower on the frontier of junk, this crane.

O

Before a landscape sprouts those giant stepladders that pump oil
or before far out iron mosquitoes attach to the sea
there is this sortilege with phones that plug into mapped soil,
the odd gelignite bump to shake trucks, paper scribbling out serially
as men dial Barrier Reefs long enfolded beneath the geology
or listen for black Freudian beaches; they seek a miles-wide pustular
rock dome of pure Crude, a St. Pauls-in-profundis. There are many
wrong numbers on the geophone, but it's brought us some
        distance—and by car.
Every machine has been love and a true answer.

O

Not a high studded ship boiling cauliflower under her keel
nor a ghost in bootlaced canvas—just a length of country road
afloat between two shores, winding wet wire rope reel-to-reel,
dismissing romance sternwards. Six cars and a hay truck are her load
plus a thoughtful human cast which could, in some dramatic
    episode,
become a world. All machines in the end join God's creation
growing bygone, given, changeless—but a river ferry has its
    timeless mode
from the grinding reedy outset; it enforces contemplation.
We arrive. We traverse depth in thudding silence. We go on.

The Mouthless Image of God in the Hunter-Colo Mountains

Starting a dog, in the past-midnight suburbs, for a laugh,
barking for a lark, or to nark and miff, being tough
or dumbly meditative, starting gruff, sparking one dog off
almost companionably, you work him up, playing the rough riff
of punkish mischief, get funky as a poultry-farm diff
and vary with the Prussian note: *Achtung! Schar, Gewehr' auf!*
starting all the dogs off, for the tinny chain reaction and stiff
far-spreading music, the backyard territorial guff
echoing off brick streets, garbage cans, off every sandstone cliff
in miles-wide canine circles, a vast haze of auditory stuff
with every dog augmenting it, tail up, mouth serrated, shoulder ruff
pulsing with its outputs, a continuous clipped yap from a handmuff
Pomeranian, a labrador's ascending fours, a Dane grown great
    enough
to bark in the singular, many raffish bitzers blowing their gaff
as humans raise windows and cries and here and there the roof
and you barking at the epicentre, you, putting a warp to the woof,
shift the design with a throat-rubbing lull and ill howl,
dingo-vibrant, not shrill, which starts a howling school

among hill-and-hollow barkers, till horizons-wide again a tall
pavilion of mixed timbres is lifted up eerily in full call
and the wailing takes a toll: you, from playing the fool
move, behind your arch will, into the sorrow of a people.

O

And not just one people. You've entered a sound-proletariat
where pigs exclaim *boff-boff!* making off in fright
and fowls say *chirk* in tiny voices when a snake's about,
quite unlike the rooster's *Chook Chook*, meaning look, a good bit:
hens, get stoock into it! Where the urgent boar mutters *root-root*
to his small harassed sow, trotting back and forth beside her, *rut-rut*
and the she-cat's curdling *Mao?* where are kittens? mutating to
    prr-mao,
come along, kittens, are quite different words from *prr-au*,
general-welcome-and-acceptance, or extremity's portmanteau
    mee-EU!
Active and passive at once, the boar and feeding sow
share a common prone *unh*, expressing repletion and bestowing it,
and you're where the staid dog, excited, emits a mouth-skirl
he was trying to control, and looks ashamed of it
and the hawk above the land calls himself Peter P. P. Pew,
where, far from class hatred, the rooster scratches up some for you
and edgy plovers sharpen their nerves on a blurring wheel.
Waterbirds address you in their neck-flexure language, hiss and bow
and you speak to each species in the seven or eight
planetary words of its language, which ignore and include the detail
God set you to elaborate by the dictionary-full
when, because they would reveal their every secret,
He took definition from the beasts and gave it to you.

O

If at baying time you have bayed with dogs and not humans
you know enough not to scorn the moister dimensions
of language, nor to build on the sandbanks of Dry.
You long to show someone non-human the diaphragm-shuffle
which may be your species' only distinctive cry,

the spasm which, in various rhythms, turns our face awry,
contorts speech, shakes the body, and makes our eyelids liquefy.
Approaching adulthood, one half of this makes us shy
and the other's a touchy spear-haft we wield for balance.
Laughter-and-weeping. It's the great term the small terms qualify
as a whale is qualified by all the near glitters of the sea.
Weightless leviathan our showering words overlie and modify,
it rises irresistibly. All our dry-eyed investigations
supply that one term, in the end; its occasions multiply,
the logics issue in horror, we are shattered by joy
till the old prime divider bends and its two ends unify
and the learned words bubble off us. We laugh because we cry:
the crying depth of life is too great not to laugh
but laugh or cry singly aren't it: only mingled are they spirit
to wobble and sing us as a summer dawn sings a magpie.
For spirit is the round earth bringing our flat earths to bay
and we're feasted and mortified, exposed to those momentary
    heavens
which, speaking in speech on the level, we work for and deny.

TIME TRAVEL

To revisit the spitfire world
of the duel, you put on a suit
of white body armour, a helmet
like an insect's composite eye
and step out like a space walker
under haloed lights, trailing a cord.

Descending, with nodding foil in hand
towards the pomander-and-cravat sphere
you meet the Opponent, for this journey
can only be accomplished by a pair
who semaphore and swap quick respect
before they set about their joint effect

CLIVE JAMES

———— ❧ ————

CLIVE JAMES WAS born in 1939 in the Sydney suburb of Kogarah, brought up by his mother, a war widow, and studied arts at Sydney University—all well-known facts because of the immense success of *Unreliable Memoirs*, the first volume of his autobiography. At university he was preoccupied with theatrical reviews, and was a prolific writer of skits. He is an admirer of Hope's poetry, and this can be seen to have influenced certain of his own poems. James went on to complete a second degree at Cambridge, and became a freelance literary and TV critic in London. He is now a television personality and humorist, and hosts his own programmes. He has written pop lyrics, three books of essays, a novel, three volumes of autobiography, four mock-heroic epics, and has published a selection of his light and serious verse. Like Barry Humphries, James is able to move with naturalness and ease between popular and high culture.

CLIVE JAMES

———— ❧ ————

CLIVE JAMES WAS born in 1939 in the Sydney suburb of Kogarah, was brought up by his mother, a war widow, and studied arts at Sydney University—all well-known facts because of the immense success of *Unreliable Memoirs*, the first volume of his autobiography. At university he was preoccupied with theatrical reviews, and was a prolific writer of skits. He is an admirer of Hope's poetry, and this can be seen to have influenced certain of his own poems. James went on to complete a second degree at Cambridge, and became a freelance literary and TV critic in London. He is now a television personality and humorist, and hosts his own programmes. He has written pop lyrics, nine books of essays, three novels, three volumes of autobiography, four mock-heroic epics, and has published a selection of his light and serious verse. Like Barry Humphries, James is able to move with naturalness and ease between popular and high culture.

JOHNNY WEISSMULLER DEAD IN ACAPULCO

Apart possibly from waving hello to the cliff-divers
Would the real Tarzan have ever touched Acapulco?
Not with a one-hundred-foot vine.
Jungle Jim maybe, but the Ape Man never.
They played a tape at his funeral
In the Valley of Light cemetery of how he had sounded
Almost fifty years back giving the pristine ape-call,
Which could only remind all present that in decline
He would wander distractedly in the garden
With his hands to his mouth and the unforgettable cry
Coming out like a croak—
This when he wasn't sitting in his swim-trunks
Beside the pool he couldn't enter without nurses.

Things had not been so bad before Mexico
But they were not great.
He was a greeter in Caesar's Palace like Joe Louis.
Sal, I want you should meet Johnny Weissmuller.
Johnny, Mr Sal Volatile is a friend of ours from Chicago.
With eighteen Tarzan movies behind him
Along with the five Olympic gold medals,
He had nothing in front except that irrepressible paunch
Which brought him down out of the tree house
To earth as Jungle Jim
So a safari suit could cover it up.
As Jungle Jim he wasn't just on salary,
He had a piece of the action,
But coming so late in the day it was not enough
And in Vegas only the smile was still intact.

As once it had all been intact, the Greek classic body
Unleashing the new-style front-up crawl like a baby
Lifting itself for the first time,
Going over the water almost as much as through it,
Curing itself of childhood polio
By making an aquaplane of its deep chest,
Each arm relaxing out of the water and stiffening into it,

The long legs kicking a trench that did not fill up
Until he came back on the next lap,
Invincible, easily breathing
The air in the spit-smooth, headlong, creek-around-a-rock trough
Carved by his features.

He had six wives like Henry VIII but don't laugh,
Because Henry VIII couldn't swim a stroke
And if you ever want to see a true king you should watch
       Weissmuller
In *Tarzan Escapes* cavorting underwater with Boy
In the clear river with networks of light on the shelving sand
Over which they fly weightless to hide from each other behind the
       log
While Jane wonders where they are.
You will wonder where you are too and be shy of the answer
Because it is Paradise.

When the crocodile made its inevitable entry into the clear river
Tarzan could always settle its hash with his bare hands
Or a knife at most,
But Jungle Jim usually had to shoot it
And later on he just never got to meet it face to face—
It was working for the Internal Revenue Service.

There was a chimpanzee at his funeral,
Which must have been someone's idea of a smart promotion,
And you might say dignity had fled,
But when Tarzan dropped from the tall tree and swam out of the
       splash
Like an otter with an outboard to save Boy from the waterfall
It looked like poetry to me,
And at home in the bath I would surface giving the ape-call.

EGON FRIEDELL'S HEROIC DEATH

Egon Friedell committed suicide
By jumping from his window when he saw
Approaching Brownshirts eager to preside
At rites the recent *Anschluss* had made law.

Vienna's coffee-house habitués
By that time were in Paris, Amsterdam,
London, New York. Friedell just couldn't raise
The energy to take it on the lam.

Leaving aside the question of their looks,
The Jews the Nazis liked to see in Hell
Were good at writing and owned lots of books—
Which all spelled certain curtains for Friedell.

Friedell was cultivated in a way
That now in Europe we don't often see.
For every volume he'd have had to pay
In pain what those thugs thought the fitting fee.

Forestalling them was simply common sense,
An act only a Pharisee would blame,
Yet hard to do when fear is so intense.
Would *you* have had the nerve to do the same?

The normal move would be to just lie still
And tell yourself you somehow might survive,
But this great man of letters had the will
To meet his death while he was still alive.

So out into the air above the street
He sailed with all his learning left behind,
And by one further gesture turned defeat
Into a triumph for the human mind.

The civilised are most so as they die.
He called a warning even as he fell
In case his body hit a passer-by
As innocent as was Egon Friedell.

GO BACK TO THE OPAL SUNSET

Go back to the opal sunset, where the wine
Costs peanuts, and the avocado mousse
Is thick and stong as cream from a jade cow.
Before the passionfruit shrinks on the vine
Go back to where the heat turns your limbs loose.
You've worked your heart out and need no excuse.
Knock out your too-tall tent-pegs and go now.

It's England, April, and it's pissing down,
So realise your assets and go back
To the opal sunset. Even Autumn there
Will swathe you in a raw-silk dressing-gown,
And through the midnight harbour lacquered black
The city lights strike like a heart attack
While eucalyptus soothes the injured air.

Now London's notion of a petty crime
Is simple murder or straightforward rape
And Oxford Street's a bombing range, to go
Back to the opal sunset while there's time
Seems only common sense. Make your escape
To where the prawns assume a size and shape
Less like a new-born baby's little toe.

Your tender nose anointed with zinc cream,
A sight for sore eyes will be brought to you.
Bottoms bisected by a piece of string
Will wobble through the heat-haze like a dream
That summer afternoon you go back to
The opal sunset, and it's all as true
As sand-fly bite or jelly-blubber sting.

What keeps you here? Is it too late to tell?
It might be something you can't now define,
Your nature altered as if by the moon.
Yet out there at this moment, through the swell,
The hydrofoil draws its triumphant line.
Such powers of decision should be mine.
Go back to the opal sunset. Do it soon.

GEOFFREY LEHMANN

———— ❧ ————

B ORN IN 1940, Geoffrey Lehmann grew up at McMahons
Point on Sydney Harbour. His father began working in an iron
foundry at the age of ten and later owned and piloted a small motor
launch. His mother began working in a sewing factory when thirteen.
Lehmann graduated in arts–law from the University of Sydney,
where he studied German literature. He wrote poetry prolifically
when he was younger, and began publishing in literary journals at
seventeen.

While at university he met Les Murray, and they worked as co-
editors of two university literary magazines. They published a joint
first volume of their poetry in 1965. Lehmann practised as a solicitor
from 1963 to 1976, then taught law in the commerce faculty at the
University of New South Wales. He is now a partner in a major
international accounting firm in Sydney. Remarried, he has two
young children, and three children from his first marriage.

Lehmann has published six volumes of poetry; *Selected Poems*; a
novel; a book on Australian naive painters, written in association
with Charles Blackman; and co-authored a major book on taxation
law. He is an adviser to government on Australia's research and
development tax incentive and has been a member of the Literature
Board of the Australia Council.

From the early 1960s until the late 1970s, Lehmann associated with
the Sydney Push, a bohemian, libertarian group that began shortly

after the Second World War as an offshoot of aspects of the philosophy of John Anderson. It disintegrated when the women's movement developed.

Lehmann has a predeliction for exploring a subject in a series of poems. Such work includes an entire book in the persona of the Emperor Nero, and another spoken through the voice of the poet's then father-in-law, a farmer in central western New South Wales. This latter book, *Ross's Poems*, balances an acknowledgement of 'progress' with regret for the loss of a pristine and various landscape. These poems have been revised and supplemented, and are now re-issued under the title *Spring Forest*.

Lehmann's work uses a plain style, yet is always based in sensuous experience and shows a feeling for detail. He has combined something of what he admires in the Greek poet C.P. Cavafy with an aspect of Kenneth Slessor, who are his earliest and deepest influences.

ELEGY FOR JAN

I

From the bloodhouses of my youth, vagrant hotels, I see your face
Dead girl (dear Jan!) in smoke-filled rooms—glass-littered slimy
    floors.
Out of these brine-cold years, derelict houses with cracked lino
And crumbling ceilings, poems and obscenities scribbed on the
walls,
A humid wind blows from that night we met and loved as strangers,
The first night that I slept with anyone—you blushed and laughed
About the red scars on your wrists from self-inflicted wounds,
Also the deep scar on your abdomen from which the child
You loved, but gave away, had come, and then you folded me
Into a darkness better than I had dreamed, yet terrifying.

Night wind, fumble amongst the rusting cast-iron balconies,
Dank dishes in a sink and bodies on soiled mattresses,
But in a downstairs room lit by a naked globe a girl
In a red night-dress stands before a nervous, garrulous boy.
She is the night. With pale, translucent face, dark liquid eyes,
Black hair and almost oriental dignity she stands,
Says 'Tuck me into bed' and leads him into a small room.

Remember after the scalding seed, sleeping in love's sour milk
In a cramped single bed, your black hair on my naked shoulder,
Pain in our bones, a flimsy sheet across our tangled bodies,
Your breathing's sea-sound in my ears, bird-noises in your throat.
But in the silent dawn the wind stops, and I wake to hear
You grind your teeth in anguished sleep, your mind lost in cold
    rooms.

II

May 1963, eleven o'clock,
One windless autumn night
Of floodlit streamers and tooting horns
With friends you stand
At Circular Quay in Sydney
Farewelling an overseas liner.

A hundred miles away
I pace a country railway station.
The ship is leaving,
The ship you could not catch to Europe
For lack of money.
Aged twenty-two,
Drunk, high on pills,
Light-headed
(You had not eaten for eight days),
To get a better view
You climb the railing, overbalance
And fall through thirty feet of air
Onto the concrete.

III

The laundry grumbles, eats its girls.
At morning mass she faints from weakness,
Is dragged outside, hit on the face.
Frost and the older girls' cruel eyes.
Potatoes, mash and bread for meals.
The laundry hisses, thumps all day.
Nine hours each day amongst the steam
Kneeling she sweats and works for Christ
And calluses form on her knees.
Her mother gets the widow's pension,
But sends the nuns her board each week,
Once sends two extra pounds for shoes.
They get her men's shoes second-hand.
The laundry eats her mother's money.
On summer nights a hundred girls
Lie in a huge bare dormitory
And hear waves breaking on the beach.
Couples a hundred feet away
Make love, drink beer and splash each other.
The girls watch shadows on the ceiling.
They sweat and toss. Their iron beds creak.
Only the laundry sleeps at night.
'I was thirteen when I was there.

They called the place a girl's reform school.
And I'm the only girl from there
Who didn't land up on the streets . . .
The only old-girl who made good. . . .'

IV

A cheap cream fountain pen
With Chinese characters
Engraved in blue and brown,
Some old black slacks,
A couple of woollen jumpers,
A battered suitcase,
A gold watch for her twenty-first,
A scarlet night-dress,
Some photos of herself when drunk,
A small address book
Are left without an owner.

V

From old brick lavatories lit by a wavering candle flame, drab
    parties,
Songs of doomed protest drunkenly shouted to a strident guitar,
Cold nights of driving rain, the hastily swallowed pills, couples on
    floors,
Your face shines sadly, purely, and you sit all night inscribing
Black circles on a page until at dawn the page is black,
Or in a bar you sit inventing little games and laughing,
Describing a hospital tour with childish relish (and bitterness)
A funny old wooden model womb, and the white pillow pushed
In unwed mothers' faces when they take the child at birth.
Or you sit in a restaurant happily playing noughts and crosses
(I shudder as your pencil gaily disfigures the table cloth).
Outside you climb my crouching shoulders for a piggyback,
But when I stand you fall and knock your head upon the pavement.
I still bend helplessly over your bruised and curled-up body
And mutter ineffectual comfort under the glaring streetlamps—
And two years later on an autumn night you fall and die.
(The noisily waving crowds are hushed, floodlit in sudden silence.)

Out of those tangled nights, backyards of stunted weeds and cinders,
Damp walls, rain spitting through an open window, blowing
    curtains,
Dear Jan I see you so the whole world radiates around you,
Compassionate for all living things, forgetting your own body,
In bare and draughty rooms undressing slowly to the night
To hold us whimsically and tenderly upon dank beds.

OUT AFTER DARK

Out driving after dusk my headlights fumble
Through dust and trees, undulate over tarred roads.
My father somewhere in the night is plodding
Dark hills he cannot understand, loose earth,
My father innocent, frail as worn silk,
Mild at the end, not knowing he has cancer,
But knowing that he's finished; gentle, silent,
Selling bit by bit his watches, silver,
The crumbling mansion with its vast verandas,
Its palms and cedar doors with cut-glass handles
Hiving the light in honey-coloured facets,
House where we never lived, our lives unlived.
My headlights brush moths, scrub, and scan and wander,
But what I'm looking for is past not present,
A hot night twenty years ago, myself
A child reading *The Moonstone*, all of us waiting
In canvas chairs for trains eternally late,
Bells ringing as we lumber luggage aboard,
Pineapple fields lit by our passing carriage.
Reflected in the glass, our figures seated
Beneath a lamp travel dark fields and rivers.
Loving, transitory, we never existed.

from ROSES

I

At night, circling weightless, we dreamed of roses,
But woke to shrapnel whining over the tundra,
Faces drained in the time of immense bombardments,
Staggering through gas and mud, eating from tins.

Clutching the crumbling edge of nothing, our minds
Reached for the tiny bursting and popping of space.
Then the guns fell silent, men climbed from their holes,
We laboured back along the roads of pain.

To our first house and garden of the world,
Veterans of all denominations, lame
And agile, the convoys thundering back at sunset
To a place of weeds, cattle munching wild peaches.

The hybrid roses we had bred were gone
To briar, and all the simple climbing roses
Were high as houses, thick with flowers and scent.
Iron pots were hanging in an open fireplace.

In a house of fading brick on dusty floorboards
We dreamed about a ladder to a treehouse,
Girls in silk shawls, dressed in their mothers' clothes,
A marble dropped in the grass, pears drying in trays.

By our heads an old ghost stood in calico trousers,
A mattock damp with earth glittered in his hands.
'The windlass by the well needs a new rope.
This is the childhood house you never left.'

II

The mercy of the rose is simply asking.
The soldier scoops up water from the fountain.
Returning from the war, they sing in trucks
To fields rich with neglect, unkempt and shining.

His wife and child are painted ghosts, are toys,
Are motionless with too much happiness,
Transfixed by their long waiting, words or gestures
Would bruise the instant's skin, the smoky purple

Of orchard harvests dropping at a touch,
The fruit denied by war which now are his,
Glistening that doubters cannot see to have,
Pink briar rose, lichen and running water.

Amongst the motionless branches of the stars
The timbers of his house will talk all night,
A large, slow sugar ant cross his lamplit floor.
This night shall be all spring nights he has lost.

III

In an empty house we sleep by a wicker chair.
Our boots are mudcaked, mattresses are musty.
The hives murmur all night, dark fluid in the moon.
Acres of rosebeds scent the night, roots moving

Across a path, across a mountain range,
Impulsive plants growing with jerks and pauses,
In spring the new shoots almost visibly move,
Long stems of pink wax rising from old wood.

Stepping through broken windows into fields
We find beside a spring bubbling from ironstone
A jug upon an old white-painted table.
Pink and grey parrots fly up from some pines.

IV

Watching the sky for death, starved by anger
There comes a time the soldier leaves the fields
Of agony, burned rubber, sheered-off hillsides,
A time when even hatred of injustice

Must end, when we must pardon viciousness,
Before its poison can distort the mind.
Finding the wars are infinite, the soldier
Must punch the mirror, walk through broken glass,

Wash out his blood-stained garments and discard
The crutch of hatred, walk not judging
Into a landscape scoured of noise and movement,
Only amongst some distant carob trees

In limestone hills, an old man, sunburned, digging,
Is turning over dull earth, hardly noticed.
And near the trees with hanging pods are flowers,
The Changing Rose with its five petals dancing,

Ripening from yellow to buff-rose and crimson,
A butterfly amongst the ears of grass,
And Rosa Mundi's pink flesh striped with carmine,
Veined as our lives, turning upon its stem,

And in this aimless landscape is a house,
House of no argument, of sun-dried bricks,
No doors or furniture, the traveller watching
His clothes drying on a rock, birds in a bush.

V

There is no absolute rose, there are the names
And differences, the roses of a night.
The musk, the green rose, the extraordinary mosses,
Where do these strangers come from with their gifts?

Tangled in snow, the shapes, the names, the families,
No mind, no system can contain the rose.
A rose in a glass of water waits by a bed.
A child with a pencil draws a singing bird.

CHILDREN'S GAMES

I

The screen lights up as he switches it on.
The letters of the poem
are lights on a dark page,
and plastic toys, orange as summer
roar past the window
on the flagstones.

A book of games
appears on the page.
Windblown stems
blow white, blow green.

Mother where are you?
Father where are you?
says the girl in a pinafore
standing at the crumbling
edge of the path.

Mother has her lover
over the sea,
father from the bedroom
telephones a lady.

The girl sits down
and chalks on the path
a book of games.
Who will wash my dirty face?

II

As he writes at night
a black and white cat jumps
on the sill and stares in.
Slides off
and re-absorbs in the dark.

We'll play Prohibitions.
We'll dress a lady
but we can't use green,
yellow, pink or blue.

How will you dress my lady?
I'll zip the back
of her white silk dress.

How will you dress my lady?
I'll place a tortoise shell comb
in mahogany hair.

And you?
I'll get her blue silk shoes . . .

Forfeit.
The phone is slammed down.
A door crashes shut.
Feet hurry down the path
and will never come back.

Children are crying.
A telephone rings
and rings.

We'll play Prohibitions again.
In the dark of the bed
who'll undress my lady?
Forfeit.
Weeping.
And a mouth stretches in agony.

III

In the picture
the girls each touch a tree.
The trees are full of apples.
Only puss in the middle
has no tree.

Puss, puss, is the call,
give me a drop of water!
The girls change trees,
run with grim jaws,
then touch wood and compose
themselves again as a picture.

Puss in the middle.
Too slow.

IV

The girls are mocking under the tree,
his head is knocking against a wall,
she hears him as she lies in bed.

He'll kill himself in the rose garden.
His head is knocking against a wall.
She hears him and she lies in bed.

Already he's dead. The smoke of the gunshot
hovers amongst October roses.
From her bed she hears him knocking his head.

V

A rabbit is jumping and jumping
on the back steps.
Tears are in her eyes, screaming,
'Who'll sew my pantomime dress
for school, where
is my lunch and satchel?'

A rabbit is screaming
and her eyes
are red.

VI

The looking glass is shattered.
The white rabbits
have lost their silk waistcoats
and they huddle in a cage.
They squeeze up tight,
eyes closed in the wind.

Feeding them tufts of grass
the small boy bursts into tears.
'I want my green plate back.
The rabbits can't have my green plate.'

VII

When plates and doors are angry,
the cup-of-tea bird sings,
'Cup-of-tea mumma.'

The wind bells are arguing with the air,
there are raised voices in a bedroom
and the cup-of-tea bird sings,
'Cup-of-tea mumma.'

There are violet abysses in the sky,
her parents play a deadly monopoly,
smoke fumes from the kitchen oven
and the cup-of-tea bird,
fluttering to keep
the red checked curtains she knows,
is ignored as she sings,
'Cup-of-tea mumma.'

VIII

Puss has left the picture book
and become a character.
Ambling out of the frame
of two dimensional apple trees
where the girls run with set
jaws in their set piece,
he arches his tail and jumps
with soft paws onto a window sill.
He sneezes at the smell of chicken soup.

At sunrise to catch the warmth
he balances
on the rim of a cactus tub.

The woman hides in the shrubs past midnight
with wild dry eyes.
The man shakes a baby under a tree
as the moon sets, towards dawn.
Puss is the witness
of these non-events in his life.

IX

The King and Queen are fighting.
Lightning and thunder
shake the board.
In the house of cheese
the small pieces cower.

'Get-another-mother,' the two year old calls out.
The three and five year olds
giggle hysterically.
Day after day the battle goes on
and the small pieces laugh
as the two year old shouts
'Get-another-mother.'
The King becomes a father,
'What do you mean, Annie?
Do you want another mother?'
'No! You get another mother!'

X

The children play, two girls, one boy.
An apple falls in their walled garden.
The children follow the rolling apple,
run down a path and through a gate.
A clap of thunder, a sudden mist.
'Where have we been?' the smallest asks,
'All I remember is a path and a basket.'
'Our old home is gone,' the eldest says,
'Hold hands, the mist is slippery and cold.'

XI

The children are asleep.
The mother has gone to live in her own house.
The father comes home with the Queen of Diamonds.
Lying against him on a couch
she touches the buckle of his belt.

XII

The cup-of-tea bird is shut outside crying in her tantrum.
She watches the reflections of gardens and clouds in glass French
    doors.
She flies away from the house of cheese, her mother and the Jack,
Her father and his pageant of ladies. She hangs above the map,
All the clockwork lives, the children's games, the wilderness of
    roses.
There are black clouds boiling in a blue sky. Her mother is burning
    cakes.
The cup-of-tea bird sees herself after school, lying in the grass,
When her father comes to pick her up. Now in his car her grief
Empties onto her cheeks with overheard talk about her mother.
'One day, Daddy,' she says as rain begins, 'you'll find your
    princess.'
House-hunting with her mother, the two year old complains,
'Mumma, I'm too tired to walk.' 'This is a nice area,'
The cup-of-tea bird consoles. In the house of cheese the telephone
Is ringing, the wolf consults his watch, Red Riding Hood's cheeful
    clogs
Will clatter down the path in a minute, but the cup-of-tea bird
Warns the visitor, flying down on the path to drive her away.

The cup-of-tea bird discards the book of games, she calls out when
    cakes
Are burning, she flies where skies are breaking apart, she carries the
    grief
Of parents, she is the protector of the house. She is five years old.

HAROLD'S WALK

He turned and waved.
He was one year and a month.
With cobweb-light hair,
the colour of leatherwood honey,
brown poet's eyes
and refined cheekbones
burnished red like the blush
on a white Shanghai peach,
he turned and waved.
There was a graze on his left nostril,
a thin scab in the fold where it met the cheek.
He was wearing a white singlet
and plastic pilchers.
Having farewelled us
he headed off down the road
like a tottering upright tortoise.
Propelled by an unstoppable business,
his pink feet imprinted the hot soft dust
of the road that led
into that Old Testament afternoon,
the biblical vastness of southwest Queensland.

He escaped as we were placing
a small native pine in the back of the utility.
A single blow of the axe, a sharp smell of resin
and we had a Christmas tree.

But Christmas and tomorrow had no meaning for him.
His sole interest
was the random stagger of his short fat legs
and this curious ability
to distance himself from objects.

No birds or insects
announced their presence in the heavy stillness
as water and life withdrew.
The rapid and twittering dialects
of finches and wagtails, the warbling of magpies
that had made the morning into a watermeadow
of sounds and activity
were a hypothesis cancelled in the oven air
by the axeblade of sunlight.
There were no geckoes, whose ghostlike transparent bodies
attracted by insect harvests
frolicked on flywire screens at night.
They too were hiding.

But the child, an escaping particle, whose energy
had no objective,
who woke and could not be contained,
small fists hoisting the face up to look
over cot-bars
and grab for the horizon,
ran tottering and uncompromised through hot dust.
If we had tried to stop him
he would have squealed, 'No, no,'
one of his three words—
the others 'oh' for surprise
and 'mamy' for need and distress.
He ran with no sense of history
through brigalow country unreformed like himself,
that was cleared long ago with crowbar, axe and shovel,
cleared again by bulldozer and chains,
and cleared once more
by a blade cutting beneath the surface.

But the seeds and roots are unrepentant
as the tortoise-child
who runs with no fear of marks in the road
that may lead to a death-adder
in a camouflaged coil of dust.

His momentum was unadulterated by knowledge.
His hypothesis rejected our evidence.
He ran falling on his plastic pilchers
and picking himself up,
unwilling to learn
except what he could teach himself
from placing stones in his mouth
and tearing leaves apart with his fingers.

The night sky above brigalow country
is a Joseph's coat of stars,
but if your finger tracked the Southern Cross
or saucepan for him,
he grabbed at the finger and not the stars.
Because there was hot available air
into which he could run, he ran.
Balancing himself with arms apart
his stops and starts were unpredictable.
The play of free will—
liberated by chaos from classical physics.

The wild purple verbena scrambling by the road,
milk thistles,
and grasses bending with the weight of seeds
were the instantly touchable aromatic kingdom
through which he tottered,
startled only by the grasshopper's sudden parachute
of lemon splashed with a blood drop.
Some hundreds of yards further on
he turned and waved again

a last farewell
from eyes set in an oval whimsical head,
before entering his chosen land
of wilga and blue native pine.

from SPRING FOREST

THE HAPPY HOUR

It's cold, but the cold
won't wake the dead in the ground,
not even whisky will rouse them,
or the friendly glow of the lights
of the Koorawatha Hotel.
I avoid such friendship, passing
farms where they drink more grain
than they grow.

Driving my tractor home late at night,
standing up to keep warm
in my military greatcoat,
I see a figure
on a horse that has stopped,
swaying in the saddle dead-drunk.
I catch him just as he falls.

I roll up my friend in the coat
and bed him down in the roadside grass,
propping his head on the saddle,
and set out for his household of women
with its blaze of angry lights.

As I walk quickly across the paddocks
already the dogs are barking.

JACK

I've given up drink for good,
by natural evolution.
Alcohol is for the young,
out of love, in love,
young men chasing the same woman,
urinating by night among camellia bushes,
ramming trees with their cars.
Somewhere there is music playing,
glasses are breaking;
they cover themselves with grass seeds
and mud, teased by girls.

Now I've enough mental furniture
to shift around in my mind to keep it busy,
something the soft minds of the young
cannot understand
who see middle age as a shrivelling,
not a storing away of energy.
So drink is strangely irrelevant;
I say 'strangely', because unplanned.

My house is dry except for the grapevine
that loops around the veranda.
Jack would have said what a dullard I've become.
'Come on Ross,'—his ghost standing
between the grapevine and me—
'What about a booze up? Olive
and the children don't want you to martyr yourself.'

Jack and his friend Higgins,
as medical students,
swaying on the doorstep of a hostess
before a dinner invitation,
and Jack persuading Higgins, full of beer,
that a pot plant would soak up the lot
without trace.
The pot plant stood in a saucer

that was filling with tepid water
as Jack rang the bell.

Jack crash–landed in the sea
off Vanimo,
helped free his two friends from the cockpit
as the plane submerged,
and drowned himself.

Jack became a small part of history,
a pioneer doctor
bringing civilisation
with a stethoscope and syringe
to the dark people who mourned him.

I was Jack's audience,
the younger farming brother.
Jack,
fatal for girls, fatal for himself,
my mentor and guardian in the city
of wartime parties, floating populations.
The roof garden of Packie's Club
with potted palms, outlines of office blocks—
this is *my city*, a wartime city,
railway stations where we sang
and people smiled at the drunken soldiers;
but now it's gone, the T & G building,
Packie's in the starlight,
my city exists only in my mind.

But Jack bitter, unreconciled,
chasing a glimmer of phosphorus on the horizon,
stands between my grapevine and me:
the hundred possibilities as I stepped
from the train at Central Station.

BUSH KITCHENS

Here's something about our Lachlan valley
kitchen utensils:
some of the Costello camp ovens
travelled from Hill End
across the continent and back.
They'd cook a four or five gallon stew,
the lids chipped with use.
Now they're iron pots for tourists
in folk museums.

'Don't use that,'
Harry Adams said as someone
shoved a deal stick in the fire
for a pipe lighter.
'That's my custard stirrer!'

When I could run around
on tin roofs without denting them,
our river
was the mother of improvisation.
We drank the Lachlan boiled
with tea leaves.
She washed our enamel plates,
while our cardigans dried our hands
and blew our noses. (Harry Adams!)

Our only dish-washing machine
was George Grogan's:
at meal end he'd call
the dogs to lick his camp oven out.

And kitchens were a moveable
circle of light by the river.

GEOFF PAGE

꠸

G EOFF PAGE, BORN in 1940, grew up on a pastoral property
near Grafton in northern New South Wales. The family has a
political as well as a long rural tradition: Page's grandfather, Sir Earl
Page, founded the conservative Country Party (renamed the National
Party), which is the third most significant organised force in Austral-
ian politics. Page himself has been an active Labor Party supporter.
He was educated at the University of New England in Armidale and
is now a high school English teacher in Canberra. As well as eight
books of poetry he has published two novels. Married with one son,
he is an amateur jazz drummer, an interest which is technically
significant for his poetry.

Page was early attracted by William Carlos Williams' humanity,
and has been able to emulate the precision and stringency of
Williams' style. He modulates the short, strongly enjambed Williams
line into a more regular rhythmical pattern. Recently he has included
a carefully controlled version of Les Murray's rhetoric within his
range. The voice is his own, but it can become a monotone and the
rhythm reiterative. Page's work is centrally concerned with wastage:
lost opportunity and failed potential are themes that make recurrent,
diverse appearances. His cast of observed characters is wide: women
and the old, soldiers and Aborigines, suburbanites and small farmers.

GRIT

A doxology

I praise the country women
of my mother's generation
who bred, brought up and boasted
six Australians each—
the nearest doctor fifty miles
on a road cut off by flood;
the women who by wordless men
were courted away from typewriters
and taught themselves to drive—
I praise their style
in the gravel corners.
I praise the snakes they broke in two
and the switch of wire they kept in a cupboard.
I praise what they keep and what they lose—
the long road in to the abattoirs,
the stare which cures
a stockman of shooting swans.
I praise the prints, the wide straw brims
they wore out to the clothes line;
I praise each oily crow that watched them.
I praise the tilting weather—
the dry creeks and the steady floods
and the few good weeks between.
I praise each column in the ledger
they kept up late by mosquito and lamp-light;
the temerity of the banker
reining them in at last—or trying;
the machinations for chequered paddocks
swung on the children's names;
the companies just one step ahead;
the tax clerk, in his way, also.
I praise each one of their six children
discovering in turn
the river in its tempers
the rapids and the river trees;

the children who grew up to horse sweat
and those who made it to the city.
I praise the stringy maxims
that served instead of prayers;
also the day that each child found
a slogan not enough,
surprising themselves in a camera flash
and bringing no extra paddocks.
I praise the boast of country women:
they could have been a wife
to any of a dozen men
and damn well made it work.
I praise what I have seen
to be much more than this.
I praise their politics of leather;
the ideologies in a line of cattle;
the minds that would not
stoop to whisky.
I praise their scorn
for the city of options, the scholars
in their turning chairs and air-conditioned theories.
I praise also that moment
when they headed off in tears—
the car in a toolshed failing to start,
a bootfull of fencing wire.
I praise the forty years
when they did not. I praise
each day and evening of their lives—
that hard abundance year by year
mapped in a single word.

My Mother's God

My mother's God
Has written the best
Of the protestant proverbs:

You make your bed
You lie in it;
God helps him

Who helps himself.
He tends to stay away from churches,
Is more to be found in

Phone calls to daughters
Or rain clouds over rusty grass.
The Catholics

Have got him wrong entirely—
Too much waving the arms about,
The incense and caftan, that rainbow light.

He's leaner than that,
Lean as a pair of
Grocer's scales.

Hard as a hammer at cattle sales
That third and final
Time of asking.

His face is most clear
In a scrubbed wooden table
Or deep in the shine of a

Laminex bench
He's also observed at weddings and funerals
By strict invitation, not knowing quite

Which side to sit on.
His second book, my mother says,
Is always somewhat overrated;

The first is where the centre is,
Tooth for claw and eye for tooth—
Whoever tried the other cheek?

(Well Christ maybe,
But that's another story.)
God, like her, by dint of coursework

Has earned his degree in predestination.
Immortal, omniscient, no doubt of that,
He nevertheless keeps regular hours

And wipes his feet clean on the mat,
Is not to be seen at three in the morning.
His portrait done in a vigorous charcoal

Is fixed on the inner
Curve of her forehead.
Omnipotent there

In broad black strokes,
He does not move.
It is not easy, she'd confess,

To be my mother's God.

ROGER McDONALD

———— ❧ ————

BORN THE SON of a Presbyterian minister in 1941, Roger
McDonald spent his childhood in country towns, attended Scots
College in Sydney, and graduated from the University of Sydney.
He was a high school teacher; worked for the Australian Broadcast-
ing Commission as a radio and television producer; and was poetry
editor for the University of Queensland Press, publishing its suc-
cessful series *Paperback Poets* during the late 1960s and early 1970s.
Probably the best book in the series was his own volume *Airship*,
from which all but the last, uncollected poem in this selection are
taken. It is the second book of poetry he has written. He has since
published three novels: *1915*, built around the Gallipoli military
disaster; *Slipstream*, based loosely on the life of the pioneer aviator
Charles Kingsford Smith; and *Rough Wallaby*, about bush workmen.
McDonald wrote the script for the seven-part television serial of
1915, and a television series on the opera singer Nellie Melba.
He lives on a farm outside the New South Wales town of Braidwood
and is married to the poet Rhyll McMaster.

McDonald has a Flaubertian sense of the need for accuracy in the
details of his fiction. For *1915* he learned to ride (breaking his leg),
and conducted interviews with Gallipoli veterans; for *Slipstream* he
took up flying, despite an earlier fear of flight; and for *Rough Wallaby*
he became a shearers' cook. Other skills he has acquired are bee-
keeping, rock-climbing, and now sheep-farming. His poetry is

meticulous in its detail, which is always rendered surprising through imagination. There is a strange, bated, sometimes fantastic atmosphere in much of his work, somewhat like that found in certain science fiction. In McDonald's world, whether he is writing about natural objects or machines, human control is always vulnerable. His recurrent theme is insecurity.

SICKLE BEACH

Sickle beach,
bay like a wine glass.
Butterflies launch themselves
eastward from marram grass.

Lemon, the lower sky,
apricot air.
Who would believe a man
died close to here?

Came, on a blue day,
easy, on horseback.
Slipped, and broke his head
hard on a rock.

Blood in the rippled light,
a word of surprise:
Me? It is not true.
Thus a man dies.

Thus, in the empty hills,
blackberries increase,
rabbits and wild cats
run through the house.

PRECISE INVADERS

Backs in whipping broom,
high-stepping up a path of wind
that lifts from darkness in the valley floor—
unexpected, and quick, their rumps
like turned-down lanterns at a secret run—
three deer, wheeling left through broken stone

and crossing cattle grass to leap
as if to balance there
against a wall of pines, in smoky light,
alert for admiration: bounding the wire
in rapt succession, with such perfect flight
they leap inside my dreams of how they leapt.

INCIDENT IN TRANSYLVANIA

Black in a tentlike cloak, at rest
near the roots of an ancient oak on a hillside
the Count awaits a two-legged bottle.

Soon, awkward astride a mule, plunking with lurches
his winded guitar, a corpuscular friar
with lymphocytes fizzing like spa water
rides through a curtain of sweat
till his chin clicks up
on the outstretched arm of the Count who is waiting.

A surprise, like cactus clapped to his neck:

'I've been watching your ride,' lips the Count,
with ruby politeness. The friar has bubbles
of breakfast loose in his throat,
and riffles a pack of escapes:
'I'mer, willyar, issalltoo . . . too . . .' and slumps
to the pit of his belly, waiting.

But the Count draws back from capture, strangely,
and it isn't the friar's fat, or the odour of fear
that deters him, nor even a whiff of chubby religion.
There are personal bones that give trouble—
nights of competing with shadows,
the knuckle and knee-bruising hunts,

the general ascent in the land
of inferior blood.
'It's a pain in the fangs,' he snaps,
heeling the mule in the butt,
bouncing the friar in whistles downhill.

Back at the castle the groom has observed that the Count
seems no longer himself, no longer deliciously flensed
by the howl of his creatures (those slack
acres of flesh in cylindrical pits)
no longer—the servants gather and mutter—
no longer the Count of the cloak and the eye, the limp,
and the dreaded formula.

He calls for a glass of milk, he calls
for news of the world and a hot brown bun,
while a little old wife appears in the room's far corner,
clucking and knitting, nursing a cat,
blinking her blue old eyes and snicking her lips for a chat.

THE HOLLOW THESAURUS

Names for everything I touch
were hatched in bibles, in poems cupped by madmen
on rocky hills, by marks on sheets of stone,
by humped and sticky lines in printed books.
Lexicographers burned their stringy eyeballs black
for the sake of my knowing. Instinctive generations
hammered their victories, threaded a chain,
and lowered their strung-up wisdom in a twist
of molecules. But with me in mind
their time was wasted.

When the bloodred, pewter, sickle, sick or meloned moon
swells from nowhere,
the chatter of vast informative print
spills varied as milk. Nothing prepares me
even for common arrivals like this.

Look. The moon comes up. Behind certain trees are bats
that wrench skyward like black sticks.
Light falls thinly on grass, from moon and open door.
This has not happened before.

APIS MELLIFICA

In a dreamlike fall, the long
spoon in the honey-jar descends—a bubble going

down, he thinks, a silver bell.
He stands there a while,

humming, twisting the spoon
slowly from side to side. (The moon

drops from an amber-coloured cloud,
on the horizon a metal sphere rides

heavily over water, hunting the crushed ocean floor.)
Fifteen pounds of honey in the tall jar—

nectar, the fall of pollen, bees in the Yellow Box tree
filling that flowery head once a year

with a huge thought, all of it here.
Now the spoon climbs up as though something

is spoken by light
and shade in their alternating

vowels of movement, and held—as though what the tree thought
was taken away and stored,

deepened, like an old colour, and understood.

NIGEL ROBERTS

⁂

NIGEL ROBERTS WAS born in Wellington, New Zealand, in 1941 and has lived in Sydney for more than twenty years, where he is a high school art teacher. After hours he is the grand old man of the Balmain hipsters (Balmain: Sydney's Haight-Ashbury), one of the first and last exponents in Australia of Beat poetics (in which syntax and spelling are left deliberately unrevised). At the same time, he is a secret and careful craftsman, as revealed by comparing earlier and later versions of his work. Pre-eminently a satirist, Roberts is one of the funniest poets writing in Australia at present. His style reflects the vitality required of performance poetry (he has often read at pubs and similar venues), but it also survives the closer attention of a reader. He has published relatively little, being 'too busy living'.

THE QUOTE FROM AUDEN

I
at the conclusion of breakfast
in that space / moment / question
of the first cigarette
or the washing up
She / relayed
The Quote
from Auden.

I faked
message received & understood
thinking it
offering / or her
inductive incidental to
the day & its work
I knew only that
it was / a quote from Auden.

later
I found the book / publicly open
annotated
& underlined in
too true—
in her signatory agreement
with / the quote from Auden.

& again / later
in a brief drink at the pub
'R' enthusiastically
told 'M' & 'C'
who looked sharply / in
my direction
the quote from Auden.

Some deal / there was hint
was going down
I knew its key
in the quote from Auden.

II

I talked of everything but
at the Bon Gout
to affirm fuck
& deny
after dinner screw—
unsuccessfully

how could i
in a doz words / a score
be briefed
to hold the floor with
the quote from auden.

as she showered
i fed the animal computors
the encoded dactyls
broadcast on her skin
& in their readout
the quote from auden

& the gnostic glossolalia
of suck / oh jesus
fuck me bite
you're the best / on top
dont move—
She really meant
the quote from auden.

III

from then on   all speech
action   written word
in part or principle
deferred to
the quote from auden

on T shirts / the quote from auden
from umpire Brooks or the Hill to Michael Holding
after bowling
3 consecutive bumpers at Redpath

the quote from auden.
Joni Mitchell's next album / the quote from auden
& then at 11 / the news & weather
followed by the quote from auden
graffiti on the Annandale underpass
the quote from auden
every future kiss tainted with / the quote from auden
a most quotable / quote / the quote from auden
get the boot in first / the same applies
with the quote from auden

      so   i was introduced to
           her intent—
           —TO QUIT
        Sock it to me—
      The quote from auden

        I cannot
               be true
      to love
          or it
        true to me
      is one interpretation
          of the quote
      from auden

'Come live with me & be my love
& we shall all the pleasures prove'
      is not
    the quote from auden

      Sock it to me—
      one more time.

        the quote
        from auden

REWARD/FOR A MISSING DEITY

maybe / yr on sabbatical
maybe yr in the dunny / reading yr reviews
maybe yr in the Pacific / on a Women's Weekly Cruise
& maybe
yr preparing a statement for the six o'clock news
that perhaps
you were trapped in a ski hut / by an avalanche
of Betty Hutton

maybe / yr a war criminal / farming in Chile
maybe yr tapping phones / of subscribers to Dial a Prayer
maybe yr breaking that record / buried alive
12 ft underground
maybe yr weeping / in Farmer's Lost & Found
or perhaps
yr taking an angel out to lunch

maybe / yr in conference
or hitting off from the Club House tee
maybe yr demanding / a fat personal appearance fee
maybe yr on strike / & wont accept / arbitration
maybe yr being impeached / for yr crook administration
or perhaps
yr competing / in a Twist Marathon / on Taiwan

maybe / yr doing / In Service Training
maybe yr delivering newspapers
to pay yr way through Uni
maybe yr doing / Pestilence & Famine / I
& Destruction II

maybe yr on safari / collecting / for a private zoo
or perhaps
you farted / & very quickly / left the room

maybe / yr a casualty / of future shock
maybe yr in the mountains / plotting revolution
& a second coming
maybe yr the phantom of the opera / alone in the box
maybe yr wanking over Japanese woodcuts
of geishas sucking cocks
or perhaps
yr being interviewed by Frost / Fantastic / or Hef.

maybe / yr establishing an alibi
maybe yr being / held / incommunicado
maybe yr holed up / in Chicago
with a contract on yr head
maybe yr loneing it in Denver
in boxcars / boxcars boxcars

maybe you've been transferred to another branch
maybe yr in Paekakariki
maybe yr in Nimbin
maybe yr walking / nicotine desperate / up the road
& perhaps
yr going to be back in five minutes

But
& most probably
i would think—
you were horribly scarred
in a laboratory accident / &
yr too sensitive / to
show yr face.

JOHN TRANTER

———— ✤ ————

J OHN TRANTER WAS born in 1943 and grew up on a farm on
the south coast of New South Wales. He studied at an agricultural
high school and the University of Sydney, and has worked in print-
ing, publishing and as a radio producer. In the early 1970s he edited
an underground poetry magazine, and later an anthology, devoted to
work that reflected American *avant-gardism*. He has been able to prac-
tise as a professional poet over a considerable period with grants
from the Literature Board of the Australia Council.

Important influences on Tranter's poetry have been the early T. S.
Eliot, for the fragmentation and impersonality of style, and John
Ashbery, recognisable in the *non sequiturs*, the self-deconstruction,
and the allusions to pop culture. Tranter, less often, has an alterna-
tive mode, reminiscent of translations from Chinese poetry and the
modern Greek poet Cavafy, in which he writes plainly about dis-
affected middle-class urban lives.

Much of Tranter's subject matter is mediated through imagery
from films. His poetry usually has a cold, metallic surface, and is
filled with references to electronics and high-tech. But there is a
ghost in this world of the machine—sexuality here is painful, con-
fusing, betraying, and our obsession with it makes us unhappy and
human. All but one of the poems we have selected are from *Under
Berlin*, Tranter's most impressive collection. In 1992 he published
The Floor of Heaven, a book of four longer 'fictional' poems, which

are *Grand Guignol* in their content, while in a flat tone and a measured but prosaic style. 'Anyone Home?', so far uncollected, exemplifies in a playful way the deconstructionist contention about inevitable 'misreading'.

Tranter is always a highly conscious craftsman, and is the most prominent of a group of 'internationalist' Australian poets who emerged in the late 1960s and are oriented to the New York School.

COUNTRY VERANDA

I — DRY WEATHER
This country veranda's a box for storing the sky—
    slopes, acres of air
    bleached and adrift there.

From outside, a shade-filled stage, from inside
    a quiet cinema, empty
    but for the rustling view

where a parrot scribbles a crooked scrawl of crayon
    and off-stage a crow
    laments his loneliness

and six neat magpies, relaxed but quite soon
    off to a General Meeting
    stroll, chortle and yarn.

When the summer sun cracks the thermometer, laze
    there in a deck chair,
    shake out the paper

and relax with the local news: who won the cake
    in the Ambulance raffle;
    what the Council did

about the gravel concession down at the creek, who
    suffered a nasty fall
    but should be well in a week.

II — RAIN
From that open room where sheets hang out to dry—
    cool, wet pages
    whose verses evaporate—

you stare out at the trees semaphoring their sophistry:
    their tangled, pointless plots
    and obsessive paraphernalia,

drenched among the spacious palaces of vertical rain
    where no phone rings
    and neighbors are distant.

Behind that ridge of mist and blowing eucalypt tops
    the world waited once:
    exotic, inexhaustible.

You've been there now, and found that it's not much fun.
    On the veranda, silence
    fills the long afternoon.

VOODOO

From his rushing-away, from his
ever-receding throne, under a rainy
canopy of trees and scraps of cloud
that topple back, shrink and disappear,
embalmed behind his rear window in a nest of
crushed velvet plush, the flash wog's nodding dog
blinks out his witless approval to the vehicles
that shadow him forever.

His twin the dipping bird sips and sips,
tilts back, cools off, dries out,
dries out utterly, totters weakly
on the lip of philosophy
then dips again.

These two critics teach us how to live,
rehearsing the gap between the no-no
and the drink-again. Their motto? Every day
I will get better at embroidering the lingo
of the tongue-tied doctors of letters; every night,
in the lack of light, I will get better
and better at the negative virtues, telling

girls to piss off, who needs them,
swimming off the edge of the rock
ledge into the plunging broth of deeper waters,
soaring up to the stratosphere, bothering the angels
and yarning with God. My left hand does it,
my right hand tells me that it's right.

In the pre-dawn rack and bash of winter peak hour
traffic on the Sydney Harbour Bridge you notice them
hefted up over the city like ju-ju dolls
in the trance of a terrible gift. You note
the man with gauntlets and the goggled girl
on motorbikes, the nurses' giggles
in the fogged-up Mini Moke, an ambulance weaving
and howling in the rear-view mirror, the tablets
rattling in the Emergency Bucket, the icy rain
furious and seething on the road, and Noddy
and his loopy brother brooding on it all
for our sake, so that we can see it whole.

CROSSTALK

The way you lie there, it's an opinion, those
bronze medal limbs, the sheets crumpled,
your body the site and centre of conspicuous
waste. It's a vote against the mob,
the way you flick the lamp out, thoughts
akimbo, and stare at the visual display.
Sleep, says the computer.

It sounds brilliant in the dark, at 2 a.m., that
breathing in stereo, so crisp, or rain
in the mesh grille of a microphone.
Is it recording a storm, or sound effects?
The machine listens to its own astrology. Who
left the screen on? That red, that luminescent
green, I must be sleepwalking. Toast,

ham and eggs for two, all on the video.
Does a wish flicker, like that?
Then you disappear leaving a faint ghost
and go to black, as the program dumps
a bracelet of digits in the outboard memory.
The printout spelling doom, do you carry it
with you through sleep, a gift, a poison?

And when you wake at sunrise, heavy breather,
golden in the light, will you be content?
Hush—the shower's whispering, breakfast is ready,
and two expensive German microphones wait for
breath, for movement, for the trace of your desire.

ANYONE HOME?

I can hear the stop-work whistle
down at the Club, can I go home now?
Then I see Grace Kelly,
      the young Grace Kelly!
'Starlet Fever', that's what it is.
I keep hearing the word 'workaholic'.
Echoing, echoing. The Doc says
      take a tablet.
How do you feel down there? Okay?
Take a dive. Bite the bullet. It's
the jim-jams, I've got the jim-jams.
I think he said 'phenomenology'.
I keep hearing jackhammers, it's
the jackhammers, that's what it is.

Do you know Jacky Rackett?
      Do I know Jacky Rackett?
Lovely type of a feller. Dropped his packet.
I keep hearing syllables, polysyllables.
Do I know Sherelle? Young Sherelle?

Then I hear an Appaloosa, getting closer,
the clip-clop racket in the bracken, then
a clattering gallop on the gravel,
        I hear the hullabaloo.
How d'you do, sir. Jacky Rackett?
Top o'the Paddock, sir, the witch's cat.
Then I can see Grace Kelly again,
up close, it's getting warmer.

Down here in Third Class it's getting warmer.
Pull the toggle. No, blow the whistle.
I keep hearing the word 'histrionic'.
Is that better? Snug in a rug?
        Clacketty-clack.

Do you know Gary Langer? Barry Langer?
They were both practising solicitors.
I keep hearing polysyllables,
        then jackhammers.
Now that's a clavier sonata!
That's the cat's pyjamas! No,
it's the Appaloosa! Barry! Gary!
How are you going, you old bastard!
I keep hearing these unpredictable
polysyllables, it's like the Name of God.
Isn't God indelible? Indivisible?

I can see a Californian kitchen, I'm
visiting Gidget, isn't she cute?
I can almost reach out and touch her,
gently. I pour us a Coke and it bubbles.
Is this Paradise? Is it really Paradise?

Hey, there's Jack Napier. Jack Napier!
Absolute type of a gentleman. Wouldn't
hurt you with a barge pole. Jack's
a jumper. Jack invented the calculus.
Then I hear a rustling noise,
        highly magnified.

I think I snapped the tape
at the pain threshold, then stumbled.
Oh Sherelle, will it ever diminish?
Will it ever diminish, and fade away?
Gidget, I'm carrying Gidget, on the beach,
and I stumble! Bugger it!

Down at the Club, the Workers' Club,
the stop-work whistle, should I go home now?
Spots in front of me, spots all over,
Black Friday, Over, for Black Friday
read Man Friday, Man Overboard.
Do you read me? Try again.

I keep hearing 'intelligent,
        very intelligent'.
Push the toggle-button, the green one,
the illuminated one, no, not that,
the other one! You'll feel
worse at first, considerably worse
at first, until the medicine. Oh boy,
some party! Were you there?
        Was I there?
I keep hearing 'medical, paramedical'.
Don't you think it's time to pull the plug?
Push the button? I can see Paul de Man,
Paul de Man, is he in Heaven?
I keep hearing 'shoot, parachute'.

Okay, what odds would you give me?
Push the toggle-button, bird-brain.
This one, or that one?
Go home, time to go home.
Quick, put on the Nazi uniform.
He says 'Quick, Sherelle, do as I say!'
Why should I?
        Why should I?
Who do you think I am? He says—

famous Chinese proverbs—he says
'Quick philosopher, dead solicitor!'
Who do you think I am? Paul de Man?

I can hear a whistle, an emergency whistle.
Now I can see the tropical effluent.
I think it's moving in our direction.
Dark stain.
    Dog paddle! Back-pedal!

That's funny, I can't hear a thing.
Ding-dong.
             Anyone home?

CAROLINE CADDY

———— ❧ ————

C AROLINE CADDY WAS born in Western Australia in 1944, but spent part of her childhood in the United States. After finishing school in Western Australia, she worked throughout the state as a dental nurse with the Road Dental Unit. She has been married and has two children. She now lives reclusively on a farm on the southern coast of Western Australia, and is publishing her poetry, which has appeared in four books, with increasing regularity.

Caddy's work makes a strongly felt use of physical space on the page, in the manner of the American 'projectivist' poets. Recently she has taken to squaring her stepped-down lines at the right-hand margin, as well as the left, which gives her poems a solid, pictorial appearance—the irregular, overlapping lines and extensive open space producing at times a strong visual rhythm. She is often elliptical and abbreviated, and the emotion can be elusive.

STUDY OF A SQUID

There is a point in the ganglia of a squid
where it might be said
                          to approach a brain—
right between the eyes!
And it would take something more
                          to coordinate
the view from those guillotined planets
          ringed with the flash of lagoons.
Dead innocent/evil eye.
          The pure concentration of universe
at you.
Squid just looks its prey to death.
Centurion   spear-helm—
              octopus could be its innards.
On my kitchen sink now—
                          bled dragon's tail.
Stretch its mesenteric camouflage
and tiny freckles spread pale or bunch
                    into flames and cinders.
Scraped clean
          it's the skull of a god of wisdom—
computer pod with a crotch of tentacles
      that stick like miniscule new-borns.
Cut the sculpted tofu—
            dollops of ink on stainless steel.
Pull a finger through and I'm writing
kana
                    with no effort at all
or understanding.
Sometimes they are found
                    stranded in shallows
by their fondness for moon-gazing.
I remember one summer night
              a white glow out to sea . . .
can there be a mirage at night—
                      antarctic inversion?
                              it was
                          a sea-market!

Boats of strung incandescence that lure
                squads of them into the nets
finishing as vellum rockets
                    or this unusual pasta.
Thumb and finger grip
             slides out the welded quill.
What organ queasy inside me
   recognises this celluloid goose feather?
Every thing anticipates every thing.
     I make a meal of soft compendiums.

MOONVIEWING

One thumbprint
above the horizon it covers
the sewage ponds
with foil
pumps streetlights full
of bottled gas.
Now it's herding
bright barrettes of herring
into nets
and slicing the gills
from beached dingies.
Sand electroplates to sand.
Neon swells flicker—
go out.
On my face   on my arms
no heat at all.
Moonlight is remission.
     Now you can tell me
      now can you tell?—
while we are zinc
titanium   manganese.

ROBERT GRAY

———— ❧ ————

ROBERT GRAY, BORN in 1945, was brought up on the north coast of New South Wales. This coastline, and landscape in general, have been an abiding theme in his poetry, and from his youth he has had close friendships with landscape painters.

Gray's mother was a north coast farm girl who worked for a while in domestic service in Sydney. His father was from a well-off family, which established him numerous times on plantations, that grew bananas and other tropical fruit. When the last of these was lost to gambling debts, Gray's parents and their four children moved into a Housing Commission house on the outskirts of a nearby country town. Gray's father obtained a pension as 'totally and permanently incapacitated' by war service, although his state of health was more the result of alcoholism. His mother joined a fundamentalist Christian sect, involving her children, but Gray broke away from this in his mid-teens.

Perhaps an even more important influence on him was the diagnosis in childhood of a rare congenital heart disease, which was inoperable. He remembers his mother being told, in front of him, that he could not hope to live beyond thirty. Gray responded by training for sports, becoming a newspaper delivery boy, and taking long hikes through the bush. He always insisted there was nothing wrong with him, and in his twenties more advanced tests confirmed either that this was the case, or that the hole in the inner wall of his heart had completely healed.

In the meantime, Gray dropped out of high school and became a cadet journalist on a country newspaper. After a year he moved to Sydney, where he wrote for a magazine, then worked as an advertising copywriter, mail sorter, and in a bookshop, while writing poetry. His work has now appeared in five separate volumes, and in *Selected Poems*, which has gone through several (always revised) editions. (Most of the poems here are again slightly revised.) He was awarded a travelling scholarship which took him to the United States and Europe, and has been a writer-in-residence in Tokyo. Married briefly in the 1970s, he now lives with a long-time partner and her daughter. He has had numerous awards from the Australia Council. For over twenty years, since first encountering it through Japanese poetry, he has studied Zen Buddhism, which he finds is compatible with a scientific materialist philosophy.

Gray's earliest enthusiasm in poetry, an abiding one, was for Kenneth Slessor's work, discovered while at school. He has also felt a strong attraction to the poetry of D. H. Lawrence, and later to that of William Carlos Williams. The Bible, which was compulsory study as a child, has had an influence on his style. More recently, he often writes what might be called a loosely formal poetry, which in the irregularity of its rhythms and its half-rhymes shows a fundamental loyalty to free verse.

Jamie Grant has commented on Gray:

The strength in his poetry arises from a minutely fastidious attention to the facts of physical existence . . . *Claritas* is the essence of his poetry . . . the imagery he uses is an explanatory device, rather than a decorative one. Each simile is drawn in order to bring a picture more clearly into focus . . .

TO THE MASTER, DŌGEN ZENJI

(1200–1253 AD)

Dōgen came in and sat on the wood platform;
all the people were gathered
like birds upon the lake.

After years, home from China,
and he had brought no scriptures; he showed them
empty hands.

This in Kyoto,
at someone-else's temple. He said, All that's important
is the ordinary things.

Making a fire
to boil the bathwater, pounding rice, pulling weeds
and knocking dirt from their roots,

or pouring tea—those blown scarves,
a moment, more beautiful than the drapery
in paintings by a master.

'It is this world
of the *dharmas* (the momentary particles)
that is the Diamond.'

O

Dōgen received, they say, his first insight
from the old cook of some monastery
in China,

who was on the jetty
where they docked, who had come down
to buy mushrooms

among the rolled-up
straw sails, the fishnets, brocade litters,
and geese in baskets.

High sea-going junk,
shuffling and dipping
like an official.

Dōgen could see
an empty shoreline, the pinewood plank of the beach,
the mountains

far off
and dusty. Standing about
with his new smooth skull.

The horses' lumpy hooves clumped on those planks,
they arched their necks
and dipped their heads like swans,

manes blown about
like white threads from off
the falling breakers;

holding up their hooves as though they were tender,
the sea grabbing at
the timber below.

And the two Buddhists in all the shuffle got to bow.
The old man told him, Up there,
that place—

The monastery a cliff-face
in one of the shadowy hills.
My study is cooking;

no, not devotion. No,
no, not your sacred books (meaning Buddhism). And Dōgen,
irate—

he must have thought
who is this old prick, so ignorant
of the Law,

and it must have shown.
Son, I regret
that you haven't caught on

to where it is one discovers
the Original Nature
of the mind and things.

O

Dōgen said, Ideas
from reading, from people, from a personal bias,
toss them all out—

'discolourations'.
You shall only discover by looking in
this momentary mind.

And said, 'The Soto school
isn't one
of the entities in Buddhism—

don't even use such names.'
The world's an incessant transformation, and to meditate
is awareness, with no

clinging to,
no working on, the mind.
It is a floating, ever-moving, 'marvellous emptiness'.

Only absorption in such a practice can release us
from the accidents, and appetites,
of life.

And upon this leaf one shall cross over
the stormy sea,
among the dragon-like waves.

FLAMES AND DANGLING WIRE

On a highway over the marshland.
Off to one side, the smoke of different fires in a row,
like fingers spread and dragged to smudge:
it is an always-burning dump.

Behind us, the city
driven like stakes into the earth.
A waterbird lifts above this swamp
as a turtle moves on the Galapagos shore.

We turn off down a gravel road,
approaching the dump. All the air wobbles
in some cheap mirror.
There is a fog over the hot sun.

Now the distant buildings are stencilled in the smoke.
And we come to a landscape of tin cans,
of cars like skulls,
that is rolling in its sand dune shapes.

Amongst these vast grey plastic sheets of heat,
shadowy figures
who seem engaged in identifying the dead—
they are the attendants, in overalls and goggles,

forking over rubbish on the dampened fires.
A sour smoke
is hauled out everywhere,
thin, like rope. And there are others moving—scavengers.

As in hell the devils
might pick about through our souls, for vestiges
of appetite
with which to stimulate themselves,

so these figures
seem to wander, disconsolate, with an eternity
in which to turn up
some peculiar sensation.

We get out and move about also.
The smell is huge,
blasting the mouth dry:
the tons of rotten newspaper, and great cuds of cloth . . .

And standing where I see the mirage of the city
I realize I am in the future.
This is how it shall be after men have gone.
It will be made of things that worked.

A labourer hoists an unidentifiable mulch
on his fork, throws it in the flame:
something flaps
like the rag held up in 'The Raft of the *Medusa*'.

We approach another, through the smoke,
and for a moment he seems that demon with the long barge pole.
—It is a man, wiping his eyes.
Someone who worked here would have to weep,

and so we speak. The rims beneath his eyes are wet
as an oyster, and red.
Knowing all that he does about us,
how can he avoid a hatred of men?

Going on, I notice an old radio, that spills
its dangling wire—
and I realize that somewhere the voices it received
are still travelling,

skidding away, riddled, around the arc of the universe;
and with them, the horse-laughs, and the Chopin
which was the sound of the curtains lifting,
one time, to a coast of light.

PUMPKINS

What in novels is called 'a grizzled stubble'
on these pumpkin leaves.
The leaves shuffle
as you wade amongst them, their bristles
rustling.
One is slowly stepping upon
egg shells,
pagodas of orange peel,
on heaps of tea slops.
And the pumpkin flower,
a big loud daffodil.
You push about darkness, parting the leaves.
A rooster is on this slope, also;
come to peck
outside, in the late afternoon.
It is putting down its spur
with care,
and its eye is flickering about.
The rooster is red
and lacquered as a Chinese box;
a golden hood
down to its shoulders, like a calyx, flexible
upon its body, as it pecks,
flicks,
flicks, and blinks,
pecks. I'm holding one foot up, looking for
somewhere
amongst this vine. And find
the pumpkin—
segmented like a peeled mandarin
or leather
on the back seat of a thirties tourer.
I break the stem
and lift the heavy, warped pumpkin,
just when the vine's become
too dark.

In between pink and yellow,
its orange tone
can be added easily to the sunset
that's been going on.
I take the pumpkin beneath my arm.
Like a bad painting, this magnificent sunset.

The Dusk

A kangaroo is standing up, and dwindling like a plant
with a single bud.
Fur combed into a crest
along the inside length of its body,
a bow-wave
under slanted light, out in the harbour.

And its fine unlined face is held on the cool air;
a face in which you feel
the small thrust-forward teeth lying in the lower jaw,
grass-stained and sharp.

Standing beyond a wire fence, in weeds,
against the bush that is like a wandering smoke.

Mushroom-coloured,
and its white chest, the underside of a growing mushroom,
in the last daylight.

The tail is trailing heavily as a lizard lying concealed.

It turns its head like a mannequin
toward the fibro shack,
and holds the forepaws
as though offering to have them bound.

An old man pauses on a dirt path in his vegetable garden,
where a cabbage moth puppet-leaps and jiggles wildly
in the cooling sunbeams,
the bucket still swinging in his hand.

And the kangaroo settles down, pronged,
then lifts itself
carefully, like a package passed over from both arms—

The now curved-up tail is rocking gently counterweight behind
as it flits hunched
amongst the stumps and scrub, into the dusk.

DIPTYCH

I

My mother told me how one night, as would often happen, she'd
    stayed awake
in our weatherboard house, at the end of a dark, leaf-mulched drive,
waiting for my father, after the pubs had closed,
knowing he would have to walk
miles, 'in his state',
if no one would drop him home
(since, long before this, he had driven his own car off a
    mountain-side,
and, becoming legend, had rode
on the knocked-down banana palms
of a plantation, right to the foot, and someone's door,
the car reared high on a great raft of mutilated, sap-oozing fibre;
from which he'd climbed down, unharmed, his most soberly polite,
and never driven again).
This other night, my mother was reluctant to go out, and leave us
    kids asleep,
and fell asleep herself, clothed, on the unopened bed,
but leapt upright, sometime later, with the foulest taste—
glimpsed at once

he was still not there—and rushed out, gagging,
to find that, asleep, she'd bitten off the tail
of a small lizard, dragged through her lips. That bitterness (I used to
    imagine),
running onto the verandah to spit,
and standing there, spat dry, seeing across the silent, frosty bush
the distant lights of town had died.

And yet my mother never ceased from what philosophers invoke,
    from 'extending Care',
though she'd only ever read the *Women's Weekly*,
and although she could be 'damned impossible' through a few
    meal-times, of course.
This care for things, I see, was her one real companion
in those years.
It was as though there were two of her,
an harassed person, and a calm, that saw what needed to be done,
    and
seemed to step through her, again.
Her care you could watch reappear like the edge of tidal water
in salt flats, about everything.
It was this made her drive out the neighbour's bull from our garden
    with a broom,
when she saw it trample her seedlings—
back, step by step, she forced it, through the broken fence,
it bellowing and hooking either side sharply at her all the way, and I
five years old on the back steps calling
'Let it have a few old bloody flowers, Mum.'
No. She locked the broom handle straight-armed across its nose
and was pushed right back herself, quickly, across the yard. She
ducked behind some tomato stakes,
and beat it with the handle, all over that deep hollowness of the
    muzzle,
poked with the millet at its eyes,
and had her way, drove it out bellowing; while I, in torment,
stood slapping into the steps, the rail, with an ironing cord,

or suddenly rushed down there, and was quelled, also,
repelled to the bottom step, barracking. And all,
I saw, for those little flimsy leaves
she fell to at once, small as mouse prints, amongst the chopped-up
    loam.

II

Whereas, my father only seemed to care that he would never appear
    a drunkard
while ever his shoes were clean.
A drunkard he would define as someone who had forgotten the
    mannerisms
of a gentleman. The gentleman, after all, is only known,
only exists, through manner. He himself had the most perfect
    manners,
of a kind. I can imagine no one
with a manner more easily, and coolly, precise. With him,
manner had subsumed all of feeling. To brush and dent the hat
which one would doff, or to look about, over each of us, and then
    unfold a napkin
to allow the meal, in that town where probably all of the men
sat to eat of a hot evening without a shirt,
was his passion. After all, he was a university man
(although ungraduated), something more rare then. My father, I see,
    was hopelessly melancholic—
The position of those wary
small eyes, and thin lips,
on the long-boned face
proclaimed the bitterness of every pleasure, except those of form.
He often drank alone
at the RSL club, and had been known to wear a carefully-considered
    tie
to get drunk in the sandhills, watching the sea.
When he was ill and was at home at night, I would look into his
    bedroom,
at one end of a gauzed verandah,
from around the door and a little behind him,
and see his frighteningly high-domed skull under the lamp-light, as
    he read

in a curdle of cigarette smoke.
Light shone through wire mesh onto the packed hydrangea-heads,
and on the great ragged mass of insects, like bees over a comb, that
    crawled tethered
and ignored right beside him. He seemed content, at these times,
as though he'd done all he could to himself,
and had been forced, objectively, to give up.
He liked his bland ulcer-patient food
and the big heap of library books I had brought. (My instructions
    always were:
'Nothing whingeing. Nothing by New York Jews;
nothing by women, especially the French; nothing
translated from the Russian.')
And yet, the only time I actually heard him say that he'd enjoyed
    anything
was when he spoke of the bush, once. 'Up in those hills,'
he advised me, pointing around, 'when the sun is coming out of the
    sea, standing amongst
that tall timber, you can feel at peace.'
I was impressed. He asked me, another time, that when he died
I should take his ashes somewhere, and not put him with the locals,
    in the cemetery.
I went up to one of the hills he had named
years earlier, at the time of day he had spoken of, when the half-risen
    sun
was as strongly-spiked as that one
on his Infantry badge,
and I scattered him there, utterly reduced at last, amongst the wet,
    breeze-woven grass.
For all his callousness to my mother, I had long accepted him.
After all, he'd given, or shown me, the best advice,
and had left me alone. And I'd come by then to think that all of us
    are pathetic.
Opening his plastic, brick-sized box, that morning,
my pocket-knife slid
sideways and pierced my hand—and so I dug with that one
into his ashes, which I found were like a mauvish-grey marble dust,
and felt that I needn't think of anything else to say.

CURRICULUM VITAE

I

Once, playing cricket, beneath a toast-dry hill,
I heard the bat crack, but watched a moment longer
a swallow, racing lightly, just above the ground. I was impressed by
        the way
the bird skimmed, fast as a cricket ball.
It was decided for me, within that instant,
where my interests lay.

And the trajectories at dusk of random moths and lone decisive
        swallow
will often still preoccupy me, until dew occludes the air.

II

I can remember there were swallows that used to sew together
the bars of a cattle yard.
I would be sitting in morning sunlight
on the top rail, to feel its polished surface
beneath my hands.
A silvery, weathered log that had the sheen of thistle's flax.

III

A cow was in the stocks with the calm expression of a Quaker;
and my father stretched his fingers,
a pianist seated on a chopping block. He bent his forehead to an
        instrument
out of Heath Robinson—
a dangling bagpipes, big as a piano,
that was played by tugging on organ stops.
The cow began to loosen its milk: its tits were disgorged,
the size and colour of small carrots;
and milk was flourished in the bucket, two skewer-thin daggers
sharpened on each other underhand.
Then, as the bucket filled, there would be the sound of a tap running
into deep suds at the end of a bath.
Finally, the calf was let in to have its turn,
and this sounded like a workman building-up a big lather between
        his hands.

The concrete in those bails was shattered, but lay together
as though a platform of river stones; and water ran there constantly
from a hose, breaking up and bearing off
the hot lava of any cow-pats. That water was delicate and
    closely-branched—
a long weed fluttering, on such a breezy morning.

IV

There were big dents of cloud-shadow on the blue-forested
    mountain;
and far off, over
the paddocks, through midday heat, the fluttering silk scarf
of a light purple range.
Our mountain was the kite, and those in the distance, its tail,
through all the heat-wavering days.

And many broken, dead trees had been left standing about,
like stone ruins: pillars that held out the remnants
of cloisters and fine stonework,
with rubble beneath them. But the air was so clear; so uncrowded
with any past—
arbitrary corridors, unpeopled, through the air.
Room for the mind to travel on and on.
I used to have to stop, often, to stand there, in that immense
    amphitheatre
of silence and light.

V

I remember watching our three or four geese let loose and rushing,
with their heads beating sideways like metronomes,
towards a dam where the mountain-top hung;
and when they entered the water, the mountain's image came apart
suddenly, the way a cabbage falls into coleslaw.
Everything was changed, as easily as that.

VI

Since then, I have been, for instance, in Petticoat Lane—pushing by
through narrow, stacked alleys,
among the tons of rotting garbage for sale,
and have seen the really poor.
Those people seemed just dangling paper dolls, threaded onto
a genetic string—
the characters of poverty, starch, lack of sun,
and stunted, hopeless spirit everywhere. Their crossed eyes, warts,
twisted faces, snaggle teeth,
drunkenness were Dickens still, in '70 something,
again in '82. — People in greasy rags, on crutches, weeding wet butts
from the gutters, wild-eyed,
spiky-haired, foul-muttering.
The women were shaped like slapped-together piles of clay. They
        scrabbled
amongst junk, scratching themselves viciously,
shouting and oblivious . . .

What is such an evil, but the continuing effect
of capital's Stalinism?
Enclosure, as John Clare has said, lets not a thing remain.

And then, an hour later, in the West End I found
how much worse I thought the fleshy,
askance, meringue-coloured, prissy-lipped upperclass face—so sleek
in its obliviousness.
People go rotten with culture, also.

VII

Another time, in Washington, when my girlfriend had gone
to see someone,
and while I was sitting at an upstairs window, I watched the bald
        man
who lived next door, after he'd argued once more
with his wife, come out to stand alone
in their backyard—round as a pebble, in his singlet,
but nowhere near so hard.

He was standing with chin sunk,
holding the garden hose—a narrowed stream
he felt around with
closely, like a blind man's cane.
It disturbed me to see him like that—and then, as I started to
    consider myself,
I saw I was walking
in those silver paddocks, again,
which as a kid I'd known.

VIII

Or, travelling alone in Europe once, and staying in a provincial city,
indolent and homesick of an afternoon,
I turned, as ever, to the museum.
In such a mood, though, the masterpiece will often no longer serve:
it seems too strenuous and too elevated;
it belongs in a world too far beyond one's own.
From experience, one has learned at these times to follow that arrow,
    Ecole française
XIXe siècle. There, on an attic floor,
unnoticed by the attendant, a newspaper crumpled
over his boots, or along the deserted outer corridors,
before tall windows, in the light from which
many of them are cancelled,
hang one's faithful mediocrities—in sympathy with whom
one had thought to be borne through until dinnertime.
Armand Guillaumin, Léon Cogniet, Jules Dupré, Félix Ziem:
no artistic claims can be made for these. Their sluggish or
    bituminous pigment,
greasy sheen, and craquelure,
their failures, so complex and sad, have earned them
'an undisturbed repose'.
And yet, even these harmless,
unassuming, and forgotten, as I glanced among them, on this
    occasion,
were forgotten
by their arbitrary idle re-creator,
and the landscapes that came far more vividly before my eyes
were all memories.

IX

Into my mind there has always come, when travelling,
images of the twisted Hawkesbury bush
crackling in the heat, and scattering its bark and twigs about,
white sunlight flicked
thickly on the frothy surges
and troughs of its greenery; and within those forests,
great pools of deep fern, afloat
beneath a sandstone rock-lip; and of the Platonic blueness
of the sky; and recollections of Coledale and Thirroul
on their clifftops, where sea-spray
blows among the pines and eucalypts; and, most of all, of those
     forests,
cool, light-flouncing, with white female limbs,
and the yeasted green pastures,
where my mind first opened, like a bubble from a glass-blower's
     tube,
and shone, reflecting
things as they are—
there, where I have felt, anxiously, I would find them
a while longer,
after passing Kempsey, once more, on the mail train of an early
     morning.

DESCRIPTION OF A WALK

In the shape of long sand-dunes, but apple green,
the pastures that I'd crossed. A quivering rain
hung above them. One currawong somewhere, warbling
happily as a hose within a drain.

The forest was cumulus on stilts, from afar;
everywhere within it, leaf-splatterings and spar;
the leaves, paint clots, or a fringe of trickling.
Angry as a burned insect, a distant car.

The forest closed. I climbed amongst sandstone—
great gouts of lava, petrified as iron;
puffed like fungi, or with a broken iceberg's edge;
all of a rusty red or burnt orange tone.

About the plinths and mantels was an artful
pebble-scatter; on its pedestal, an eccentric bowl.
Rose-coloured sandstone syncopated salt.
Blown rain was being emptied by the bushel.

Uphill, warped arcades of bush, rack on rack,
reiterative as cuneiforms. Bacon redness of bark,
or smooth wet trunks of caterpillar green,
and some with a close dog's fur, greyish black.

Other colours: Brazil nut kernel, an unfired pot.
In the wet, tart as bush smoke, a sweet rot.
The air rain-threaded, as though with insect sounds.
My heart flapped like a lizard's, by the top.

Underneath a clay bank, an old grey gutter,
sealed with rare smoked glass. A claw of water
flexed nearby, on rock ledges, and over roots—
its wide-toothed, vibrating cane rake clatter.

Sprigged trees, and vista of Pre-Raphaelite shine:
beneath gentian hills, a billiard table green;
ploughed land, pumpernickel; the road, a fracture;
the shapes of coral in a dark tree-line.

Rain shaded to silence. To cicadas' shekel
sound. — Emptied from a bucket, a pile of shell
poured with the numerous headlong pour of sand
onto other shells. A dry calcite rattle.

And this merely the start — warming of an engine.
Each opens a row of gills; if you find one
you see almost through the body. Their joined hums'
ascendant power, an electricity substation.

I walked on and on, in such vibrance. Wet light
gave the leaves' undersides a stainless glint.
Ragged bushland. The white arms raised, dangling
cloth; that chant. What it was all for I forgot.

MARK O'CONNOR

———— ✤ ————

MARK O'CONNOR, THE son of a Melbourne judge, was born in 1945 and educated at a private school. He began a degree in engineering, but switched courses and graduated from the University of Melbourne in English and classics. While in Canberra as a post-graduate student, he began a friendship with A. D. Hope, with whom he shares an interest in scientific discoveries as subjects for poetry. O'Connor is a knowledgeable amateur biologist. However, Les Murray, rather than Hope, is his strongest stylistic influence. In 1976 O'Connor received a travelling fellowship and spent the next four years in Europe, surviving 'by minding houses and winning literary competitions'. Back in Australia he has made an independent living entirely as a poet, particularly through being writer-in-residence at many tertiary institutions across the country. Recently he has extended his itinerary to include universities in Russia and China.

O'Connor's poetry covers a wide range: the culture of the classical world, problems of population and ecology, and religion (from a critical standpoint). His main subject, however, is the natural environment of Australia, and, like Judith Wright, he is a passionate conservationist. He believes it is his duty as a poet to draw our attention in this country to 'places . . . we have scarcely begun to notice, much less revere'. He has been a particular critic, in his book *Modern Australian Styles* (1982), and in reviews, of those poets who have ignored Australia for the sake of an abstracted internationalist *avant-gardism*. His work might be seen to prove the continuing vitality of the Jindyworobaks' ideals. He draws on an old (and largely disused) classical tradition in regarding poetry as a means of communicating important information, but he seems at times to be impatient with style and form. In his successful poems he is able to present his strong subjects in language that is fully alive.

THE PAIRING OF TERNS

Human lovers know it only in dreams
the wild mating flight of the terns;
riding the weird and unguessable surf of the air
blown round the compass, locked
in pairs by invisible steel; wings taut
as the sharp stretched skin of a pterodactyl;
now criss-crossing moon-high in an evening sky,
and now outskimming the wind on the waves of a twilit bay
now rising, now falling tumultuous heights
and cackling their random delirious laughter.

Sometimes they hover
motionless, high in a half-gale torrent of air
unmoved yet sustained by the stream that surrounds them
then suddenly and sharply they break
quick as a kite
when the string snaps
plunging down and across the sky

then low against wind they row back hard
plying with swift strokes their strong feathered oars,
beating into curd the thick vortices of the air;
then turn and take the gale under their wings
running fast as the wind without moving a feather
driven miles from their haunts, yet unworried,
they know there is nothing they cannot do.

Their love is everything for which we have only metaphors,
peaks and abysses, stallings and dizzying speeds
wild oceans of distance, and feathertip closenesses,
and wingbeats that answer so swiftly none knows
which struck first, which called and which answered.
They were circling the globe when our fathers still
cringed from the monsters beyond the next hamlet.

from PLANTING THE DUNK ISLAND BOTANIC GARDENS

I

THE JOB

Sometimes the perfect tree will seed itself
  into a spot owned by the man
who didn't think of it, but lets it be.
  More often nurture helps what Nature
marred. The loquat in the wilderness, schoolyard
  mango, or coconut by the little sandy cove
have all been sponsored. Strong forces work
  to heel a slip-stone under, though you know
the fruit will be another's—is it some itch
  to be creation's partner? or
those peasant generations seething in the genes?
  We each in our time aspire to nourish
the seed of life in children, ground or art.

I found Coonanglebah, old Banfield's home, first
  gardened by that one-eyed man, tough, English
and ant-vigorous, like all islanders that last.
  In thirty years he brought, described and grew
the fruits that brutal Queensland still rejects:
  the pummelo with savage spines; breadfruit
(Bligh's curse) that drops a dinner on your head;
  durian, whose taste is heaven and whose smell
is hell; the sweet-fleshed litchi; mangosteen for which
  his Queen once gave a hundred guineas;
the spikey lime; starfruit, monsteria; and three
  once fed to pigs: the oil-pear, avocado; pawpaw,
the island-wife, whose gentle juice disjoins all flesh;
  and India's choicest mango strains. His work
remained, hacked, bulldozed, overgrown, and known
  to only two or three.

I came in a later, greedy time,
   chasing work on the tourist farm.
Found the manager. Delivered myself
   a perfect barman, chef's hand—or gardener.
He saw the place as a marlin fisherman's hide-away,
   but it needed shrubs. The job was mine,
with a brief to prove all arts are learnt by doing.

III

'THE BOSS'

Managers are island kings: they get great powers,
   no thanks, and little time; moved on
if too good, too bad, or anyway. The cheery
   jungle hermit here in his fourteen years
weaving the jungle in his tapestries
   had seen some thirty of their kind
come roaring in and go miaowing out. His word
   to each new one, 'Drop round before you go.'
So here, when I thought the way was smoothed:
   'Y'know the new manager?' 'Which one?' 'One
that gave you yer job last week. He's sacked. Resigned
   this morning when the Board flew up. The new one's
heavy, real professional.' Next week he came. Was both.
   A fat man with a boy's loud voice, a mouth of commercial
tropes, a shrewd head, and broad lard face on which
   sweat showed like water-drops on butter.
'My first job here's to show a profit. Been running pubs
   since most of you were born. I don't chase hassles.'
Evenings, as if the heat could melt him, he inhabited
   the swimming pool like a giant frog
—a curse on midnight nudists. To him I made my pitch.
   He listened, asked a thousand things:
trees, climate, Banfield's history; then spoke an hour
   on finance, brochures, how to make it pay.

'You'll want two thousand bucks for plants—thank God
    you can write your own submissions. We'll build
a Botanic Gardens. Name tags on everything.' Through fuzz
    of business talk we planned a kindred dream:
new strains of mango on the hill, the native Queensland
    orchids mixed with all exotic ones.
So then; license to chase the rarest, brightest
    plants, and the job desperate to be done
before the wet was over. From week to week
    he jogged me on with thoughts. 'Bamboo,' he'd boom,
'why have we no bamboo? Did Banfield slip up there?'
    I told him of the types. Giant green, that grows
to twenty metres in wet soil, and the easier giant yellow,
    banded, elegant, to ten. Or he'd bring
a picture book of trees. 'That's a bloody beautiful
    one. We must get that! And that! (with stubby finger
underscoring names). 'Here's one that perfumes
    a whole garden.' I chased, and got.

IV

THE WET

The monsoon struck. It poured by night and steamed by day
    —good gardening weather. I greened the beach-dune
where plants once died in half an hour's sun, raking
    hibiscus clippings in. After a week
they struck and pushed up free; plumerias too.
    But roads were cut. Few plants arrived.
My plane was booked for Greece, and soon the wet
    would end. I filled in time
transplanting the monsterias, quisqualis, philodendrons
    Banfield had loosed last century
to grow rampant in the jungle. Vanilla orchids which I tied
    air-rooted to the palms, would make
a trellis for mere tendril-creepers. I had plans,
    spoken most quietly in their hearing, to de-top
the smaller palms and wedge young figs above. (I knew
    all figs will strangle: the squat-boled *Moreton Bay*,
giant *Watkinsiana*, savage *destruens*, placid *carica*,

or *religiosa* that in tilled Java, where scarce
a wild ant survives, towers above all temples; yes even
   the banyan, walking shore-tree, fig of the Fall
said Milton, that less than any other knows root from bough
   —from its sightless canopy roots drop
like plumb-lines to the ground, then strike, draw
   taut as harpstrings, thicken into columns,
trunks and buttresses of the walking wood.)
   The nights were spent in noting catalogues
while friendly girls with one-week passes from
   the South were left on bar-stools. Once
in a life one plants a garden properly. And then,
   what plans swam through the drub of rain!
Names that rolled in the mouth from scented pages:
   pompelmo, litchi, tamarillo, rambutan
(the drought-dry cockscomb rind around the inner
   sweet implosion), *Macadamia ternifolia*, or butter-nut
Hawaii stole; black mulberries—dwarf, and Downing's
   ever-bearing; deadly cashew; cumquat; custard-apple;
spiny spectacular Bunya nut (that came a contemptible
   seedling); okari, jakfruit, whose flesh
feeds households, whose mere seeds are roasting chestnuts;
   cinnamon the ornamental spice; and live coffee known
as a scented shade-dweller; taro, the lush-named *Colocasia*
   esculenta, a deadly feast uncooked. And the soft
ones: feijoa; tangerine; *Garcinia X*, the mangosteen's
   sour willing cousin; the mangoes—'Bowen', 'Peach',
'Black Java'; dates; pawpaws; and the eugenias, 'appled'
   and 'plummed' around the tropic world; with
Austromyrtus dulcis, the sweet native 'midyim' fit
   for a blazing salt-front. Reading I marvelled—the
manifold chromosomed patterns fighting for place in my garden.

VI

BEGINNINGS

Slowly, between floods and strikes, stuff came.
   Twice a cyclone passed that could have blown
my shrublets all away: the tides by luck stayed low.

   First came creepers for the walls and trunks;
a smother of scented beauty: gay allamandas,
   scented rangoon creeper, jasmines,
convolvulus, tecomanthe, bougainvilleas,
   petrea's lilac statement, climbing cactus (night-
blooming, scented, large), jade-vine, clitoria (a perfect
   replica of the thing in china-blue), great granadilla
the melon-passionfruit on trellis-breaking vines—
   a crop to lure me back—then bamboo liana
that ties whole groves together, the fish-tail
   palm, caladiums, watery aglaonemas,
plus *Cassia fistula* the weeping golden-shower
   that brings giant bumble-bees, bananas,
birdsnest-ferns, dracaenas, umbrella-tree the strangler
   whose crimson spikes drip a daily gallon
of nectar for birds, bats, bees to quarrel over,
   plus native tree-ferns. I turned that dusty
street of boxes to a glen, a labyrinth where dazed couples
   maundering home of nights could lose their way
a minute from their doors.

VII

THE BUTTERFLY TUNNEL

   The isle had two giant butterflies:
Cairns Birdwing, a psychedelic eight-inch insect fit
   for a fairy toadstool; and *Papilio*
Ulysses, blue as a flake of heaven, a summer day's
   epiphany of azure coruscations;
alarmed they fly like sparrowhawks, yet come
   to a blue umbrella or dead comrade's wing.
Banfield described how on calm days they flocked

round rowboats in the bay; today
more seen on resort stationery than in the wild. The boss:
   'Each bastard who comes here expects
to drown in 'em. I've seen just four myself'.

We had an alley-valley-way between twin rows of palms
   where seepage from a bank ran down in shade.
Knowing the *Ulysses* loves to court and hover over
   a stream bed, I planted it with honey-giving trees
for double-shade, making the 'Butterfly Tunnel'—
   one long cool avenue down which their pairs might dance
delirious with leafy scents. Next I assembled there
   food-plants of every bright-winged butterfly
the North contains. Then came the Boss's
   finest hour—he had a mind to send
Mucuna, 'flame-of-the-forest', giant Niugini firebean,
   racing up quailing palms. The books
named it a rare monstrosity, giant liana python-thick
   that in its nuptials turns the forest crimson.
'If we could get that here!' We did. Planted
   in scrub-hen compost they rose a foot a day, and
mixed with their gentler yellow brethren *Tecomanthe*
   that hung below the canopy, sun-scared, they fed
a deeper shade on the broad-foliaged plants below
   —the dracaenas, difenbachias, calatheas, ferns
through which *Ulysses* danced.

VIII

'SIMMO'

   Yet in every Terran garden you appropriate
lurks the offended snake whose turf you've taken.
   Mine was the works-foreman, earth-machinery-master;
not one in whom Queensland's jungles raised
   a larger admiration, but a sandy twisted kid,
bred to the inland like the spinifex, bullied by class,
   school, bigger boys, and then brain-eating sun
on plains where your horse's wind-lee side is black with flies
   that change when you round a corner. Chasing work

he'd drifted here where his 'dozer card and willingness
    to stay bought promotion. Immune to green
and gardens, a creature of drought; like a mole
    he'd built and unbuilt the resort's terrain
to a dozen manager's whims, content only to stay.
    Single in his unfixed forties ('Gave up that
nonsense years ago'), a model employee he recycled
    his wage, less a slave's pittance,
through the bar-room till; his sole extravagance
    and topic his pet rabbit—'stupid bloody bitch
with a mind of her own'—that he saw as wayward daughter.
    Only when drunk would he play country music
on the guitar in his rough room, singing 'It takes
    a hard man to tame a hard hard land'.
He had the up-jumped habit of blaming coarseness
    on his men. 'My boys don't like to hear
Latin names . . . I'd have saved some scrub from the dozer
    but the boys don't understand.' 'Don't ask
my boys to do what you can't do yourself' was his phrase
    for refusing help with the machines. So I worked
unaided on a mighty front, putting the unwished crown
    on his labours. An inch of topsoil and a bag
of couch seed was his notion of completed
    work. Mine was two feet of windrowed soil
and an edible forest. He stalled the manager
    till the wet, then crowed to me 'Thought
you could walk around and tell us what to do!
    You're a bludger, worthless'. Each tantrum
took two hours' drinking, just-so's, rabbit-chat,
    to be resolved. He tried to have me sacked.
No dice. We both were needed, but got lectures on
    'wet-season nerves'. He cramped my plans,
robbed me not of success but something of the calm
    current joy in it. Later, in Italy when I heard
how he got T.B., lost a lung, and left for Alice Springs
    the bounce in my heart made pretence of finer
feelings useless. He, and the short, short time were what
    I'd fought against to make my garden.

IX

DEFEATS

There came a weary time of cyclones;
the dark palms swept the ground, nuts bounced
    like shrapnel. We huddled with the guests
in one wood-house (termited, Harry said)
    and watched from its creaking lee
the ridge-top forests flail like meadow grass. Some
    of our senior trees (the Boss's phrase) came down;
the new ones, rightly staked, stayed put. No cyclone kills
    a garden utterly. But the boats were gone,
moored high up creeks. We turned to what could come by plane,
    and first to orchids, those tough miracles
that cling on trunks, eat rainy air, and rot
    at touch of soil: to pour Earth's pick
upon our little forest, turning its lamp-post palms
    to barky gardens hung with scent and flowers.
I went to mainland gardens, orchidariums, talked
    with white-coated men who grew the airy spawn
twelve months in jars before it seemed the size of moss;
    then spent a risky week on ladders checking
shade and North; worked all the hours God made.
    Often at dusk would meet the manager, rolling
his weight along the jungle path, well pleased
    with the results. Then crazed with lack of stock
I moved giant pawpaws, roof-top high, and had them live.

But, still in my last week
    the shipments were delayed. Five hundred plants
on Wednesday waiting on the wharf; Thursday, no boat;
    then on the last day—everything. The island trucks
threw down a nursery that blocked our roads.
    A month, and not a day, would go to plant them all.
Queensland is littered with men's broken dreams. Throat
    lumped, like a failing examinee, I saw how time
ran out. Yet there they stood, the landmarks
    of my plan: caladiums; episcias; lilies;
pandanus; white plumerias; ginger; bromeliad flowers;

the scented perfect orchid-tree, *Bauhinia*; *Bombax*
wine-blooming, tall; the leafless flame-tree;
    bottle-tree; swift giant-leaved teak, the labelled
legend in my hand; sweet date; litchi; and leopard
    tree; pink, yellow *Cassias* and aperient *fistula*;
fern-foliaged *Poinciana* whose tresses sweep the ground;
    breadfruit, a five-foot sprig with plate-size leaves;
bamboos; the *Cerbera*, ever-blooming poison-tree;
    and edible *Cordia* to stand the wash of tides;
plus eucalypts—rose-gum that grows twelve feet a year,
    and weeping *tesselaris* with its smooth-barked symphony
of white then autumn-gray . . . The heart sank sampling them.
    The day half gone. No one but I
knew where an Edenful of plants should go.

X

FINISHING

What could be done, we did; tagged by a team of cooks
    with spades, I ran like a Christmas waiter
dropping each pot in its position. Print-outs of shade,
    salt, growth-rate, water, colour, height
flashed up in answer to each label. The exam
    was strictly now. Nothing of all I knew
would count tomorrow. Under cruel sun sweat flowed in pints
    to cool our melting brains. One bucket of mound-builder
soil, a splash of water, and one rapid stake each protege
    received, as each flashed first and last time by.

Among them: milky pine, the eagle-giant; new strains of the
    hibiscus miracle that grow on sand and give delight
for nothing; Grevillea whose red spider-flowers drip honeydew
    into delicious mouths; towering *Ficus benjaminii*
that brings the spirit of an Indian cobra shine
    to dry Australian churchyards: *Melaleuca leucadendron*,
'white-wooded honey-white', the paperbark whose bulk
    beats cyclones; *Solanum* tree-potato that grows
twelve metres in two years; the cassie-wattle whose flowers
    are fried in brandy-batter; Jacaranda, *acalypha* . . .

I dare not think what slips I made; but at dusk recall
   still dropping pots for morning's labourers,
with always further groups to place, until under the moon
   I found myself with one last pot for which there seemed
no place—*Ficus religiosus*: in Bali I have seen it hold
   two hundred watchers at a temple show.
It went at last between two paperbarks, gaunt
   veterans that might have seen their day.

So my commission ceased. The fostering spirit
   that builds houses, nations, farms,
mixed with an awe of nature's spiral genes,
   had had its due from me. I left a letter
full of necessities and schemes; but guessed the best
   my plants could hope would be neglect—
foresaw the plans all changed, forgotten trees
   bulldozed for Simmo's roads, botanic tags
soon worn away. My faith was in the sun, that good
   black soil around the roots, and the ten feet
of rain a year. And now, remembering how
   the island tree-of-life can kill,
I thanked the deadly palms that shaded all
   my work. Then a short bull's rush along the strip
tore all away. Circling I saw on a green isle
   a strip of palms with softer greens below. The sea
spun round and turned the world to blue, before
   a flock of islands speckled into sight. My mind
wiped off its knowledge, turned to poems, talks,
   the strange non-answers we give city folk
whom poetry consoles. In front, all peaked and snarled,
   loomed Hinchinbrook the monster. We banked away
on a blue plain towards the distant smoke.

XI

HOME THOUGHTS . . .

Later, in Italy, I heard the news:
'Your trees are well', the Hermit wrote, 'except
    some unstaked ones the cyclone got. There
was lots of neglect after you left—it still
    goes on. New staff—new manager—new plans
—all too depressing. But round this side *my* garden
    grows, and life is good. Bananas great!' I see him
carry in a shoulder-bowing bunch; a green pawpaw, secure
    from fruit-bats, matures beside his loom. Happy
who live among their riches . . .! I guessed without interpreter
    my vines left wire-less, orders cancelled, trees
unknown before in Queensland rotting on dry wharves,
    and in some bright board-member's mind the thought
that doubling guests and golfcourse is the way
    to make investment pay. All was foreseen, and known;
since gardeners are suspicious patient men; only
    the trees go on growing in my mind.

RHYLL McMASTER

❧

RHYLL MCMASTER, BORN in Queensland in 1949 and raised and educated in Brisbane, was working as a secretary when she married the poet and novelist Roger McDonald. While later living in Canberra with her family, she qualified as a nursing sister. She and McDonald have since moved to a property outside Braidwood, where she farms sheep. They have three daughters.

McMaster's poetry is oblique, quirky and highly inventive. Much of her work is a strong-minded, wry reminiscence. She has published two books of poetry, a decade apart, and uncollected short stories.

PROFILES OF MY FATHER

I

The night we went to see the Brisbane River
break its banks

my mother from her kitchen corner
stood on one foot and wailed, 'Oh Bill,
it's *dangerous*.'
'Darl,' my father reasoned,
'don't be Uncle Willy.'

And took me right down to the edge
at South Brisbane, near the Gasworks,
the Austin's small insignia winking
in the rain.

A policeman helped a man load
a mattress on his truck.
At a white railing we saw the brown water
boil off into the dark.
It rolled midstream higher than its banks
and people cheered when a cat on a crate
and a white fridge whizzed past.

II

Every summer morning at five-thirty in the dark
I rummaged for my swimming bag
among musty gym shoes and Mum's hats from 1940
in the brown hall cupboard.
And Dad and I purred down through the sweet, fresh morning
still cool, but getting rosy
at Paul's Ice Cream factory,
and turned left at the Gasworks for South Brisbane Baths.

The day I was knocked off my kickboard
by an aspiring Olympian aged ten
it was cool and quiet and green down on the bottom.
Above the swaying ceiling limbs like pink logs,
and knifing arms churned past.
I looked at a crack in the cream wall
as I descended and thought of nothing.
When all of a sudden
Dad's legs, covered in silver bubbles,
his khaki shorts and feet in thongs
plunged into view like a new aquatic animal.

I was happy driving home;
Dad in a borrowed shirt with red poinsettias
and the coach's light blue, shot-silk togs.

WOMAN CROSSING THE ROAD

It's cold, wind gusty,
I can smell rain.
She crosses toward me
her mouth asking something.

At a certain point
our eyes are forced to meet.
Do I smile?
Wave?
You could take away everything
except the feet
self conscious, steady
edging the pavement.
She moves and looks with care to right and left
('She was run over coming to say hullo').

You could slide all the pieces
out of the picture
except her arms
and her eyes and mouth smiling—
her arms hug her tight,
are posed.

She wants to come over just for a minute.
Half way across now
assured, determined.
(Overhead two crows are fighting with a blue jay)
She says, 'I meant to . . .'
but the backwash from a car fades her words away.

ALAN GOULD

———— ❧ ————

A LAN GOULD WAS born in London in 1949, his father British, his mother Icelandic. His father was in the British Army and the family lived in Ireland, Germany and Singapore before coming to Australia when Gould was seventeen. He graduated from the Australian National University in Canberra, and was involved there in resisting the draft for the Vietnam War. He has written six books of poetry, two novels, and a book of three novellas. He is a builder of model sailing ships, and much of his poetry and fiction is concerned with the sea and the age of sail. He lives in the inland city of Canberra, is married, and teaches part time.

Gould's poetry is often written in sequences, and can show a great enjoyment of language. It suggests an admiration for virtuoso stylists such as W. H. Auden and Les Murray.

A Change of Season

after a newsreel of a Himalayan spring ritual

Sleepless on Capricorn;
outside an equinox moon
hangs like a skull's dome
above the orchard where
our peaches and apricots
sweat their sugars; the grass
is electric with reptile movement;
the carnal, murderous traffic
hurtles north through canefields
toward the Sunday headlines.
Inside a fan revolves,
lazily disintegrating
the headlights into cinema
on the roof. The newsreel
of the girl and cobra flickers
back across the decades.
She, an oblation attended
by plantations and film-crew
has arrived and placed the sweetmeats.
Now from the rock issues
eleven yards of liquid
obsidian, a head puffed
and big as the moon. Last year
a sister died here, her neck
encompassed by these jaws,
her trachea pierced, stifling
a shriek you might have heard
in Tibet, in Brisbane. They sway,
each the other's hypnotist,
a minute, a lifetime, gazing
on the gimlet-eye of death,
till she becomes the cobra's body,
and solemn as a bride, bends
thrice to kiss the lipless

mouth. Thirty years
cannot break the trance,
and we would go as far,
hunched before our screens,
learning to know this vicarious
appetite for darkness,
amazed by the daybreak
that reddens on Capricorn,
on Cancer, where the plantations
tremble their luminous heads.

GALAXIES

Hamburg: the clock hands move upon their star.
A liner glides along the Elbe, its lights
move through the city's lights, a galaxy
passing in silence through a galaxy.

My girl's behind me on the bed. She smokes
and minutes tick. Her time is waiting for
a time to end, a time to start. As mine is.
We are the flowers of our lineage,

were sinuous, bluff-mannered in the wine room
with all our company at like pursuits,
transactions that the liquor tantalised,
that led into this silence and this calm.

Yes, here I took myself, yes here was taken.
And here she chose to lie and here was lain.
Our choices and our fates, we house them both
like galaxies that pass through one another.

The liner's disappeared behind the docklands:
my girl is getting dressed again behind me.
I'll close the curtain on this night sky's map,
step out into the dark I know knows me.

Taffy Evans

Time and your gym, that girdered firmament,
make small the ardent boys of nineteen sixty.
   In togs of downy white we gawp
as you, untender angel in a tracksuit,
    hold before our eyes the grail,

the pilch, the ball, the egg. 'All life,' you boom,
'begins inside the egg.' Thus rugger came,
   dressed in its fierce theology,
gravely ranked us, made of me a hooker,
    to hug and hook though ears be shorn

and shinbone hacked, though bootstuds etch my back
at each collapse of scrum on afternoons
   not good, not clean, not fun. Alas,
not in six years did I convert or score:
    butterfingers and knock-knees

won me many shields against admirers.
The game meant bruises, freezing toes and yearning
   deep as winter for full-time.
Yet I blazed with reverence for the heroes,
    for Coutts who danced through fifteen tackles,

for Coe, carried senseless from the field
after he scored in extra time for Johnston's.
   Happier for me the summer mornings.
As you instructed how to hurl the javelin
    I was dreaming the school's defence,

white schoolboys armed with javelins, discoi, shot,
manning the balustrades on Orwell Field,
   hurling the Commies back on Chelmo.
Athlete and dreamer, sir, we shared too little,
    though when you read us Tales of Terror

you had the ghoulies stalking in my brain.
Despite my prayers, your regimen fell short
  of making my biceps burst their sleeves.
What of you have I kept? One tour de force—
  the time you showed us the flying vault,

showed us the brio of a man near fifty,
to grin, to run, to bounce, to launch and flash
  at speed along our near horizon,
white fighter skimming beneath our radar, to thump
  a perfect landing on the mat.

It left us breathless. Vivid still that risk,
that trust of splittable flesh to air and timing.
  Would I try? No Sir! Enough
to praise and give you back the nerve, the flaunt
  that leapt self-doubt, that leaps these years.

THE SCISSORS

They have become her fingers.
Her present thoughts
possess no closer friends.

Silver twins, dividing their estates,
they find the invisible trails
she laid there, years ago perhaps.

No stone will break them now.
They've come too far:
absorbed in their decisive task

they are the slish and slish
that parts one stillness from another.
They also are that stillness.

And though this room grows dark
they draw all light toward her.
There is, as well, her smile,
so calm, so frightening, so remote.

JAMIE GRANT

———— ❧ ————

J AMIE GRANT WAS born in 1949 in Melbourne, his father a
    company director, and boarded from the age of eleven at Geelong
Grammar. It was an experience he did not enjoy, until his last year
there, when he became interested in poetry. He graduated from
La Trobe University with a BA, had a brief career in advertising,
and then worked for ten years with Cambridge University Press in
Melbourne. During this time he published a shared volume of poetry
and worked on his second collection, *The Refinery*, but he was
best known for his reviews. His criticism has been thought by some
to be too often acerbic, but it is admired (or acknowledged) for its
prose style.

In 1984 Grant moved to Sydney and managed a bookshop for a
year. He has since become a freelance literary editor. His third book
of poetry, *Skywriting*, is as cool and ironic as his satirical early work,
and as sceptical and agnostic in its viewpoint, but is an advance in its
imaginative and striking imagery. These poems are influenced by the
'Martian' style of English writers like Craig Raine; however what
is a playful use of simile and metaphor in Raine, meant to produce
a freshening of perception, becomes in Grant's work a feeling of
alienation. The almost capricious similes suggest the world is a more
or less arbitrary conglomerate, and such an impression is assisted by
the use of imperfect rhymes and by the 'inorganic' organisation of
many poems into syllabics. At the same time there is a fastidious
prose exactitude to his work. The style in itself powerfully conveys
an attitude to life.

Grant plays shires cricket, as a medium-paced swing bowler (a fact
not irrelevant to his poetry), and has co-edited a book of literary
writings on Australian cricket.

ANTS IN THE SHOWER RECESS

Tiny black-skinned warriors,
   the aboriginal inhabitants

of this suburb do not require
   a land-rights movement, having not

moved from it. The modest cuisine
   of the coloniser (that's who

I am) fuels their factories:
   the soldiers carry head-sized

sugar boulders, and crumbs bigger
   than loaves, back underground; their ranks

marching through the kitchen look like
   columns of refugees.

The scouts they dispatched to my shower
   have found some of yesterday's

personality, washed up in
   the grouting. Their scientists proved

it edible: why not devour
   Gulliver? And now they're waiting.

One day the daily monsoons
   will not happen; the mountain-range

of food-ore will rest from earthquakes.
   Then they can send the miners;

I will be excavated, with ants
   like a chain of firemen passing buckets

to each other, when their one thought
   comes about—all of my skin

become a crowded market-place,
    my picked-clean skull swarming

with more ideas than ever
    it contained before, except

that every one is this one idea.

STILL LIFE WITH DESKS

Dust-yellow light slants
all over the city,
a new coat of paint
for the upper stories;

it lies across sports-fields
in narrow lanes, the aisles
of a floodlit, cold
pavilion. Tiles

on the imitation
church spires of take-away
chicken operations
deflect the neon-bright rays

which scatter among
oil-slicks on the river,
and cling to the long
stems of fever-

coloured aniseed plants
on the railway's
stony embankments.
The train has been delayed

near the end of its journey,
the city centre's wedge
of oblong forms, that vary
in height like the ridge-

line graphs at the stock
exchange. We're up close
to one high-rise block,
watching its precipice

of glass blink back even
more light than the polished
leaves on a eucalypt. Then
a square-edged

shadow moves up the side
of the building, like
a rising water-level. Lights
turn on inside

as offices submerge.
Windows, losing
their blankness, emerge
to frame a painting:

*Still Life With Desks
And Clerks*; another becomes
a television set,
screening some Board Room

Drama. The woman
sitting opposite
jerks awake: the train
has begun to pull out

from the shade. The light
touches her ankle,
that's swelled-up in the heat,
and prickly with stubble.

DAYLIGHT MOON

'Genius is next to madness,' said my mother,
'and your cousin is the living proof.' The talent
which provoked this much-used maxim was a bent
for arithmetic: in any decade after
the 1950s, we would have compared his mind
to a computer, but then computers remained

to be invented. Intricate multiplications
and long-divisions were performed in his head,
promptly and accurately, as if he had
long been prepared for each calculation,
a matchless party trick, wasted in a person
who was not invited to parties by reason

of madness. His condition was no shameful
family secret, but a source of anecdote
and wry group-humour—it amused us to quote
the latest findings from his search for fanciful
place-names in the Sydney street-directory,
one of the two volumes in his library,

the other being Melbourne's telephone book. Rhyme
appealed to him, and alliteration,
but the purpose of all his investigation
was specific: he was in quest of the sublime
music of numbers. 'What is map seventy-two,
D-4?' he'd ask, his voice a swift staccato

monotone, like the speech of a teller-machine,
knowing the answer was always *Lilli Pilli*,
his favourite suburb for its rhyme with *silly*.
'Christopher Codrington,' he'd continue, '16
Seventh St Sptswd.' Mostly his conversation
consisted of abrupt interrogation

compelling a numerical reply: 'How old
are you? What do you weigh? How tall? What year
were you born?' His gift could not be used in a career
just because he would always do what he was told
should not be done. The life he endured instead
was that of a prisoner. His parents were dead;

he hardly noticed, held in institutions
from the age of five. The specially assembled
family he had sprung from might have resembled
a closed-off hospital ward, into which, once
in a while, he was released, to a shower of names.
The asylum—we supposed—was the same

as a boarding-school, only more severe.
Whatever he suffered there must be deserved,
as his actions were deliberate and perverse:
this was my mother's view, one not founded on sheer
cruelty, only on the age's innocence.
It was far too late for my cousin, when science

identified autism. He was called a lunatic,
for all that the full moon's influence on the brain
had been disproved. Ignorance can generate pain,
though knowledge is often as cruel to eccentrics,
and on purpose. In our parents' gravel driveway
an unfamiliar car would announce the day

of his visit: he'd wander round the house,
shuffling in oversize boots like a pensioner,
half-stunned with motion-stunting tranquillizer,
his expression a bare-gummed grimace. He'd drowse
and then wake up, in a cushion-plumped living room
which had been stripped of every breakable heirloom

before he came. A pebble-shaped daylight moon hung
above my father's lawn, a left-over Christmas
decoration, suspended near an isthmus
of cloud in the picture-window; his brother's damaged son
held court in the lounge, greeting everyone he knew
with a robot-voice question: 'How old are you?'

SKYWRITING

Cool, clear autumn morning, so still
the knock of someone hammering
a nail rebounds from the floor
of the valley, with its shimmering

metal rivulets: that shadowy
vale in fact is a railway yard.
For some reason, on a Sunday,
a jet pilot has expelled a hard

stream of smoke behind his aircraft,
so precisely outlined
it could almost be a steel rail.
It's chilly, and there's no sigh of wind.

Flying high and fast, the pilot
has drawn a straight line, an arrow
of exhaust from one horizon
to the other, a path whose narrow

course is seen from the ground as curved,
so that it appears an enormous
basket-handle has been attached
to the land. Unlike the mischievous

Air Force trainee who, in the skies
over Perth, etched out in smoke form
his own private parts, as if he were
a vandal on a railway platform,

this pilot has not diverted
himself, leaving a colourless
rainbow arched over the city,
and over those suburban palaces

secured by the Bank. A rainbow,
though, is never as wide an arc
as the flowery canopy stretched
there now, like an archway in the park

arranged for a wedding. Beneath
its bridal bower, an airliner
coming in low resembles
a clumsy groom, cutting it finer

than he should, arrived with buttons
unfastened. An unhappy man
in Melbourne years ago rented
a skywriter, in desperation,

to advertise for a wife: people
always look at the sky. The track
made by this morning's jet may be
a less intricate message, yet its lack

is not of import: its simple
curve is the curve of the face
of the world, and hence it implies
all things within its embrace.

Like the world, the smoke meridian decays
before your eyes. Out of vision
an engine roar persists, sounding
like a far-distant storm's reverberation,

and like the football crowd I heard
once in a garden, a commotion
which could only be accounted for
as the shimmering pulse of the ocean.

SUSAN HAMPTON

B ORN IN 1949, Susan Hampton grew up in suburban New-
castle in New South Wales, and now works part time as a
teacher of writing in tertiary education in Sydney. She has published
a book and a pamphlet of poetry, and a collection of stories, fables,
monologues and poems on women's lives, called *Surly Girls*. She
co-edited an anthology of twentieth century Australian women's
poetry.

Hampton has two approaches in her work: a realistically detailed
one, and a style which plays language games. Her output so far has
been small. Her poetry has warmth and humour, and she is able to
express emotion with a lightness of touch.

YUGOSLAV STORY

Joze was born in the village of Loski Potok,
in a high-cheek-boned family. I noticed
he had no freckles, he liked playing cards,
and his women friends were called Maria, Malcka, Mimi;
and because he was a handsome stranger
I took him for a ride on my Yamaha
along the Great Western Highway
and we ate apples; I'd never met anyone
who ate apples by the case, whose father
had been shot at by Partisans in World War II,
who'd eaten frogs and turnips in the night,
and knew how to make pastry so thin
it covered the table like a soft cloth.
He knew how to kill and cut up a pig
and how to quickstep and polka. He lifted me up in the air.
He taught me to say '*Jaz te ljubim, ugasni luc*'
('I love you, turn off the light')
and how to cook *filana paprika*, *palacinka*,
and *prazena jetra*. One night in winter
Joze and two of his friends ate 53 *palacinke*
(pancakes) and went straight to the factory
from the last rummy game. Then he was my husband,
he called me '*moja zena*' and sang a dirty song
about Terezinka, a girl who sat on the chimney
waiting for her lover, and got a black bum.
He had four brothers and four sisters,
I had five sisters.
His father was a policeman under King Peter,
my father was a builder in bush towns.
Joze grew vegetables and smoked Marlboros
and he loved me. This was in 1968.

STRANDED IN PARADISE

Your fuselage, your entourage,
your wingtip. now your eyes.
your feet which touch the ground.
stranded in Paradise
I'm climbing over your body
the hill of your breast
stranded. what god put me here.
my time with you. will you
kiss me again. like this. here.
now here. hold my head.
hold my feet down, I'm levitating.
it's so easy. when you roll over
onto me, I hold your fuselage.
I pat your wingtip. I touch your teeth
and your shoulders. you are sinking
into me. I balloon under your hand.
                                    The night sky
is humming with crickets. and humming birds,
which only live in Paradise. which only exist
here. soon they will stop. the noises will stop
and we'll lie still. only the sound of the cars
and the clicking inside the metal boxes
for the traffic lights. someone slowing up
for a hitchhiker. and off again.
another person who'll be stranded.
will it be in Paradise, at the corner shop,
the fruit stall. will she hover over
the apples. delicious or jonathan.
she can't decide. it's because she's stranded,
and thinks it's only the fruit stall, or the corner shop.
it's only Paradise, I want to say. it's only here.
the planes going over. the traffic passing by.

VICKI RAYMOND

———— ❧ ————

BORN IN VICTORIA in 1949, Vicki Raymond grew up at Geeveston in the isolated south-west of Tasmania, where her parents ran a small, almost self-sufficient property. She studied English at the University of Tasmania in Hobart when James McAuley was there, and her poetry, although more witty than his, suggests his influence. On graduating, she edited the staff newspaper of the university's English department for some years. Her first poems were published at this time in *Quadrant*, the magazine of which McAuley was the founding editor. She went to London in the early 1980s and found work at Australia House as a secretary. She married in England.

Raymond's poetry, though often witty, is always tough-minded in its content and its formal severity. This is apparent in 'Roaring Beach', a self-aware comment on her determination not to play the poetess. Her book *Small Arm Practice*—which includes poems from an earlier volume, *Holiday Girls*, all of them brief—is particularly satisfying in the cumulative effect of its tone.

ON SEEING THE FIRST FLASHER

Grey-coated, solitary stranger, hail!
Thou harbinger of summer's lusty days,
tracing through country parks thy mazy trail,
or lingering by some brook to catch the gaze
of passing schoolgirl, who, with scornful eye,
remarks upon thy manhood's lack of length,
then vanishing, before her angry cry
shall summon to her aid the studded strength
of forty skinheads, or, with deadly aim,
her dainty foot shall plunge into thy crotch—
when shalt thou find a partner to thy game,
a maid whose pleasure is to stand and watch?
As soon, alas, as poets shall enthrall
commuter crowds, or fill the Albert Hall.

KING PINEAPPLE

Of all minor deities, remember
fat Pineapple, swinging complacently
in string bags along the Harrow Road.

You know he's male by his sudden
rude spiking of ladies' buttocks
in crowds. His crown is a jester's cap.

Guest of the rich, he sometimes presides
over linen antarcticas, shoals of silver;
but he is Poverty's true friend-in-need,

and will feed you from his sugary paunch
for seven midnights, in dripping communion
with sunlight, over the frosty sink.

OFFICE DRUNKS

In offices, you may find someone
who doesn't wash enough,
or drinks too much, or spends

his spare time in ways
that rumour guesses at.
Obscurely unsackable, such men

persist from year to year,
like the old gods, malodorous
Jacks-in-the-green, failed Pans.

In secret underground rooms
they drain their hip-flasks,
are sent home after lunch,

and stay away for days.
When they return, they look
sheepish and oddly smart,

like oaks you'd thought were dead,
in April, holding out bunches
of new leaves, foolishly.

DON'T TALK ABOUT YOUR CHILDHOOD

Don't talk about your childhood.
Anyone can do that.
We were all sensitive once,
and most of us hated school.

That man who made his millions
from guns: even he
can recall the smell of his mother's dress,
rain on leaves.

And as for the dark cupboard
and what you did to the cat,
confession of childish guilt
is a form of boasting.

You risk nothing, singing
your song of a small ghost.
Don't talk about your childhood:
say what you are now.

Roaring Beach

for Edith Speers

The sea was cold enough to burn you,
in spite of sun. We plunged
under the waves, and came up cursing,
lungs crushed. That was at first.

Later, we could relax neck-deep.
Our heads bobbed like apples on the surface,
as we talked—about what? Not poetry,
I think. There was, as well,

a smell of smoke from illicit fires
somewhere on shore. We could see,
looking down, clear to the wrinkled floor.
One of us, surely, must have mentioned that.

JOHN FORBES

———— 🌿 ————

JOHN FORBES WAS born in 1950 in Melbourne, but because of his father's work as a meteorologist he spent much of his early life in New Guinea and Malaya. He graduated from the University of Sydney with a thesis on the American poet John Ashbery. Forbes's own poetry also shows the marked influence of another New York school poet, Ted Berrigan. He has rejected the 'bourgeois' way of life and has worked, amongst other jobs, as a petrol pump attendant and furniture removalist. He edits an occasional magazine, *Surfer's Paradise*, and now lives in Melbourne where he is an editorial assistant on the above-ground literary magazine *Scripsi*. He has received Literature Board grants.

Forbes's work might be described as combining the determinedly party-going jokiness of the pop art influenced Frank O'Hara with the deflation and vulnerability of Philip Larkin. In his poetry, relationships with women, rather than some more general *angst*, are the ostensible reason for the sometimes melancholy tone. Forbes's persona is that of an intellectual who asserts the superior value of bodily pleasures—of the beach, sex, pop music and alcohol—over Art. He has published four individual volumes and a *Selected Poems*, which maintain his wittiness, bounce, and mockery of an intellectual manner.

Rrose Selavy

for Julie Rose
'a transistor & a large sum of money to spend'
—Steely Dan

Julie the beauty of a tooth
& from the red & white checked tablecloth's back garden
             where we're quietly avoiding lunch
                 Julie begins to somersault
O facelift sing of Julie!
O mascara croon!
And Ireland green as hair let every crystal drop of whisky
                    flow to me
   as a fish knife's clatter falling sounds the name of Julie—
               the blue day collects her
               & disappears
Julie breathing like a T-shirt after a swim
        in Crete, Julie
      in Rangoon a Chevrolet Impala
   & in it Julie. She watches osmosis on television combing
      her hair
      & FLASH!
appears like an ice-cream to Fragonard, aeroplane bliss Julie
              helping the air of London get cleaner
      Julie, her watch stopped exact
      sneeze balloon happy griefs
      of the portmanteau
Julie, passing exams
Julie the hand-made spine of rare first editions sunburns
               under the Eiffel Tower
          Golfball of insomnia!
Julie the wedding dress cries like an Italian face
& when the aftershave factory explodes the Spirit of Alcohol
               beams on Julie.
Imagine an iceberg's ideal form
or an escaped embrace (!) Avoid such horrors with Julie

           and on a weekend hike with Julie
      the snapshot of a bear!
Julie invites a drop of foam to eternity as a blood bank
                       bursts pulpily,
             every corpuscle dying in love
                with Julie,
       more luminous than a burning patio /
                more tasteful
          than a day at the zoo.
Julie, surfing the night away
and in the dark beauties of drugs on the pension, Julie,
     a crazed spanner in the intricate works of death!
O bored cigarette Julie!
Julie the myth of beauty where sex is 'concerned'
and Julie the myth of ugliness where helicopters are learning,
                    slowly,
       to dance (their feet are clumsy but tender
                      tender!)
Even the windscreen wipers on their electric stage swivel
     for Julie, even the Enos bubbling in its glass.

         More precise than a stocking,
    Julie lounges at the pool
she moves like a heatwave in December. It's the year slipping by
it's the strange coast of Mozambique I've never seen—
         no it's Julie
           buying a blazer.
      O abhorrent sunglasses!
I peel an orange listening to the fridge erupt in the night
      & in the morning I go to the movies,
          with Julie.

Angel

not serious about drugs
and into the sky that's
open like a face and
when night arrives the
smiling starts we being
our own stars as the days
pass in their cars and
the stereo fills with mud
we don't care   we walk
in the rhythm of a face
that's awake in the air
and I'd like to kiss you
but you've just washed
your hair. the night goes
on and we do too until
like pills dissolving
turn a glass of water
blue it's dawn and we
go to sleep we dream
like crazy and get rich
and go away.

PETER GOLDSWORTHY

B ORN IN 1951 at Minlaton in South Australia, his father a teacher, Peter Goldsworthy grew up in country towns of that state and in Darwin in the Northern Territory. He qualified as a doctor at the University of Adelaide in 1974. He now has a medical practice in suburban Adelaide that he shares with his wife, an arrangement which gives him time to write. They have three children.

Goldsworthy has written two collections of poetry, three of short stories, and two acclaimed novels: *Maestro*, which draws on his study of classical music, and *Honk If You Are Jesus*, a 'romance' with a scientific setting. In his poems, Goldsworthy combines witty anecdote with the minimalist form and moral concerns of modern Polish poetry (he particularly admires Rozewicz). His output is small, but all of it is honed and concentrated. His very slim *Selected Poems* (1991) is without a failure.

Memories of Kampuchea

My first rabbit was the hardest.
Unscrewing the neck,
flipping gut-things between my legs.
Later I developed forehand,
and the traps set themselves.

And then my first two-legged corpse,
my first day in dissection.
There was cold pork for dinner, inevitably—
but coming up hot later,
I never ate meat again—till the next week.

I should mention also a slaughterhouse
downwind from memory.
A place I might have visited,
or might have not. It was all long ago.

Because always this forgetting.
This bringing kill home in butcher's paper,
picked like fruit off a shelf.
Smothered with herbs and euphemisms
till it could be anything.

At times I seem almost to remember
the sealed trucks arriving,
the sheep hurrying to be meat.
At times I count them at night,
trying to stay awake.

Alcohol

You are the eighth
and shallowest
of the seven seas,

a shrivelled fragmented ocean
dispersed into bottle, kegs, casks,
warm puddles in lanes behind pubs:
a chain of ponds.

Also a kind of spa,
a very hot spring:
medicinal waters to be taken
before meals, with meals, after meals
without meals,

chief cure
for gout, dropsy, phlegm,
bad humours, apoplexy, rheumatism
and chief cause of all the same.

At best you make lovely mischief:
wetter of cunts,
drooper of cocks.

At worst you never know when to stop:
wife-beater, mugger of innocents,
chief mitigating circumstance
for half the evil in the world.

All of which I know too well
but choose to ignore:
remembering each night only this advice:
never eat on an empty stomach.

For always you make me a child again—
sentimental, boring
and for one happy hour very happy—
sniffing out my true character like a dog:
my Sea of Tranquillity
always exactly shallow enough to drown in.

SUICIDE ON CHRISTMAS EVE

After the doctor, the steam-cleaners,
more usefully. I drive home to bed
through intersections sequinned with glass:
it's Christmas Eve, season of donor organs.

What is the meaning of life? I shake you
gently awake. What answer would satisfy?
you mumble, yawning, from Your Side.
To understand is to be bored, you say,
practising, perhaps, for Speech Night.
Knowledge is a kind of exhaustion, you say.

A child enters our room: is it morning yet?
Not Yet. In another room the lights of the Tree
wink colourfully, and when the telephone rings
again, it is almost, but not quite, in time.

A STATISTICIAN TO HIS LOVE

Men kill women in bedrooms, usually
by hand, or gun. Women kill men,
less often, in kitchens, with knives.
Don't be alarmed, there is understanding
to be sucked from all such hard
and bony facts, or at least a sense
of symmetry. Drowned men—an
instance—float face down, women up.
But women, ignited, burn more fiercely.
The death camp pyres were therefore,
sensibly, women and children first,
an oily kind of kindling. The men
were stacked in rows on top. Yes,
there is always logic in this world.
And neatness. And the comfort
of fact. Did I mention that suicides
outnumber homicides? The figures
are reliable. So stay awhile yet
with me: the person to avoid, alone,
is mostly you yourself.

KEVIN HART

———————— ✺ ————————

K EVIN HART WAS born in London in 1954 and came to live
in Brisbane at ten years of age. His father was a factory em-
ployee and a union representative. Hart has been interested in reli-
gion from his youth, first as a Baptist, then an Anglican, and since
his twenties as a convert to Catholicism. He graduated *cum laude* in
philosophy from the Australian National University in Canberra and
received a scholarship to Stanford University, California. He has
been a secondary school teacher and is now Associate Professor of
English at Monash University in Melbourne.

Hart has published four books of poetry, as well as a study of
deconstruction and theology, *The Trespass of the Sign*, which finds an
affinity between certain intellectual strategies of Jacques Derrida and
those of medieval negative theologians such as Meister Eckhart. In
his most recent collection, *Peniel*, Hart utilizes something of negative
theology, which refuses to conceptualise religious experience, through
poems made up of 'constellations' of things and incidents, precisely
presented but 'open' or imprecise as to their content. Much of Hart's
earlier poetry is more obviously religious. He uses generalised sym-
bols, such as rocks, shadows, sun, moon, and clocks, in poems that
are extremely bare (often reading like translations) and that rely almost
entirely on conceptual brilliance for their effect. Although rigorously
intellectualised, his work is always founded in emotion.

NADIA COMANECHI

Montreal, 1976

Yet there are consolations, she chooses a point
in the hush-swept stadium
straightens arms, legs, attracting us to watch

as, first, she hesitates, then rises—
as if some law
suspended itself to witness her grasp

a point five feet above,
coil, and then unwind, relaxing into mathematics
as a chameleon

darkens to become
one with the earth. Soon, when she lands,
a score will flash,

those leaning against the rails will note
her hair now ruffled,
officials will hear the thud as energy

soaks into the mat,
a pureness will escape, a light from a dying star
or lamp that sheds a curve

across a wall where Rheticus rams his skull
against the stone,
or Kepler, disease crawling through his hand,

drops his chalk,
an abstract love unfolds, inflames his mind,
and thirty years

wrinkle into his face before perfection.
She does not play,
perfection recedes from her, a curve

never to touch its axis:
her instant dissolves, the past expands, she lands
smiling without warmth, entirely human.

A HISTORY OF THE FUTURE

There will be cities and mountains
as there are now,

and steeled armies
marching through abandoned Squares
as they have always done.

There will be fields to plough,
the wind will shake the trees, acorns
will fall,

and plates will still crack
for no apparent reason.

And that is all we can truly know.

The future is over the horizon, we cannot hear
a word its people say,

and even if they shout to us
to make us cease
bombing their lands, destroying their cities,

a shout from there would sound like an acorn
dropped on cement,

or a plate on the shelf
beginning to crack.

THE GIFT

One day the gift arrives—outside your door,
left on a windowsill, inside the mailbox,
or in the hallway, far too large to lift.

Your postman shrugs his shoulders, the police
consult a statute, and the cat miaows.
No name, no signature, and no address,

only, 'To you, my dearest one, my all . . .'
One day it fits snugly in your pocket,
then fills the backyard like afternoon in Spring.

Monday morning, and it's there at work—
already ahead of you, or left behind
amongst the papers, files and photographs;

and were there lipstick smudges down the side
or have they just appeared? What a headache!
And worse, people have begun to talk:

'You lucky thing!' they say, or roll their eyes.
Evenings find you combing the directory,
(a glass of straw-colored wine upon the desk)

still hoping to chance on a forgotten name.
Yet mornings see you happier than before—
after all, the gift has set you up for life.

Impossible to tell, now, what was given
and what was not: slivers of rain on the window,
that gold-tooled *Oeuvres* of Diderot on the shelf,

the strawberry dreaming in a champagne flute—
were they part of the gift or something else?
Or is the gift still coming, on its way?

PHILIP HODGINS

———— ✤ ————

BORN IN 1959, Philip Hodgins grew up on a dairy farm at Katandra West, a flat, pastoral area of inland Victoria. An only child, he helped on the property from an early age, and farming life, viewed pragmatically, has been an important subject for his poetry. For his high school education he went to a private school in Geelong. The vehemence and independence of his work were already apparent in his personality: he was twice expelled from school in his last year. He then worked for seven years with a publishing company in Melbourne as a sales representative.

In 1983, at twenty-four, Hodgins was diagnosed as having leukemia, and was given three years to live. His first book appeared in 1986, while he was a full-time student at the University of Melbourne. Since then his disease has been in remission, and he has published two more collections of poetry, in 1988 and 1990. He has also in that time travelled in Europe and the United States. In 1990 he married the writer Janet Shaw (whose first collection of short stories was published that year). They moved to the country and are restoring a derelict mudbrick farmhouse, against all advice. They have one child.

Hodgins has said that his poetry is mainly influenced by that of Robert Gray and Les Murray, but its confident reliance on an Australian colloquial voice also suggests the example of Bruce Dawe. The carefully structured, succinct poems of his first book, expressing bitterness about his illness, raised the question whether the subject was the sole *raison d'être* for his poems. Later volumes have answered that question, as the subject matter has broadened and his skill diversified and become continually more impressive.

THE BIRDS

The time was going five a.m.
and all the birds were on the go.
They sounded like the frequencies
of many twiddled radios.

It's really bad the way it's gone—
I always used to sleep OK
and dream and miss the rural life
and never see the break of day.

But since I got the only part
in cancer's tragic dialogue
I've heard those birds a million times
and seen the sun come up a lot.

I've been rehearsing death each night,
and still I haven't got it right.

WALKING THROUGH THE CROP

It doesn't matter any more
the way the wheat is shivering
on such a beautiful hot day
late in the afternoon, in Spring.

I couldn't care about the sound
of insects frying in the heat
or how a flock of cockatoos
has gone up in a brilliant sheet.

I had a list I tried to keep.
Sometimes I even wrote it down.
It had all sorts of private things
like images, sensations, sounds . . .

There's nothing in these dying days.
I've given everything away.

CHOPPED PROSE WITH PIGS

There was one old barrel-size boar
who just couldn't hold off
until the gate had been dragged open.
On that evening, after milking,
when we reversed down the lane
with a load of reject peaches from the cannery
this pig charged the electric fence
like some quixotic warrior whose time
had come. Knowing what the wires held
he started screaming with metallic vigor
way back before he got to the pain.

We stood on the trailer in filthy stasis
like two ham actors
upstaged by a member of the audience.
When it arrived the moment
was wonderful. The scream
went up to an ecstasy and the pig,
soaking with mud, hurled and dragged
itself frighteningly under the wires
while at the arch of contact
blue sparks burned into the twilight
and into my memory.
I had never seen so much intensity
for so many small peaches.

But pigs will eat other things as well,
including their offspring and you.
There was a farmer up at Yabba North
who came unstuck in a pen
full of pigshit and duplicitous saddlebacks
one ordinary morning in January.
When they hosed out the place
they found about half the things
he had been wearing

plus all the bigger bones.
I saw his widow doing some shopping in town
not long after the funeral.
She was loaded down with supermarket bags
and grief.

Another time we found a bloated cow
tipped over in a far paddock.
The dead-cow truck wasn't coming round
so my father tied her to the tractor
and lurched her down the lane
like a small ship in a gentle swell.
We stopped in the smell of pigs
and while I rolled a cigarette
he broke her into half a dozen pieces
with an axe
and threw them over to the pigs.
When I went back early the next day
I stood rolling another cigarette
and looked at all the bigger bones
and the pigs lying round in the innocent mud.

It was one of those same pigs, a sow,
who got out of the churned-up paddock
and went down to the dairy one afternoon.
In the passageway there was a cattledog tied up
to keep cats out of the milkroom,
but he didn't worry about the pig.
She got in there
and tipped over an eight-gallon cream can
and then licked it all up.
We found her three days later
lying very still in an empty drain
with a relentless cream hangover.
Her eyes were so bloodshot
that whenever she opened them
it looked like she would bleed to death.

She recovered
but later on she did go out that way.
It happened early in the Spring.
I coaxed her into a single pen mechanically
and smashed her between the eyes
with a hammer.
After pushing a knife through the jugular
I rolled her to one side
until most of the blood had pumped out.
It spread across the concrete
like an accident
and made me think how the cream
must have spread the same way.

I scalded and scoured her thoroughly
and when I hung her up
and drew the knife down her front
some of the guts pushed out
like odds and sods from an overloaded cupboard.
Reaching in for the rest
had me disgorging handfuls of animal warmth.
When the job was done
I hoisted her out of catreach
in muslin as clean as a bridal veil
and threw the chopped shinbones
to the cattledog.
I can still hear him
outside his tipped-over forty-four
chewing them with a sloppy broken rhythm.

SHOOTING THE DOGS

There wasn't much else we could do
that final day on the farm.
We couldn't take them with us into town,
no one round the district needed them
and the new people had their own.
It was one of those things.

You sometimes hear of dogs
who know they're about to be put down
and who look up along the barrel of the rifle
into responsible eyes that never forget
that look and so on,
but our dogs didn't seem to have a clue.

They only stopped for a short while
to look at the Bedford stacked with furniture
not hay
and then cleared off towards the swamp,
plunging through the thick paspalum
noses up, like speedboats.

They weren't without their faults.
The young one liked to terrorise the chooks
and eat the eggs.
Whenever he started doing this
we'd let him have an egg full of chilli paste
and then the chooks would get some peace.

The old one's weakness was rolling in dead sheep.
Sometimes after this he'd sit outside
the kitchen window at dinner time.
The stink would hit us all at once
and we'd grimace like the young dog
discovering what was in the egg.

But basically they were pretty good.
They worked well and added life to the place.
I called them back enthusiastically
and got the old one as he bounded up
and then the young one as he shot off
for his life.

I buried them behind the tool shed.
It was one of the last things I did before
we left.
Each time the gravel slid off the shovel
it sounded like something
trying to hang on by its nails.

JEMAL SHARAH

JEMAL SHARAH WAS born in 1969, of Irish and Lebanese descent. Her father, who was at the time Assistant Secretary to the Treasurer, was killed in a car accident near Canberra in 1975. She was brought up by her mother in Sydney, and has been an outstanding student at Sydney Girls High and at the University of Sydney, where she is now working for a master's degree in English. 'Kristallnacht' was written when she was nineteen.

KRISTALLNACHT

Alone in the bush.
Before, they had been singing,
when the car was given a great push
off the road; rain tinkling.

And then she got a fright—
the only one awake;
the others' eyes stayed shut tight
no matter how she'd shake

and shove their arms.
She didn't think of death—
sleep wasn't any harm—
and there was her father's breath,

though harsh, asthmatic, sore.
Locked in a foggy sleep
it might have been a snore.
Except it seemed so deep.

But she—she was awash
with cubes of window-glass,
with one leg safely squashed
in a metal cast;

and such neatly shattered crystal.
Her father loved to buy
goblets, clear as the distilled
water from an eye.

Its rhinestones chained her wrist.
She waited as time passed:
one car sped by—missed
seeing them, it was so fast.

Then desperation changed to hate,
she knew everything was wrong:
soon it would be too late
(it had already been too long).

And no-one came to help
in spite of all her cries;
she was stuck there by herself,
and adult blandishments were lies—

that to cry help was proof
against perverts, loss, distress,
that the boy who had cried wolf
was gobbled through excess.

Vague rain, sickness in tides;
neither offered any answers.
Nor, later, did the pride
of howling ambulances.

A SMALL SONG

There is a sparrow frozen on the lawn,
in the snow that lasted through the night
and the cold dawn
that killed it. Now sunlight
drops about the corpse a pall of white.

So ends an unimportant life, and brief.
It spent some seasons lightly on the earth,
then doubtless with relief
found one lungfull of breath
was all that stood between itself and death.

ACKNOWLEDGEMENTS

———— ❧ ————

F OR PERMISSION TO reprint work used in this anthology, grateful acknowledgement is made to authors or estates, and to the following publishers and copyright-holders: Collins/Angus and Robertson, for poems by Christopher Brennan, Shaw Neilson (from *The Poems of John Shaw Neilson* and 'Eva Has Gone' from *Witnesses of Spring*), Hugh McCrae (from *The Best Poems of Hugh McCrae*), Mary Gilmore (from *Selected Verse*), Lesbia Harford (from *The Poems of Lesbia Harford*), Kenneth Slessor (from *Selected Poems*), R.D. Fitzgerald (from *Forty Years' Poems*), A.D. Hope (from *Collected Poems*), Ronald McCuaig (from *Selected Poems*), Elizabeth Riddell (from *Selected Poems*), William Hart-Smith (from *Selected Poems 1936–84*), Roland Robinson (from *Selected Poems*), John Blight (from *Selected Poems*), Douglas Stewart (from *Collected Poems*), David Campbell (from *Collected Poems*), Judith Wright (from *Collected Poems* and 'Smalltown Dance' from *A Human Pattern*), James McAuley (from *Collected Poems*), Rosemary Dobson (from *Collected Poems*), Gwen Harwood (from *Selected Poems* and 'Naked Vision' from *The Lions Bride*), Lex Banning (from *There Was A Crooked Man*), Nan McDonald (from *Selected Poems*), Francis Webb (from *Cap & Bells*), Vivian Smith (from *Selected Poems*), Barry Humphries (from *Neglected Poems*), Les Murray (from *Dog Fox Field*), Geoffrey Lehmann (from *Children's Games*), Geoff Page (from *Selected Poems*), Robert Gray (from *Selected Poems*), Alan Gould (from *The Twofold Place*), Jamie Grant (from *The Refinery*), Peter Goldsworthy and Philip Hodgins (from *Blood and Bone*); University of Queensland Press, for poems by John Manifold ('The Tomb of Lt. John Learmonth, A.I.F.' from *Collected Verse*, 1978), Roger McDonald ('Sickle Beach', 'Precise Invaders', 'Incident in Transylvania', and 'The Hollow Thesaurus' from *Airship*, 1975) and John Tranter ('Country Veranda', 'Voodoo' and 'Crosstalk' from *Under Berlin*, 1988); Curtis Brown, for a poem each by A.D. Hope, James McAuley, and Eric Rolls, and for poems by Vicki Raymond; Charles E. Tuttle, for the poems by Harold Stewart; Oxford University Press, for the poems by Peter Porter; Longman Cheshire, for the poems by Bruce Dawe; Jonathan Cape, for the poems by Clive James; Hale and Iremonger, for the poems by Nigel Roberts, Mark O'Connor, and John Forbes; Fremantle Arts Centre Press, for the poems by Caroline Caddy; Penguin Australia, for the poems by Susan Hampton (from *The Penguin Book of Australian Women Poets*); Lothian Books and Mr R.J. McKimm, for poems by Shaw Neilson; Richard Scott Simon, for the poems by Randolph Stow ('Ruins of the City of Hay', 'The Embarkation', 'The Land's Meaning', 'Convalescence' and 'The Singing Bones' from *Selected Poems: A Counterfeit Silence* by Randolph Stow, © Randolph Stow 1969, published by Angus & Robertson, 'Endymion' from *Outrider* by Randolph Stow, © Randolph Stow 1962, *Selected Poems: A Counterfeit Silence* and *Randolph Stow*, published by University of Queensland Press, 1990, 'Frost Parrots' from *The Literary Half-Yearly* © Randolph Stow 1979 and *Randolph Stow*, published by University of Queensland Press, 1990; Golvan Arts and Kevin Hart, for the poems by Kevin Hart; Chris Wallace-Crabbe, for his poems; John Tranter, for one of his poems; and Jemal Sharah, for her poems.